DATE DUE

12/9			
GAYLORD			PRINTED IN U.S.A.

ESSENTIAL TIBETAN BUDDHISM

Essential Tibetan Buddhism

དམ་ཚིག་ཀྱི་སྐྱིང་པོ།

ROBERT A. F. THURMAN

CASTLE BOOKS

Grateful acknowledgment is made to the following for permission to
reprint previously published material:
Bantam for excerpts from *The Tibetan Book of the Dead*
by R. A. F. Thurman.
Library of Tibetan Works and Archives, which published earlier versions
of translations of "Three Principles of the Path" and "Transcendent
Insight" in *Life and Teachings of Tsong Khapa* by R. A. F. Thurman.
Princeton University Press, which published an earlier version of "Praise
for Relativity" in *The Central Philosophy of Tibet*
by R. A. F. Thurman.
Snow Lion Publications for the Nobel Prize lecture in *A Policy of
Kindness* by H. H. Dalai Lama.
Wisdom Publications for an excerpt from *The Door of Liberation*
by Geshe Wangyal.

The painting on the cover is *The Refuge Tree,* an array of enlightened
beings like the wish-fulfilling gems on the mythical tree of life.
Tibetan Buddhist meditators visualize such a tree in vivid details as present
before them in the sky of the mind's eye, showering them with liquid
jewel light-ray nectar blessings that fill up body and mind with light
and understanding. One imagines one's own mentor as the
Shakyamuni in the center, who has the Tantric
Buddha Vajradhara in his heart.
Tibet, eighteenth century, gouache on cotton.
Courtesy Shelley and Donald Rubin collection.
Photograph courtesy of Mokotoff Asian Arts.

This edition published by arrangement and with permission of
HarperSanFrancisco, a division of Harper Collins Publishers, Inc.

This edition copyright © 1997 by Castle Books.

Published by CASTLE BOOKS
A Division of Book Sales, Inc.
114 Northfield Avenue, Edison, New Jersey 08837

ISBN 0-7858-0872-8

MANUFACTURED IN THE UNITED STATES OF AMERICA.

Contents

To His Holiness the Dalai Lama of Tibet

"You are Lama!
  (all my mentors)
You are Archetype!
  (all my deities)
You are Dakini!
  (all enlightened women)
You are Protector!
  (all fierce angels)
For now 'til enlightenment,
No Savior other than you! . . .
Be my eternal friend!"

May His wishes all come true!

ESSENTIAL TIBETAN BUDDHISM

Introduction

1. The Tibetan World and Its Creators

The Three Most Gracious

To look for the essence of the Tibetan worldview, a popular Tibetan saying is a good place to start: "There were three who were most kind to Tibet: the Precious Guru (Padma Sambhava); the Lord Master (Atisha); and the Precious Master (Tsong Khapa)." The Tibetan titles that come before the names of these three—*Guru Rimpochey, Jowo Jey,* and *Jey Rimpochey,* respectively—could apply to any of the tens of thousands of other great figures in Tibetan history. But any Tibetan, of whatever persuasion or affiliation, knows immediately who is meant by the *Precious Guru,* the *Lord Master,* or the *Precious Master.* The key to the whole matter is that all three of these names indicate that their bearers are considered *actual* Buddhas in their own right. They are not thought of as mere human beings, albeit extremely holy, wise, or capable, who brought to or propagated in Tibet a teaching *about* Buddhas. They are clearly considered by the mass population as examples of the real thing.

The essence of Tibetan culture is defined by this experience of real Buddhas dwelling among them. It is thus a civilization that feels itself touched by Buddhas, marked by having experienced the living impact of real Buddhas. Tibetans have even come to take for granted the constant presence of many Buddhas around the country. Tibetan Buddhism is thus a reorientation of individual and social life to account for the reality of Buddhas, the possibility of becoming one oneself, and the actuality of a methodical process of doing so.

This is the characteristic that distinguishes Buddhism in Tibet from the Buddhisms in other civilizations, though Indian civilization in its classical heyday of roughly 500 to 1000 C.E. enshrined the human possibility of Buddhahood more and more openly in its core, as did the Ch'an, Son, and

Zen subcultures of East Asia. Theravada Buddhism of South Asia, a form of what Tibetans call Monastic or Individual Vehicle Buddhism, believes that a Buddha is a purified being, a saint or *arhat*, who has attained cessation of embodiment in Parinirvana, a realm of absolute freedom, and so has definitely departed from the world. According to this view, there were a few other Buddhas prior to Shakyamuni, there are other purified saints following in Buddha's footsteps, and any human who has the teachings and makes the effort can become one of those. But there are no living Buddhas around until Metteya, the next Buddha, comes to the world thousands of years from now.

The Universal Vehicle, or Messianic, Buddhism now remaining in East Asia has many forms, but in general it has a different view of Buddhas. It teaches that there are infinite numbers of Buddhas. All have a Truth Body, a Body of Absolute Reality (which is undifferentiated; they all share it in infinite peace), and a Form Body of relative, compassionate manifestations. This Form Body subdivides into a Beatific Body, an immeasurable body of infinite bliss, color, and light, imperceptible to ordinary beings, and an Emanation Body, a body of boundless manifestations. This Emanation Body has three forms: the Ideal, of which Shakyamuni is the example in our epoch; the Incarnational, which manifests limitless examples who appear like ordinary humans and other kinds of beings, even inanimate objects like planets, oceans, continents, islands, bridges, and buildings; and the Artistic, which includes all kinds of representations of Buddhas in all art forms. Thus all Universal Vehicle Buddhists consider that the Buddha's final Nirvana was a kind of instructional show and that Buddhas can manifest any time, any place. However, except for the Tibetans, they do not expect any Buddhas to show up here and now, except in other dimensions (a pure land such as Sukhavati or the visionary world of the *Lotus*, for instance). They remain more or less attached to an originally brahminical cosmology wherein the planet is experiencing a "Dark Age" (*kaliyuga*), and Buddhas have given up on it for the time being. The Ch'an/Son/Zen Buddhists are one exception to this. They consider perfect Buddhahood to be a mental enlightenment, the direct result of the practice of their methods of contemplation and understanding; yet they have only a weak sense of the emanational richness, the embodiment potential, of Buddhahood. The Shingon Tantric Buddhists of Japan are the other East Asian exception, in that they also cultivate a sense of the immediacy of the Buddha presence and potential.

Tibetan Buddhism, almost alone among Asian Buddhisms, preserved the huge treasury of Indian Buddhist Tantric traditions. The Tantras emerged from the third Vehicle of Indian Buddhism, the Tantric, Mantric, Adamantine, or Apocalyptic Vehicle. This Vehicle is the esoteric dimension of the Universal Vehicle, and it emphasizes practices based on the cultivated sense of the immediate presence of the Buddha reality. It teaches methods for the attainment of complete Buddhahood in this very life, or at least within a few more lives, thus vastly accelerating the Universal Vehicle evolutionary path on which a Bodhisattva transforms from a human to a Buddha over three incalculable eons of self-transcending lifetimes. A major component of these accelerated methods is the accessibility of beings who have already become Buddhas.

Thus for the Tibetans, Shakyamuni Buddha, the foremost Buddha of this world-epoch, is not just a dead hero. He is not just an object of belief, a divine being encounterable in another dimension or an altered state. He is a being believed to have conquered death, just as Jesus Christ is. But Tibetans are not awaiting Buddha's triumphal return; they feel He is right now utterly available to them, that in a real sense He never left them when He withdrew the Ideal Emanation Body known as Shakyamuni. Tibetans think that Shakyamuni Buddha Himself taught both the Universal Vehicle and the Apocalyptic Vehicle, as well as the Monastic Vehicle, and that every human can become a Buddha. They find the proof of this teaching in the presence and deeds of the many people they consider living Buddhas.

Padma Sambhava was the earliest and most legendary: He was born by miracle from a lotus blossom, millennia ago, at approximately the same time as Shakyamuni Buddha. He was adopted as a prince of Afghanistan, then called Odiyana, at the time a cultural part of the Indian subcontinent. He became a perfect Buddha, practicing all three Buddhist Vehicles, the Monastic, the Messianic, and the Apocalyptic. He visited Tibet toward the end of the eighth century of the common era, in the twelfth century of His already long life. His impact in Tibet was crucial; without Him, Buddhism would never have taken root there. He is presented as not only conquering the minds of the kings and warlords of Tibet by extravagant displays of magical power, charismatic kindness, and astounding wisdom, but also as capable of "taming" the savage war gods of Tibet, the wild and powerful deities of the tribes, the Tibetan equivalents of the gods Odin, Zeus, Thor, Indra, and so on. Padma eventually left Tibet but is believed to be still alive today in a hidden paradise, Copper-colored Glory Mountain, somewhere in the vicinity of Madagascar.

Another important Buddha, Atisha, was born naturally as a prince of the Zahor kingdom of the Pala dynasty Bengal, in 982 C.E. At the age of twenty-nine, after extensive Tantric studies, He renounced His throne and became a monk, soon becoming a famous teacher of all levels of Buddhism. At the prompting of the Goddess Tara, He traveled to Java to recover the essential teaching of the messianic spirit of enlightenment of love and compassion. He went to teach in Tibet in 1040 C.E., where He had an enormous impact on the people. He died there around 1054.

A later Buddha, Tsong Khapa, was born in 1357 C.E. in the far northeast of Tibet, in the province of Amdo. He was a child prodigy, recognized early as an incarnation of Manjushri, the god of wisdom. He spent his life from the age of three in study, contemplation, and social action, attaining His own perfect enlightenment in 1398, after a five-year meditation retreat. He founded a progressive movement in Tibetan Buddhism that looked toward the advent of the future Buddha Maitreya, the "Loving One." He revitalized the practice of monasticism through revision of the Vinaya Rule in 1402. He universalized the messianic spirit by founding the Great Miracle Prayer Festival that brought the whole nation together around the Jokang Cathedral in Lhasa for two weeks every new year, beginning in 1409. He refined and spread the wisdom teachings by writing master treatises and establishing a definitive curriculum for cultivating insight in the monastic universities. Above all, He facilitated and energized the Apocalyptic Vehicle, Tantric ritual and contemplative practice and attainment, by giving inspiring and penetrating teachings, writing critical, comprehensive, and lucid treatises, building exquisite three-dimensional mandalas, and initiating hosts of well-prepared disciples. He passed away with a demonstration of miracles in 1419.

The Founding Teacher and His Angelic Disciples

All Tibetans would agree that the kindness these three great men showed the Land of Snows would never have been possible if the most important human of our world-epoch had not first demonstrated the highest evolutionary perfection accessible to humans, the mental and physical enlightenment of Buddhahood. That human being was the prince Siddhartha of the Shakya nation in northern India, who became the unexcelled, perfectly fulfilled Enlightened Lord under the tree of enlightenment in around 536 before the common era. Once a Buddha, His name was Shakyamuni, the "Shakya Sage," considered to have become a form of life beyond the human or the divine, the "Human-Lion" (*Narasimha*), or the "God Beyond Gods" (*Devatideva*). By definition, no being can possibly be more kind to all other beings than a perfect Buddha; such kindness is ultimately something superhuman.

Among the Buddha's many human and divine disciples, there were four great celestial or angelic Bodhisattvas, "Enlightenment Heroes," who are believed to have taken a special interest in Tibet and the Tibetans. These are the female Bodhisattva Tara, Lady of Miraculous Activities, and the usually male Bodhisattvas Lokeshvara, Lord of Compassion, Manjushri, Lord of

Wisdom, and Vajrapani, Lord of Power. These Bodhisattvas are only in one sense disciples of the Buddha; in another sense they are themselves already perfect Buddhas. They became perfect Buddhas innumerable world-eons before our universe and vowed to manifest as disciples of all Buddhas in all world systems in order to mediate between those Buddhas and the human populations of those worlds.

Among these, Lokeshvara and Tara are a kind of divine, or archangelic, couple, a father and mother for Tibetans. He is the mythic Father of the Nation, siring the first six Tibetans during a mythic life as a Bodhisattva monkey in the prehistoric past. Later he reincarnates repeatedly as the emperor, king, or lama (mentor) ruler of Tibet. She is the ever-present Mother of the Nation, a fierce female who unites with the monkey to bring forth the human children who start the race. Later she serves as empress, queen, and defender of the ruler. She manifests numberless incarnations in every walk of life to help Tibetans overcome their difficulties and meet the challenge of making human life meaningful.

Lokeshvara incarnated as the thirty-third emperor, the first great Dharma king of Tibet, Songzen Gambo (ca. 617–698 C.E.). He unified the land, built the first network of Buddhist shrines, had the Tibetan alphabet and grammar created on the model of Sanskrit, and promulgated the foundational Buddhist law code of Tibet. Both of his chief empresses—Bhirkuti, princess of Nepal, and Wencheng, princess of Great T'ang—were incarnations of Tara.

Manjushri was a Buddha countless eons ago who vowed to incarnate in every world a Buddha visited, to ask the hard questions about the profound teaching of selflessness and voidness. His aim is to help people develop the transcendent wisdom that is the sole cause of the ultimate freedom from suffering that is enlightenment. He is a pervasive figure in Buddhist literature, being a god of learning and a patron of literature as well as the archetype of enlightened realization. He incarnated as the thirty-seventh Tibetan emperor, Trisong Detsen (ca. 790–844 C.E.), who built the first monastery in Tibet, inviting the Abbot Shantarakshita and the Adept Padma Sambhava and commissioning the first great wave of translations of Indian Buddhist texts. Later came the "three Manjushris" among teachers: the great scholar, mystic, and first lama ruler of Tibet, the Sakya Pandita Kunga Gyaltsen (1182–1251); the great Nyingma philosopher and mystic Longchen Rabjampa (1308–1363), and the greatest of Tibet's "Renaissance men," scholar, mystic yogi, and social activist Tsong Khapa Losang Drakpa (1357–1419).

Vajrapani, the "Thunderbolt Wielder," is quite fierce in appearance and represents the adamantine power of enlightenment to ward off evil and bring about the good. He incarnated as the fortieth and last Buddhist Tibetan emperor, Tri Relwajen (ca. 866–901 C.E.), who completed the early dynasty's work of unification and cultural transformation. Later he reincarnated as many rulers, ministers, and lamas.

From the time of Lord Atisha, Lokeshvara reincarnated as Dromtonpa (1004–1064), Atisha's main disciple, who founded Radreng Monastery. During the time of Tsong Khapa, he incarnated as Jey Gendun Drubpa (1391–1474), who later became known as the First Dalai Lama. The Dalai Lamas became important spiritual leaders, first of the New Kadam or Geluk Order and eventually, from the coronation of the Great Fifth (1617–1682) in 1642, of the entire nation.

Lokeshvara's continuous reincarnation as the Dalai Lama of the Land of Snows sealed the Bodhisattva's covenant with the Tibetan people: He would always serve them, reborn in many regions, in families of various levels of society, skillfully preserving their realm as a special sanctum of the Buddha Dharma, building a culture that maintained relatively ideal conditions for individuals to educate themselves in Dharma.

Today Tibet has been shattered almost beyond recognition, suffering horrendously for the first time in its two-thousand-year history under the oppressive domination of an outside invader and occupier. Tibetans within and without Tibet still regard the Fourteenth Dalai Lama as their legitimate leader, the current reincarnation of Lokeshvara, and they look with pleading glances to his Ganden Palace government in exile to represent their plight to the world community.

Of course, Lokeshvara, Tara, Manjushri, and Vajrapani are believed to manifest themselves in countless other ways at the same time, and the Tibetan imagination is waiting for their activities to surface in a new era. Lokeshvara manifests himself as other lamas who do not have such political responsibilities, lamas such as the Karmapa incarnations. Manjushri is evident in the manifestations of the Sakya lamas and in many a great scholar, artist, and spiritual teacher. Tara has numerous female incarnations, both formally recognized and informally active. Vajrapani is thought to be exercising his indomitable protective power in some currently unfathomable way. And there are innumerable other messianic figures.

The rich tapestry of the activities of these enlightened beings constitutes the Tibetan sense of history itself. Tibetans live in a multidimensional universe; they are quite aware that a single event appears quite differently to different beings. Thus in history they posit an "ordinary perception" (*thun mong pai snang ba*) and an "extraordinary perception" (*thun mong ma yin pai snang ba*); or sometimes "outer," "inner," and "secret" levels of history. These need not be contradictory. For example, on the ordinary or outer level, Siddhartha was a human prince who was too intelligent to accept an unawakened mode of mechanical living, so he renounced his inherited identity, strove mightily to understand his own innermost essence, and succeeded in attaining complete awakening. At the same time, on an extraordinary or inner level, Shakyamuni had attained Buddhahood many eons earlier and chose this time to incarnate as Siddhartha and manifest the deeds of a Buddha-life in order to educate and liberate the beings of this world.

In the case of the taming of Tibet, on the ordinary level, Songzen Gambo built on the conquests of his ancestors and expanded the Tibetan Empire to its maximum feasible size, spilling over a bit in all directions beyond the gigantic Tibetan plateau. He then began the process of transforming a warrior empire into a peaceful civilization, importing an alphabet, traditions of learning, and a nonviolent ethic, fashioning an appropriate law code, and initiating peaceful relations with neighboring states through treaties sealed with marriages. On the extraordinary level, Lokeshvara and his two Tara consorts looked down into Tibet from their vantage in the South Indian paradise called Potalaka and saw the time was right to bring Buddhism to the Tibetans. A light-meteor streaked from his heart and landed in the womb of the queen of Tibet; similar meteors went from the hearts of the two Tara goddesses to the wombs of the queens of Nepal and T'ang China. Nine months later the prince Songzen was born in Tibet, as was Wencheng in China and Bhirkuti in Nepal, the two princesses destined to become his brides, who brought Buddha icons, books, and learned teachers in their dowry trains. Tibetans believe that every event in the life of an individual and of a nation is susceptible to such a multileveled analysis of meaning.

In a last, extremely poignant, example, on the ordinary level, in the last forty-six years, Tibet has been invaded, occupied, and annexed by the People's Republic of China. This Chinese communist government has made a systematic effort to exterminate Tibetan religious belief and cultural identity, resulting in the deaths of over a million Tibetans and the destruction of all but 13 of Tibet's 6,267 significant monasteries. It has established large colonies of Chinese settlers throughout Tibet, defended by up to half a million troops, whose presence and abuse of land, wildlife, and natural resources have badly damaged the fragile Himalayan ecosystem (the Tibetan plateau has an average altitude of about fifteen thousand feet). How can this be explained on the extraordinary level?

There are various theories. The most compelling one, if somewhat dramatic, is that Vajrapani emanated himself as Mao Tse-tung and took upon himself the heinous sin of destroying the Buddha Dharma's institutions, along with many beings, for three main reasons: to prevent other, ordinarily human, materialists from reaping the consequences of such terrible acts, to challenge the Tibetan Buddhists to let go of the trappings of their religion and philosophy and force themselves to achieve the ability to embody once again in this terrible era their teachings of detachment, compassion, and wisdom, and to scatter the Indo-Tibetan Buddhist teachers and disseminate their teachings throughout the planet among all the people, whether religious or secular, at this apocalyptic time when humanity must make a quantum leap from violence to peacefulness in order to preserve all life on earth.

This all happens within the context of the advent of Shambhala upon the entire planet, according to the prophecy originating with the *Kalachakra Tantra*, a central component of the national cult of Tibet since the seventeenth century. The prophecy emerges in Indian and Tibetan literature in the eleventh century, dating itself from the Buddha's time fifteen hundred years earlier. It shows the Buddha as emanating himself in the form of a "time machine" or "history machine," an embodiment of what the unenlightened perceive as the flow of time, adopting such a form to show his commitment to the future enlightenment of all beings.

Thus this Tantra contradicts the outer or ordinary cosmology that says that the Buddha's teaching lasts for a few thousand years and then disappears until the next Buddha, with the condition of life on the planet worsening until it becomes unimaginably horrible, something like the brahminical notion of a "Dark Age." The Time-machine Buddha rather proclaims that all beings are evolving in a positive or progressive manner, beneath the surface events of a planet apparently dominated by the egoism, militarism, and materialism of gods and humans. Finally, some three thousand years after the Buddha's time, when the outer world is completely dominated by a single materialistic dictatorship, the country of Shambhala emerges from behind an invisible barrier. The dictator's military forces are destroyed trying to conquer this new land, and the enlightened people of Shambhala emerge and share their high-tech, liberated, enlightened style of living with all the other peoples of the planet, ushering in a golden age that lasts for at least eighteen hundred years. Tibetans believe that this age of Shambhala is only a few centuries in the future, and the destruction of the Buddhist institutions in their homeland is a sign of the nearing of the age of liberation, for the whole world, not just for Tibet.

Thus at least one of the levels (the highest, most would say) of the Tibetan sense of history sees the planet as progressing positively toward a time of unprecedented fulfillment. Tibetan Buddhist society therefore is perhaps unique among Buddhist societies in that the people live within a consciously articulated myth of historical progress, carrying within itself a fascinating complexity. The last three centuries under the Dalai Lamas were a kind of millennial time for the Tibetans, since their messiah returned regularly and remained a tangible presence preserving the community. They saw Tibet as a kind of holy land, a pure realm of the highest opportunity for the individual's evolutionary fulfillment. At the same time they understood that this millennial moment itself would perish in a planetary holocaust, only to be reborn one further time during a planetary time of fruition in the age of Shambhala.

Tibetans thus believe that anyone who looks upon the color-particle mandala of the Kalachakra Buddha with reverence and faith will be reborn advantageously during the era of Shambhala. That is why they undertake arduous pilgrimages and make intense efforts to attend performances of the Kalachakra initiation ritual.

2. The Essence of Buddhism Itself

To appreciate essential Tibetan Buddhism, we must look for the essence of Buddhism itself. The Tibetan genius did make its own distinctive contribution to the great river of Buddhism. But Tibetans considered it their discovery, achievement, and special offering to find, embody, preserve, and extend the deep and magnificent Buddha Teaching.

The enlightenment of the Buddha was not primarily a religious discovery. It was not a mystical encounter with "God" or a god. It was not the reception of a divine mission to spread the "Truth" of "God" in the world. The Buddha's enlightenment was rather a human being's direct, exact, and comprehensive experience of the final nature and total structure of reality. It was the culmination for all time of the manifest ideals of any tradition of philosophical exploration or scientific investigation. "Buddha" is not a personal name; it is a title, meaning "awakened," "enlightened," and "evolved." A Buddha's enlightenment is a *perfect omniscience*. A Buddha's mind is what theists have thought the mind of God would have to be like, totally knowing of every single detail of everything in an infinite universe, totally aware of everything—hence by definition inconceivable, incomprehensible to finite, ignorant, egocentric consciousness.

No matter how preposterous it may seem to us at first, it is necessary to acknowledge the Buddha's claim of the attainment of omniscience in enlightenment. It is foundational for every form of Buddhism. It is rarely brought to the fore nowadays, even by Buddhist writers, since this claim by a being once human is uttermost, damnable sacrilege for traditional theists and a primitive fantasy, an utter impossibility, for modern materialists. But it is indispensable for Buddhists. A Buddha is believed to have evolved to a state of knowing everything knowable, evolving out of the states of ignorance of the limited and imperfect awareness of animals, humans, and gods. Therefore the purpose of one's own life, seen as a process of infinite evolution, is to awaken such omniscient awareness within oneself, to transcend the egocentered animal condition to become a perfect Buddha.

Everything in Buddhism follows from this single chain of propositions that the Buddha is believed to have exemplified: Life has the purpose of achieving supreme happiness through total awareness of itself and the universe; every being has been working at this from beginningless time in life after life; the human life-form is itself the result of inconceivable evolutionary efforts and is relatively quite close to ultimate evolutionary fulfillment; this fulfillment, this blossoming, this butterfly awakening, occurs by means of perfecting the understanding, through sensitivity and wisdom; upon such awakening, suffering is no more and happiness is unimaginably complete; and the infinite numbers of beings who have already become such Buddhas are naturally moved to share that happiness with all other beings, which they are doing all the time, effortlessly yet effectively.

In spite of this ultimately rosy picture of evolution, even Buddhas cannot simply force ignorant beings to become wise and therefore free and happy. While the Buddha did, on numerous occasions, calmly mention His attainment of Godlike omniscience, He emphatically disclaimed the possession of the Godlike power of creatorhood. He critically rejected the plausibility of any being having total power and control over all other beings and things. This does not mean that He disbelieved the existence of gods—the Buddha was not an atheist. He not only believed in gods but, like Moses or Jesus, He personally met a great number of them, including Brahma, the god credited with creatorship by many Indian theists, Indra, the Father of the Vedic pantheon, and Yama, the Lord of the Dead. (By definition, Tibetan Buddhists believe that He certainly would have met the Jehovah of the Bible, as well as every god of every nation on the planet.) He gave various accounts of his encounters with this wide variety of gods, angels, and even devils. He found them to be just as real as any other living beings. He simply discovered that no one of them had created the universe, no one of them possessed the key to salvation or liberation, no one of them had attained omniscient awareness. Beyond their immense pride in being powerful gods, they themselves ultimately needed help to save themselves from their own entrapment in suffering, just as humans and other egocentric animals do. They all needed the teachings of perfected Buddhas who have evolved the omniscient awareness of enlightenment. Among a Buddha's most important names are God Beyond Gods and Teacher of Gods and Humans.

As a Buddha, one discovers the unity of one's awareness with the omnipresent awareness of all beings and things. One actually experiences the reality of absolute voidness, one's own and other beings' freedom from a fixed individual and substantial self and all things' freedom from intrinsic identity or objectivity. One integrates this experience of cosmic unity with the realization of one's ability to manifest freely a responsive interactive presence among other beings as a supple, open, happy, blissful, and powerful Buddha person, or even multitude of persons. One lives this realization as the happy relaxation of futile servitude to the illusion of being a fixed subject in a real objective world, enjoying an infinitely fresh and boundless continuum of loving and liberative relationships with others.

Buddha liberation is so happy and complete that it can effortlessly include without distortion or separation the infinite realm of interconnected beings and things. From there one has the experience of all beings as inseparable from oneself; one feels the condition of others. One is sensitive to the continual suffering that arises from their imprisonment within a rigid self-image opposed to an apparently overwhelming objective and alien universe. One's beatitude thus naturally reacts against the self-created suffering of other beings. For them one manifests educational events that help them see through their beginningless delusions and arrive at freedom by coming to an understanding of their own deeper nature. This natural and inexhaustible reaction energizes the Buddhist liberative arts and the teachings of the way of freedom through exact intuition of the nature of all things.

3. The Teaching:
The Buddhist Enlightenment Movement

Tibetans believe then that Buddha Shakyamuni's enlightenment is not mystical, in the sense of "contrary to reason." It is rational, guided by a critical inquiry into the nature of the reality of self and of the world, and experimental, proceeding from solid conclusions to the experiential verification of those conclusions. Indeed, the Buddha considered beings' ignorance, their insistence on the illusion of an intrinsically established world of beings and things, to be "mystical" and "nonrational." He did not consider irrational faith, even in good things such as liberation and enlightenment, to be powerful enough in itself to bring a being to liberation.

It is thus clear that His compassion for beings forced Him not to offer them a religious solution to their predicament, a redemptive belief in Him, or any dogma, deity, salvific rite, or membership in a group of elect. Since

He knew that the only means for beings to gain freedom was their individual understanding of their unique situation, He was forced to try to help them come to such an understanding. Simple faith cannot produce such understanding. Blind faith in implausible things blocks understanding, preventing the open experience of reality itself, and rational faith becomes obsolete once understanding takes over. Buddha was thus compelled to create methods of *education* for beings, "education" in the true sense of eliciting in beings the understanding of which they are capable, without indoctrinating or conditioning them. As the celebrated verse of Matercheta, a well-known author of the third century C.E., says: "Buddhas do not wash away sins with water, They do not heal suffering by laying on of hands, and They do not transmit their understanding into others' minds; They introduce beings to freedom by educating them about reality."

According to this perspective, Shakyamuni had to face a monumental task: He had to found an educational movement in a society that was organized only for professional training and religious indoctrination. He rejected the Vedas, the brahminical Scriptures of the day, not in order to found an opposing religion but because He found religion itself to be of limited value, even of negative value, in His enterprise of educating beings for freedom. He lived in a world wherein a healthy secularity had begun to develop only among the merchant classes of the cities, those who generated the Indian traditions of "the good life"—namely, materialists, economists, and political scientists.

Shakyamuni was brought up by His father to become a military general and ruler of men, the first duty of a city-state monarch being military organization and social discipline. Thus when His beatitude moved Him to offer an educational process to His contemporaries and posterity, He began His work in a skillfully organized manner. His organization was militant in a way precisely opposite to the prevailing militancy of military organizations.

His enlightenment showed Him a new meaning and purpose for human life. It should not be wasted on relatively unsatisfying egocentric pleasure, on procreation, economic productivity, conquest, the amassing of riches, fame, glory, or even on religious piety, purity, or sanctity. He found Himself infinitely intertwined with the fates and feelings of infinite beings. He recognized that human beings are biologically best suited to awaken, to discover their own ultimate freedom and immortal beatitude. He had the powerful interest of His infinite altruism in redirecting humans' investment of their life-energies, shifting it from mundane preoccupations toward evolutionary and liberative ends.

He built on the existing Indian tradition of ascetic, wandering truth-seekers (*shramana*) and founded the monastic Community (*Sangha*). Alert to the tensions this would create with the warrior-kings, He proclaimed the Community to be an "other world," a sacred realm, a spiritual society outside ordinary society. He pledged the continuing obedience to the king's law of anyone still within the king's realm of ordinary society. He asked only for exemptions and special support for those who moved outside into the extrasocial Community: exemptions from duties of productive labor, procreation, family, military service, and taxes, and special support in the form of free time for self-development, free food for subsistence, free land for temporary shelter, and free cloth for robes, all limited to the minimum necessary. He was alert also to the danger of threatening too strongly the religious priesthood of the times, so He prohibited His mendicant monks and nuns from performing priestly services. They were not allowed to perform rites of birth, blessing, marriage, funerals, or divinations and were forbidden to perform miracles or healings.

4. *The History of This Movement in India and Its Spread Throughout Asia*

This militant organization of the previously loose-knit ascetic traditions was utterly revolutionary. The Buddha's near contemporaries such as Confucius and Socrates had no such luck in organizing their movements; nor did the much later Mencius, Chuang Tzu, Jesus, Paul, or Peter. The mainstream activity in all the Eurasian city-states of this time was the opposite—namely, the organizing of professional armies, in the manner of Darius of Persia, Ajatashatru of Magadha, Alexander the Great, Ashoka Maurya, Chin Shih Huang-ti, and the caesars. Like the monk or nun, the professional soldier also left ordinary occupations in the service of a universal ideal—world conquest, the very one prince Siddhartha had abandoned to become a Buddha. Like a renunciant, the soldier also shaved his head, donned an impersonal uniform, and trained himself to face death unflinchingly. Like an ascetic, the soldier abandoned ordinary social constraints for the frenzy of battle, dropping all normal concerns in the *samadhi* of slaughter. The language of the Buddhist Sangha was a mirror image of military language: The monk was to conquer his inner enemy, face death moment to moment, and give up attachment to comfort and even the sense of personality in order to find the victory of liberation and transcendent bliss.

In sum, the Buddhist monastic, educational movement was the only major universally expanding institution in ancient urban India other than the universally expanding military organizations and mercantile trade empires that gradually developed the sixteen city-states of the Buddha's time into the Magadhan and Mauryan empires. The monastic organization was a kind of inversion of the military organization: a peace army rather than a war army, a self-conquest tradition rather than an other-conquest tradition, a science of inner liberation rather than a science of liberating the outer world from the possession of others. If we understand this perspective, then the later, millennia-long encounter between monasticism and militarism throughout Asia, and especially in Tibet, emerges in an entirely new light.

In its role as universal educator, the Buddhist Sangha can be seen as a powerful "taming," or civilizing, force in ancient India. It was the one multinational institution, opposed to the conquest army and the trade empire, that could provide the individual some bulwark against the power of the monarch and his state. It also was the engine of the inward-looking bent of Indian science, which, in contrast to the sciences of Greece, Iran, or China, found the inner world of the mind and its energies more important than the outer world of natural elements and forces. The systematic effort of monastic education to measure, understand, and control the mind for the purpose of human betterment resulted in India's unique refinement of various kinds of *yoga*, technologies for harnessing mind and body to achieve happiness more effectively. Once we glimpse in this way how the Buddhists created the main institution outside the state and developed the curricula of taming, liberating, and empowering education, we can better assess its key constitutive role in the formation of classical Indian civilization, its arts, philosophies, religions, state institutions, and social ethics. This then changes the way we look at Buddhist institutions in relation to social development in later societies where Buddhism became even more influential.

5. The Three Stages of Buddhism in India and Beyond

Most modern historians of Indian Buddhism have seen "early" or "pristine" Buddhism as the monastic Buddhism known from the Pali literature, the only one they consider close to credibly attributable to Shakyamuni Buddha. The messianic Buddhism of the Universal Vehicle is viewed as later Buddhism's desperate attempt to compete with "Hinduism," with its popular worship of gods. These historians' account puts Tibetan Buddhism in the worst possible context, as the extension of a degenerate form of Indian Buddhism. According to this depiction, Buddhist monks were losing ground with the people, so they made up a "Universal Vehicle," which put monks in a lower place (odd that they would demote themselves!), deified the Buddha, preached an almost nihilistic philosophy of voidness and a social gospel of universal love and compassion; then they attributed this new Vehicle to the Buddha. This strategy kept Buddhism's head above the flood of popular Hinduism for a while, so the story goes, somehow persuading the people to continue to support the newly devalued monks. A few centuries further down the slope, popular magic and mysticism became more irresistible, and so this universal, messianic Buddhism compromised even further by developing an esoteric Adamantine or Apocalyptic Vehicle. Buddhism now incorporated Vedic fire-sacrifice rituals, mantras, mandalas, feasts, sexuality, breath control, and yoga, along with an even more imaginatively lush deification of the Buddha, on top of the inclusion of women in the ranks of religious virtuosi. After reaching this lowest level of popularization, so the account goes, nothing was left for Indian Buddhism but to sink into the swamp of Hinduism, submerging its own identity forever and disappearing from the land of its birth.

The main difficulty with such a rendering of Indian Buddhism's evolution—the inexplicable mystery of it—is, if Buddhists kept needing to compromise to compete with Hinduism for survival, why didn't they simply forget the whole thing and become Hindus? They were all born Hindus. Since the Buddha was apparently such a detriment, such a killjoy, why keep bothering with him at all century after century?

Obviously there must have been something more satisfying about being a Buddhist than developing elaborate ways to compete with Hindus.

The evidence in fact supports a view of Buddhism as a powerful social movement with a definite educating and civilizing program. During its fifteen-hundred-year sojourn in India, the Buddhist education movement was a catalyst for liberation and progress. The three Vehicles (Monastic, Messianic, and Apocalyptic Vehicles) so crucial to Tibetan Buddhism were manifestations of a progressive development.

Its first five hundred years were primarily monastic, solidifying the extrasocial society of the Sangha and providing the educationally oriented individual an asylum from economic, social, political, and religious demands. During its next five hundred years—with the addition of the Messianic Vehicle—Indian Buddhism moved aggressively outward from a solid monastic base in the economy, society, and culture (already changed by five centuries of feedback from the thriving educational community) to tackle the more violent aspects of society and to teach a social ethic of love and compassion. Its last five hundred years were culminatively apocalyptic: Insisting on a more evolved level of behavior in developed society, Buddhists entered the marginal areas of society among the lower castes, tribals, and foreigners, such as the Tibetans. They used magical and charismatic means to teach people who could not be approached within the literate conventions of the by now highly refined, urbane, peaceful, and civilized Sanskrit society.

In sum, we can see the Three Vehicles or styles of Buddhism as products of the gradual improvement of an entire civilization. That society had originally responded to the basic egocentrism of individuals not by questioning it but by controlling it through a system of beliefs, rituals, duties, and manners that required individuals to sacrifice themselves for the group. The evolving goal, by contrast, was a condition where individuals challenged the egocentric outlook and actually went on not only to experience freedom from it but also to live and flourish within that freedom. The table included here summarizes this new account of the development of Buddhism in India.

VEHICLES OR STYLES
OF BUDDHISM IN INDIA

A. INDIVIDUALISTIC STYLE, MONASTIC BUDDHISM—
DOMINANT CA. 500 B.C.E. TO 0 C.E.

    1. Emphasizes monasticism as necessary for individual liberation.

    2. Socially revolutionary, stressing ethical dualism, though antitheistic.

    3. Ideal of monks and nuns is *arhat*—sainthood.

    4. Urges lay community toward tenfold path of good and bad evolutionary action.

    5. Warrior training reversed produces tamed person, free of wild, egocentric drives.

    6. Social result: tamed-warrior society, values supporting urban, merchant classes.

    7. Spreads outside India—mainly to Sri Lanka, central Asia, Iran, and west Asia.

B. UNIVERSALISTIC STYLE, MESSIANIC BUDDHISM—
DOMINANT 0 TO 500 C.E.

    1. Incorporating core monasticism, reaches out nondually into lay society to transform social ethic through love and compassion.

    2. Socially evolutionary; monasteries develop into universities.

    3. Ideal of the Bodhisattva, hero/ine who aims to liberate all beings from suffering and to transform the universe into a buddhaverse; doctrine of the Three Bodies of Buddha, Truth, Beatific, Emanation.

    4. Nondualism of Nirvana/samsara undergirds nonduality of wisdom and compassion, monastic Sangha and lay society.

5. Conscious adoption of the process of evolution, wherein one embarks on a career of millions of future individual lives to evolve to Buddhahood.

6. Social result: moves a more civilized society toward a universalistic orientation; frees the popular imagination to envision a colorful cosmos of infinite buddhaverse.

7. Spreads to wherever monastic style spread and farther to China and the Mediterranean.

C. APOCALYPTIC STYLE, ESOTERIC, MAGICAL BUDDHISM — DOMINANT CA. 500–1000 C.E.

1. Socially culminatory, monastic universities reach out beyond the literate state into marginal areas. Unpacks furthest implications of messianic style.

2. Ideal of the Mahasiddha, female or male Great Adept, the "psychonaut" of Indian inner science, actual perfect Buddha maintaining ordinary human form in history, latent kingship of individual explicated ritually and artistically.

3. Nondualism elucidated to include everything, including sexuality, death; wisdom-compassion union becomes wisdom-bliss union, Buddhahood as male-female-sexual-union-orgasmic reality.

4. Apocalyptic insistence on accelerating history and evolution, realization of individual Buddhahood and universal buddhaverse here and now, in this lifetime preferably, through magical, high-tech means.

5. Social result: elevation of women; expansion of culture to marginal low castes, tribals, aliens; permeation of high culture with aesthetic values; loosening of rigidities; living beyond this-life identities; unilateral disarmament.

6. Spreads everywhere monastic and messianic styles spread, though in subtle streams, reaching farther to Indonesia, Korea, Japan, and Tibet, uniquely kept in total integration with two previous styles in Tibet and later Mongolia.

The first of these five-hundred-year periods, the monastic Buddhist period, established its main foothold outside India in Sri Lanka, where it continues today. The second, the messianic Buddhist period, spread also to Sri Lanka in the same way it was integrated with monastic Buddhism in India, but it also opened up new territory in central Asia and from there into China. The third, apocalyptic Buddhist, period was integrated with both monastic and messianic institutions and spread everywhere through the

Buddhist world in small streams. But then it transplanted itself wholesale into Tibet, especially at the end of Indian Buddhism, due to the Islamically driven cultural transformation of India from the eleventh century. After the loss of Buddhist India, as the matrix civilization within which the three styles or Vehicles were nested, Sri Lanka rejected apocalyptic and messianic styles and became a bastion of the monastic style alone. East Asia emphasized monastic and messianic styles, allowing only a trickle of the apocalyptic to survive. Only Tibet attempted to incorporate all three styles in their originally integrated pattern.

6. The Advent of Buddhism in Tibet

It apparently took the efforts of living Buddhas to establish Buddhism in Tibet. Great Adepts such as Padma Sambhava and Atisha were archetypes of the apocalyptic style of the Tantric Vehicle. They had to manifest direct control of the processes of nature, of life and death, to impress the Tibetans, who were used to shamanic priests of intense charisma and who had no literate culture as India and China did. Tibetans were tribalistic theists and fierce militarists, having developed the technology and social organization necessary for large-scale campaigns of conquest. They had an elaborate cult of divine kingship, probably modeled on what they had learned of Persian imperial customs, including large-scale sacrificial rituals, elaborate tumuli, court priests and magicians, and family, tribal, regional, and national gods. It is likely, however, that the authority of the royal family still relied on continually renewed success in conquest, holding together the alliance of regional warlords on the basis of the common advantage of extending dominion and increasing spoils. As in Japan during the same centuries, there was probably no clear-cut ideology of imperial supremacy internalized by the nobles or the people that could guarantee the survival of the central dynasty in times of hardship.

The royal dynasty therefore found that its spiritual inspirations coincided nicely with its political interests in its multigenerational drive to import Buddhism from India. By doing so, it imitated regimes in India, central Asia, and China, creating spiritual legitimacy for the dynasty as defenders of the Dharma, developing systems of writing, education, mythology, law, scientific and humane medicine, literature, and art modeled on the sophisticated traditions of India. Of course there were strong tensions inherent in a warrior dynasty becoming the sponsor of a peace-cultivating, nonviolent educational system, pattern of religious beliefs, and social norms. While these would ultimately prove unsustainable by that dynasty, for more than two centuries the new import was considered highly beneficial for both the regime and the people.

Buddhism was accepted in Tibet only because they perceived it as delivered by some sort of superior being, whom they learned to call a Buddha. It arrived in Tibet full-blown, with its monastic education, universalistic social ethic, and apocalyptic vision of reality. It had to confront and overcome an already developed priestcraft capable of addressing every aspect of life and death—birth, marriage, economic ethics, magic, protection against demons, and so forth. In the mid-seventh century, an emperor named Songzen Gambo (a near contemporary of the Japanese culture-transformer Prince Shotoku Taishi) began the attempt to transform the civilization from feudal militarism to peaceful monasticism. In a systematic process of culture building, he sent a team of scholars to India to learn Sanskrit, to create a written language for Tibetan, and to begin to translate the vast Buddhist literature. He married nine queens from neighboring countries, requesting each to bring Buddhist artifacts and texts with her to Tibet. He built a system of imperial temples laid out in a geomantic grid, centering on the Jokhang and Ramoche cathedrals in his new capital at Lhasa, thereby creating a geometry of sacredness to contain the nation.

For the next two centuries, subsequent emperors continued his work, defending Tibet internationally against Arab, Turkish, and Chinese powers, sponsoring translations, holding conferences, building Buddhist institutions, and educating the people. Around the turn of the ninth century, the Emperor Trisong Detsen, with the help of the magical intervention of the Great Adept Padma Sambhava and the monastic knowledge of the Indian Abbot Shantarakshita, built the first monastery at Samyey. He thus imported the Indian Buddhist university curriculum and began a sixty-year process of collecting all useful knowledge then available. Mathematics, poetry, medicine, the art of government, fine arts, and architecture—all these branches of learning were cultivated, not only Buddhist philosophy and psychology. Scholars were invited from Persia, India, the Turkish and Mongolian silk-route states, and T'ang China. Tibetans developed their genius at comparison and combination, looking for the best understanding of humanity and nature.

Padma Sambhava spent this time ranging around the country, imparting to the most capable disciples the most advanced teachings, taking them on long retreats, and even wrestling with and "taming" the tribal gods of Tibet, gods of mountains, rivers, and sacred springs, gods of sky, and gods of earth. He thus planted the seeds of the internal transformation of the people, starting a chain reaction of changing individual hearts from egocentric violence and insensitivity to openness of identity, altruism of sensibility, and peacefulness of fulfillment.

After the high point of Samyey's ascendancy during the ninth century, a period of confusion ensued, brought about by the contradictions of a military dynasty sponsoring a national pacification campaign. There was a revolt within the royal family itself. Assassinations and coups d'etat ended with the collapse of the dynasty, the regional fragmentation of the nation, and the suppression of Buddhism as the official culture. However, the twenty-five major, and numerous minor, lay teachers who had become Great Adepts under the tutelage of Padma Sambhava evaded the suppression and preserved many of the teachings in a countercultural movement that endured. These lineages of masters of inner knowledge persisted through the next century, and a sense of the power and benefits of Buddhism, a longing for the beauty of its vision of a higher world, was kept alive at the grassroots level. In fact, after a little more than a century, when regional rulers returned to official patronage of Buddhism, their efforts resonated with a groundswell of popular support that was the flowering of the seeds planted by Padma Sambhava.

7. The Later Dissemination of Buddhism

The second major phase of the spread of Buddhism began with the advent of Atisha Dipamkara Shrijnana (982–1054) in 1042. Atisha's impact on Tibet was profound: It was possible, as in the case of Padma Sambhava in the early period, only because he was perceived as a superior being, as a Buddha.

In the new climate of the eleventh century, Atisha was able to bring to Tibet the living synthesis of mature Indian Buddhism, a Buddhism that had fully integrated the Monastic, Messianic, and Apocalyptic Vehicles of practice. Other Indian teachers visited Tibet around Atisha's time, but he alone became known as *Jowo Jey*, "Lord Buddha Master," meaning "a spiritual master who is himself a Buddha." (The other major figure in Tibet called *Jowo* is Jowo Rinpoche, the national icon of Lord Buddha, the sacred statue of Shakyamuni Buddha that was installed by Songzen Gambo in the Jokhang Cathedral in Lhasa.) This superlative honorific indicates the immensity of Atisha's importance. It is not just that he was a great pandit, not just a "reformer" backed by the king of the west, not just a dean from Nalanda Monastic University in India. He must have been seen by contemporary Tibetans as a Buddha in human form, a fully evolved yet perfectly adapted being who made the Tibetans realize that the door to their own full evolution and perfect adaptation was open wide.

Atisha was from Bengal, he knew Sanskrit, he had a pleasing appearance and a royal manner, and he was sixty years of age when he arrived in Tibet and had spent many years in Java. All of these attributes are important in understanding the impact Atisha had on the Tibetans. But these attributes pale in importance next to the apparent fact that Tibetans thought they saw in him a living Buddha.

Tibetans by this time were widely familiar with the Buddhist narratives wherein Shakyamuni Buddha's presence seemed to lift people to their feet, put them in a state of heightened awareness, bring out their strongest emotions, and often stimulate them to unprecedented understandings. The five ascetics, companions of young Siddhartha, were forced to stand up against their will when the Buddha came back from Bodhgaya to Saranath. Yashas, a young "yuppie," attained sainthood in eight hours, despite a serious hangover, due to the power of Buddha's calming and inspiring presence. It invariably impressed the most willful kings, quite used to doing as they pleased, even though all too often they were pleased to chop off heads and conquer countries. Buddha's presence always inspired gods and demons with a determination to do better, even with their own cosmic powers. In the Mahayana texts in particular, the Buddha was constantly performing amazing miracles that stimulated extraordinary visions and transformative insights in vast audiences. Tibetans were fully steeped in the literature of such accounts.

Thus a Buddha embodiment was supposed to be a manifestation of compassion with no other purpose than to open people up to their own higher potential. It seemed natural to Tibetans, therefore, that the field of a Buddha should create a space for people to change, an atmosphere wherein anything was possible and the loftiest aspirations seemed accessible. This is because the consciousness of a Buddha is divined to be quite opposite to our ordinary consciousness. A Buddha has directly experienced selflessness and so feels of one body with an infinite peace and freedom, not apart from things and beings but enfolding them all completely. Thus a Buddha feels other beings in his or her field as intimately as they feel themselves. This means that a Buddha has no solid sense of center as we do, and so when we meet one, we feel something indefinably different than when we meet another ordinary being, in whom we sense a self-center as solid as we feel our own to be. This introduces a new dimension to relating and changes the pressure of the encounter. A Buddha's energy is entirely with and for us when we encounter it; there is in it no energy scoop or surge opposed to our own.

Tibetans say that an Ideal Emanation Body Buddha appears only at certain moments in certain societies, when people are able to bear the alien aspects and benefit from the intensity of such an Emanation. An Ideal Emanation is believed to exhibit a brain-dome called an *ushnisha,* light-webbed fingers and toes, golden skin, retracted genitalia, a midbrow hair tuft called an *urna* that radiates holographic displays—an imaginative presentation. Shakyamuni is the only such fully marked Buddha to appear in our era. More usually, a Buddha Adept manifests as an Incarnation Emanation, in a relatively ordinary body, as a teacher, a scholar, a ruler, a companion, a mother, a father; "in whatever way tames whomsoever," as the verse says. Such a being, whatever his or her form, is the focal node of a field in which other beings find maximal opportunities for their own evolutionary advancement, gaining dramatically increased understanding, improved emotions, perceptions, and insights, feeling much better, often rising to the occasion and doing and understanding much better.

To return to Atisha, his stay in Tibet was rather short. He was there only twelve years. An ordinary being, just another vagrant Indian intellectual, could never have had such a powerful impact. A number of other visiting Indian masters did good works but did not leave such an extreme impression. But if we recognize that Atisha was perceived as a walking, talking, living buddha-field, surrounding the embodiment of a highly gifted Indian pandit, his impact becomes understandable.

The scope of his benefit to Tibet goes beyond the power of his example, which only enabled him to get started. His real benefit came from the fact that he established a synthesis of all the key methods of Buddhism for developing people. His teaching epitomized the integration of the methods that gave Buddhism the power and range in Tibet to respond effectively to the difficult challenge of transforming the crude, undereducated, rather violent and lusty warrior Tibetans into a nation of yogins and yoginis. His famous motto was called the Four Square Path:

All teachings should be understood as free of contradictions;
All Buddha-discourses take effect as practical instructions;
The Buddha's intention is easily discovered; and thereby,
The serious bad behavior of Dharma-rejection self-destructs.

Since the Buddhist institutions were recovering in Tibet from a period of suppression, confusion, and disorganization, Atisha was invited to Tibet to use his encyclopedic knowledge of Buddhist literature to provide criteria to distinguish between authentic Buddhist teachings and spurious fabrications. However, in a famous dialogue (see chapter 3), Atisha upheld the master's personal precept as the lifeline of the true Dharma, more important even than the authoritative canonical texts. He said that the "instruction of the Mentor" was more important than knowledge of all the Scriptures and their commentaries. This is because the authentic guru, lama, master, or spiritual mentor, is the representative of the immediate applicability of the teachings to an individual who needs methods to put into practice. General knowledge of doctrine is useful but does not automatically come with the skill to apply it. The mentor is the key element that makes the teachings practicable.

Thus, in the situation of confusion in Tibet at the time, with valid and spurious teachings mixed together in a poorly understood jumble, the first rule to lay down was that the Buddha's teachings have no internal contradiction, if properly interpreted. Second, insofar as the method of interpretation goes, we must remember that a Buddha is always speaking to a specific audience in a specific context and is always concerned with the practical impact of His teaching. He is not just spouting abstract truths that are fixed in some absolute apart from the living reality of the beings who need them. This rule of interpretation means that the enlightened mentor is necessary to extract the instructional bottom line from the discourse or Scripture, since it is his or her job to decide which teaching applies to which practitioner.

In a famous simile the Buddha Master was fond of, the practitioner is like a patient, the Dharma is like the medicine, the mentor is the physician who analyzes the patient's sickness and prescribes a specific medicine, and the practice of the Dharma is the therapy. Atisha thus emphasized the essential role of the physician, the lama or mentor, when he said that the mentor's instruction is more important than all the Scriptures. It does a sick person no good to have a suitcase full of medicines if he does not know which one to take for his condition.

In that simple statement, Atisha set down the principle of the priority of the mentor, which was the foundation of Tibetan Buddhism (the focus on the mentor is probably why it was called "Lamaism" by some observers, though they meant it as a derogatory term, intimating that Tibetan Buddhism had lost the "pure," "original" thrust of Buddhism, which they thought was to value the medicine more than the physician). But Atisha did not invent this just for the Tibetans. It was the foundation of the final Indian synthesis of Buddhism as the integration of monastic, messianic, and apocalyptic styles. It reveals Atisha's thoroughly Tantric, apocalyptic orientation. It presupposes that there is no dearth of authentic mentors. Due to the efficacy of the apocalyptic teachings, actual Incarnational Emanation Body Buddhas are plentiful, appearing as semiordinary humans, as Great Adepts, whether monastics or laypeople.

Atisha had studied and practiced Tantra as a layman and prince until the age of twenty-nine. He became ordained as a monastic at the prompting of Dakinis, the esoteric angels who guard the apocalyptic teachings, in order to integrate his deep insight with a life-form appropriate to his mission for others. He was thus able to bring to Tibet the complete synthesis of the three Vehicles already full-blown in India. Here Tantra is the supreme Vehicle of the three, the most powerful tool to accelerate the individual's evolution from common human to Buddha. Yet this emphasis is systematically integrated with the other Vehicles. As Atisha taught it, there is no motive to attempt Tantric evolution-acceleration unless the individual has the messianic determination of the Bodhisattva, for which the total commitment of the Universal Vehicle is required. And there can be no messianic determination to liberate all beings unless the individual has first gained a taste of and orientation toward liberation. This orientation can come only from the renunciative, individual Vehicle of monastic Buddhism, through which one becomes free of the worldly, "this-life" concerns of fame, gain, praise, success, and their opposites and achieves the relief of abandoning irrelevant ambitions and anxieties. Finally, the wisdom of selflessness is the foundation of the entire enterprise of Tantric transformation. Without some degree of realization of voidness or selflessness, one will not have liberated the energy of the imagination required to begin, one will be in danger of transferring the routinely frozen imagination from the ordinary objective world to a psychotic fixation on an extraordinary perfected world, and there will be no chance of becoming a successful Adept.

In sum, Atisha was by no means a dry monastic who was against Tantra, and neither was Dromtonpa (1004–1064, the first incarnation in Tibet of that series of Lokeshvara incarnations that eventually became the Dalai Lamas), who remained an ordained layman purposely in order to receive the higher initiations. When Atisha refused initiation to some nobles on a few celebrated occasions, he was merely safeguarding Tantric practice for those properly prepared for it by discerning the different aptitudes of different people and accurately gauging the teachings for them. Not everyone should be taught what is supposed to be esoteric until they have developed the foundations. Thus he kept Tantra integrated with the whole of Buddhist practice, since people need a specific foundation to succeed in the advanced practice of the Apocalyptic Vehicle.

Atisha wrote the first book by an Indian master in Tibetan, the *Lamp for the Path of Enlightenment* (also the first Tibetan Buddhist book translated back into Sanskrit for the benefit of Indian Buddhists). This book was absolutely seminal for the central genre of Tibet Buddhist writings, of which there are examples from the literature of each of the orders, the "Path of Enlightenment" genre.

Like all great Indian Buddhist masters of his era, Atisha was intensely aware of the greatness of the Tantras as the keys to the transformation of the universe into the buddhaverse and as the most high-tech and efficacious arts of liberating beings. But that did not mean that all beings were capable right away of leaping into Tantric perfections. There were different kinds of beings, each needing a precise therapy for a precise condition. All could be developed to the point where they could have the sublime good fortune to encounter Tantra. So all teachings, for the individual and for this young, frontier society of Tibet, were set within the context of the possibility and opportunity of Tantra but with precise avenues of entry according to the various levels of ability.

Some popular Tantric teachers in eleventh-century Tibet, enchanted with the beauty of Tantric visions, tended to forget about the strictures of secrecy and the careful prerequisites laid out in the Tantric texts. Less comprehensive in pedagogical outlook than Atisha, they taught the highest Tantras indiscriminately to everyone. Atisha saw that simple peasants and illiterate warriors could be seriously misled if they heard some of the shocking statements in the Tantric Scriptures (describing the unconscious long before Freud and his id) that might seem to encourage seekers to kill their parents, or even all beings, to eat human flesh, to couple with mothers and daughters or with all women or all men in order to achieve Buddhahood!

Atisha, his disciple Drom, and their successors gave a body of teachings that addressed the everyday problems of taming the mind, dwelling in a monastery, conquering an obsession with worldly concerns, cultivating love and compassion for all beings, and attaining the wisdom of the realization of selflessness. This intense concentration on the immediacy of transcendence, the universality of love, and the liberation of wisdom and insight provided the basis for the explosion of religious fervor and accomplishment that led to the mushrooming of the monasticism of all orders in Tibet from the eleventh through the fourteenth century. This movement resulted in the transformation of not merely a few individuals or only the monastic communities. It resulted in the transformation of the entire society.

8. The "Buddhicization" Process: Monasticism and Asceticism in the Medieval Period

It is said that when Atisha traveled through the southwest of Tibet, he had visions of many Bodhisattvas, especially Manjushri, at a place where the earth was yellow-gray (*sa-skya*), visions of a great Dharma activity to come there, conferring great benefit on all beings. The Khon family was the dominant nobility of the region, tracing their lineage back to Lui Wangpo, one of the seven original Tibetan monks ordained by Shantarakshita at Samyey. The spiritual traditions from those early days had been transmitted within the family down through the generations, a part of the social legitimacy of the family in the region surely being their possession of these ancient teachings, not to mention the positive qualities inculcated by those teachings.

In the middle of the eleventh century, the kings of Ngari Korsum, Yeshe and Jangchub Oeu, uncle and nephew, were themselves ordained monastics, combining in their persons the functions of ruler and priest. Their activities set a new style of unifying the religious and the political, and their popularity increased due to their sponsorship of Atisha and other masters. These kings had acquired a new vision of the purpose of human life, a vision that put the individual's self-cultivation at the center of the social system, a main priority for the society as a whole as well as for the individual concerned. This caused them to rationalize all the social arrangements of production, distribution, law and order, and ritual activities in terms of allowing the maximum number of individuals to devote themselves to educational and spiritual development for the maximum time. The Buddhist monastery was the already time-tested institution founded on such a rationalization, having delivered in India maximum free time to a maximum number of people over many centuries. Thus the kings built and sustained more and more monasteries. The monastic model of Atisha's Kadam order was typical, with Drom's main monastery, Redreng, founded earliest, between 1056 and 1064. It had the financial support of the noble Dam family of that locality as well as of Atisha's far-flung network of admirers.

The Khon family followed the same model in founding the monastery and order of Sakya in 1073. They incorporated as well the new style of leadership, combining their social status as nobility in the region with the spiritual abbacy of the monastery. The inspiration for their movement came not from the political arena but from the spiritual. The Indian Buddhist monk and Tantric Adept Virupa, having mastered his monastic studies—perfecting his self-control, extending his messianic commitment, and gaining deep insight into selflessness and voidness—entered the Tantric way of acceleration of his physical and spiritual evolution toward Buddhahood.

He focused on propitiation of the wisdom goddess archetype form Vajranairatmya. Finally he attained total Buddhahood on the subtle body-mind level, choosing to remain in the coarse world in his former gross body as a Great Adept (*Mahasiddha*), the human ideal added by apocalyptic Buddhism to the ideals of arhat and Bodhisattva. His unconventional actions in India are well known, especially his mythic wine drinking, his conquests of various groups of sacrificialists, and his propagation of Buddhism among various new populations.

Among his disciples was the translator Drogmi, who had already spent many years in India in study and practice. Drogmi was initiated by Prajnendraruchi into the Hevajra Tantra, with its sophisticated arts and sciences. He was also taught Virupa's special method of organizing all the Buddhist teachings into preparation for the Hevajra practice, a tradition known as "Path and Fruition," based on the Diamond Verse (*Dorje tsig khang*). Drogmi returned to Tibet after thirteen years of study and began to teach many disciples. After that, he hosted the pandit Gayadhara in Tibet, receiving further teachings on "Path and Fruition."

One of Drogmi's disciples was Khon Konchok Gyalpo, a scion of the Khon family. He established a hermitage at Sakya, supported by the family, which gradually grew into a major center for study and practice. Finally it became a monastic university, with a tradition of always having a member of the Khon family as abbot, usually one considered to be a reincarnation of Manjushri or another Bodhisattva. To resolve the problem of succession for celibate, childless monk leaders, they instituted the system of succession from uncle to nephew, generation after generation.

The "Path and Fruition" teachings synthesized the monastic, messianic, and apocalyptic methods into a practical system designed to lead all individuals from wherever they had evolved through the stages of transcendence, compassion, and wisdom of identitylessness toward enlightenment. The process is designed to introduce them as soon as possible to the Tantric initiation into the mandala of the archetype deity Hevajra. This enables them to use the precious human embodiment to practice the creation and perfection stages of Unexcelled Yoga in order to accelerate their attainment of Buddhahood.

The social model of an aristocratic lineage associating itself with a charismatic center of study and attainment became widely popular among all the Buddhist orders flourishing in Tibet from that time. In the thirteenth century the Mongolian warlord Godan Khan summoned the Sakya Pandita Kunga Gyaltsen (1181–1251) to represent Tibet within the Mongol Empire. His successor, his nephew Pakpa (1234–1280), was later named regent of Tibet by the Emperor Khubilai Khan, thus beginning the Tibetan innovation within Buddhism of a monastic serving as sovereign of a nation, taking responsibility for his people's social as well as spiritual welfare. During this time Tibet was divided into thirteen provinces, almost all of them ruled by a noble family associated with an important monastic center of one order or another. The main orders, all founded in the eleventh and twelfth centuries, were the Kadampa, the Sakyapa, the Kagyupa, and the Nyingmapa (slowest to form as an independent monastic order since it was based on the lay teacher lineages that had survived from the time of Padma Sambhava).

While the Khon family invested its aristocratic prestige in the development of the Sakya order, another process was continuing among the rural masses, epitomized in the history of Marpa and Milarepa and the founding of the Kagyupa orders. Marpa (1012–1099) came from a family of rich peasants and merchants in the Lhodrag region of southern Tibet. He had the ambition to adopt the highly respected profession called *lotsawa* (translator or "national eye"), seeking through knowledge of India's higher, more enlightenment-oriented culture greater knowledge and a better life for his fellow Tibetans. He began his studies with the translator Drogmi but soon decided to make the arduous journey to Nepal and India to find his destined spiritual mentors. He met many teachers, most important being his root mentor, Naropa, who had retired from his post as the head scholar of Nalanda University in order to pursue his own Tantric studies under the mentor Tilopa, and had become, after many studies and ordeals, a Great Adept in his own right.

The teachings that Marpa brought back with him from his study and practice journeys were essentially the same as those brought by Atisha and Drogmi: the monastic practice and path of renunciation and transcendence, the messianic practices of love, compassion, and universal responsibility, coupled with the wisdom of voidness, and the swift engagement in the contemplative evolutionary practices of Unexcelled Yoga Tantras. Marpa added to the Hevajra Buddha-form the archetype Buddha-forms Guhyasamaja and Chakrasamvara.

Milarepa (1040–1123) was the most important disciple of Marpa and came from another wealthy commoner peasant family. Disinherited by a wicked uncle upon the death of his father, Milarepa had made a name for himself as a successful sorcerer but was racked by guilt over having caused the deaths of thirty-five relatives with his black magic. So he sought the transformative teachings of the Dharma at the feet of Marpa the translator. Marpa forced him to go through the most terrible ordeals in order to cleanse his heavy negative evolutionary momentum from having killed so many people. After bringing him near the point of suicide, Marpa finally introduced him into the mandalas of Hevajra and Chakrasamvara, urging him to spend the rest of his life in contemplative retreat. This Milarepa did, learning to live in the high Himalayan winter with merely a cotton robe and practicing the famous yogas of Magic Body, Fury Fire, Death Ejection, Dream Yoga, Clear Light, and so forth.

Within twelve years Milarepa had become a perfectly enlightened Adept and subsequently traveled all over Tibet and taught thousands of people. He happened to be an accomplished singer, so he taught his disciples by singing his profound instructions in folk-song format. His songs were immensely popular then and have been over following centuries. While he revered his mentor Marpa as the "quintessence of all Buddhas," Milarepa himself became widely recognized by members of all orders as the "first Tibetan to become a perfect Buddha within a single lifetime." He started out an ordinary man, even a great sinner, yet his sincere practice of the Unexcelled Yoga Tantras led him to evolutionary culmination in a single lifetime. He thus became the example for generations of Tibetans who sought their own most exalted destinies. The great disciples of Padma Sambhava and Atisha, enlightened as they became, tended to be thought of as emanations of Buddhas and Bodhisattvas rather than as ordinary people who became perfected. The subliminal idea of Tibetans at that time was that Buddhas were Indian; Tibetans were disciples of Buddhas, fit only to worship them and serve them. Milarepa broke through this barrier in the first chapter of his *Hundred Thousand Songs*, where he returned to his cave, met five Indian demons mocking his contemplative practices, and eventually overcame them by realizing the nonduality of them and himself. He thus broke free of the stereotype of himself as unenlightened and enlightened beings as remote Indian icons and found the courage to assert his own potential of perfected evolution.

Here I should underline one point about the apocalyptic approach. Many people think of it as the quick and easy way to Buddhahood, and it can easily be misunderstood as an esoteric shortcut that renders unnecessary the messianic teaching of the Bodhisattva's evolution, especially if one is thinking that Buddhahood is only a mental breakthrough and not also an extraordinary physical development. All Bodhisattvas vow to be reborn infinitely, for three incalculable eons of lifetimes, in all conceivable life-forms, in order to accumulate the store of merit through generosity, morality, tolerance, and enterprise that is needed to develop the Form Body of Buddhahood. This body divides into Beatific and Emanation Bodies, which are effortlessly capable of freeing all beings from suffering and of transforming the entire universe into a buddhaverse of perfect opportunity for the happiness of all. The apocalyptic Adept determines to fulfill this very vow, never to abandon or short-circuit his or her commitment to transform the world and save all beings. Thus, when entering the mandala of Tantric initiation, he or she is not seeking a way around the eons of lifetimes of service to beings. Rather, the intensity of her compassion drives her to discover a method of accelerating the process of evolution, experiencing the lifetimes in superfast motion in the subtle virtual-reality realms of the Diamond Thunderbolt Vehicle. The reason, therefore, that apocalyptic practitioners such as Milarepa tended to spend long years in remote retreats is not just to avoid beings but to relate more intensely with more beings on the subtle, time-accelerated, virtual-reality level, rehearsing living and dying, cultivating lifetimes' worth of transcendent virtues in a night of meditation. The archetype deity forms visualized in these Unexcelled Yoga meditations represent a kind of genetic engineering that enabled the yogin or yogini to cultivate the ability to shape the body with the mind, transforming the ordinary body produced by ignorance and egocentric instincts into an embodiment of compassion produced by wisdom and artistic skill in reaching out to help other beings become free from suffering. Obviously such sophisticated technical procedures of gaining control over the processes of life and death are simply incredible for materialistic moderns; I only mention them here to show what the Tibetans themselves think their cultural heroes such as Milarepa are doing and accomplishing.

The teachings of Milarepa remain today beloved by all Tibetans at all social levels. He is thus the representative of the Buddhist transformation of the commoners, making the goal of perfect Buddhahood accessible in principle to any Tibetan. It is interesting that even though Mila had many yogin and yogini "Repa" disciples, his main successor and the real founder of the Kagyupa order was the learned monk, physician, and master yogin Gampopa (1079–1153). He had started his professional life as a physician and had become a Kadampa monk on the death of his wife. He established Kagyupa monasteries on the sound foundation of the Kadampa monastic discipline and educational curriculum, moving graduates into sophisticated apocalyptic practices utilizing the traditions handed down from Milarepa. His teaching system was called the integration of Kadam and Mahamudra teachings. Gampopa integrated within his person the roles of monastic abbot, scholastic and scientific sage, and contemplative Adept. He exemplifies the distinctive specialty of Tibetan Buddhism of integrating the monastic and the apocalyptic, since the vast majority of Tibetan Adepts of all orders were monastics as well, with the exception of the few who had reached the level of perfection-stage practice where they had to resign their monastic vows.

Among the twelve Kagyupa orders developing from Gampopa's foundation, the Karma Kagyu was an important one due to a particular institutional innovation it developed—the institution of official reincarnations. A number of great teachers in Buddhist history had attained memory of their former lives, and there were stories of a teacher being reborn in specific circumstances and accomplishing further good works and realizations. The second Karmapa was another such case; born in 1204, eleven years after his former incarnation had died, as a child he remembered events of his previous life and asked to be taken back to his monastery and disciples. He was recognized by them and again became their leader and teacher; again when he died, a third child was recognized as his reincarnation, and the tradition of formal recognition was begun.

This institution would have a profound effect on Tibetan civilization. In spiritual terms, the reincarnations proved to the people the efficacy of the most advanced apocalyptic yogas, that it was indeed possible for a human being to become a Buddha in a single life and then manifest the power to traverse death consciously and to continue to benefit other beings. Thus Tibetan Buddhists no longer needed to think of the supreme examples of the Buddhist education and evolution as having existed only in an ancient historic past in the holy land of India. Real Buddhas—living, breathing, teaching, helping, blessing—could be found among them right there in Tibet. Thus there seemed to be no deficiency in the tradition, no obstacle for any Tibetan to go as far in his or her practice as intelligence and effort would carry. On the social level, this institution created a way of leadership succession in celibate monastic communities that made it unnecessary to maintain a special relationship with a particular noble family, as in the case of the Sakya order or the Pagmodru Kagyu order. This then prepared the way for the eventual emergence of monastic governance, an institution that occurred only in Tibet and nowhere else in the Buddhist world.

Longchen Rabjampa (1308–1363) was another great genius of the later dissemination, along with Buton Rinpoche (1210–1364) a major initiatory force in the Tibetan renaissance of the fourteenth and fifteenth centuries. He was an avid scholar, an intrepid contemplative, and a prolific writer. His father descended from one of the main disciples of Padma Sambhava, Gyalwa Chogyang, who had practiced the yoga of the fierce horse-headed archetype deity Hayagriva so intensely that a small horse head emerged from his cranium. His mother descended from the clan of Dromtonpa, the founder of the Kadam order. He himself was believed to be the reincarnation of Princess Pemasel, daughter of King Trisong Detsen, who had been given, at the moment of her premature death, a treasure teaching called

"Heart-Drop of the Dakinis." He was a child prodigy, as were most of the greatest mentor figures, having learned to read and write at five and having received initiations at seven. He also memorized the *Transcendent Wisdom Sutra*. He became a novice monk at Samyey monastery at twelve, where he was educated in the rigorous Kadampa curriculum of Buddhist studies. His family education was Nyingma and his academic education was Kadampa, and he also studied Kagyu and Sakya teachings.

At twenty-seven he met his root mentor, Rigdzin Kumararaja (1266–1343), who taught him the key instructions in the Great Perfection Tantras of the Nyingma tradition. Under this mentor, he moved out of the monastery and adopted a contemplative style of life, intensely seeking meditative realization of the many teachings he had learned. He experienced many insights, visions, and realizations, remembering his former lives and receiving further teachings directly from Buddhas and angels. At thirty-two he began to give initiations and spiritual teachings to others.

He taught thousands of disciples during many years. He wrote extensive treatises, traditionally numbered at over two hundred, though quite a number have been lost. Longchen Rabjampa rebuilt temples, had mystic experiences, and had an enormous impact on future generations. He was one of the Tibetan "Renaissance men" who accomplished so much that it is hard to believe he lived only fifty-six years. His portraits present him with two lotuses above his shoulders, with a sword of wisdom on the right and a volume of the *Transcendent Wisdom Sutra* on the left, thus indicating his membership in the group of "three Manjushris," along with Sakya Pandita before him and Tsong Khapa after.

Longchenpa's main philosophical accomplishment was his synthesis of the mystic traditions of the "discovered treasure" teachings received as revelations from the Dakini-angels and the canonical teachings of the three Vehicles. His teachings of the basic path are no different from those of the Kadampa and other orders, with the methods of mind cultivation, stages, meditations, and insights. His use of the newly translated Tantras was also wholehearted; he accepted the Ritual, Action, and Yoga Tantras as Vehicles four, five, and six of his system of nine Vehicles. He divided the Unexcelled Yoga Tantras into three kinds: Mahayoga Tantras, which emphasize the creation stage; the Anuyoga Tantras, which emphasize the first two and a half levels of the perfection stage; and the Atiyoga Tantras, which emphasize the highest teachings of the Great Perfection, the last two and a half levels of the perfection stage.

This integration of Sutra and Tantra methods shared by all the Tibetan orders was the key cause of the development of Tibet's unique Buddhist culture, which I call "protomillennial" or "apocalyptic," which began to manifest more visibly in the fifteenth century. Dromtonpa, Marpa, the Sakyapa mentors, Milarepa, Gampopa, Machig Labdron, Longchenpa, and the many translators and other yogins and yoginis, scholars, Adepts—all these individuals accomplished great feats in the war against individual and national ignorance, egotism, prejudice, hate, greed, and other addictive passions. This inner struggle of theirs had a powerful effect of "morphic resonance" in the collective consciousness of the nation, turning the interest of many, each on an individual level, toward evolutionary goals. During this era, the picture of karmic evolution became common sense; karmic evolution is defined as an individual's sense of coming from many former lifetimes of biological experience, of being embedded as an individual in a great chain of vastly different life-forms, and of being subject to moving, after a relatively short instant of life, into other embodiments, other realms, other life-forms, perhaps divine forms or forms of great suffering. This sense makes the moments of this life incredibly valuable, as opportunities to positively affect those future lives. One feels naturally that one should invest the moments of this life in making spiritual efforts, working with one's subtlest mind, which is the sole thing that will determine the boundless future, for good or ill, that it be happy and not miserable.

In this era the Tibetans attained several qualities that are sociologically extraordinary, not present in most other Asian nations, and some of them not that prevalent even today in so-called modern societies. They gradually lost most interest in their ancestors, and they did not maintain any ancestral rituals as people did in ancient India and China. This is the direct result of the sense of karmic evolution, since an ancestor is more likely to be reborn as a fellow being alive today than to be sitting in an ancestral realm waiting for offerings and pious thoughts. Bit by bit Tibetans lost the intensity of their taste for war, journeys of conquest, and material development, considering the accumulation of vast treasures more or less a waste of time, a useless enterprise, since death would deprive them of the benefit soon enough. Yet they still liked to travel as pilgrims and to do business in a quiet way while on long pilgrimages to holy places. They became acutely conscious of the immediate presence of Buddhas and Bodhisattvas, as deities and angels and other spiritual agencies that help human beings and even as other human beings, living persons reincarnated to teach the way to enlightenment.

Because of these three qualities (the universalization of ancestor feelings, the loss of the taste for war, and a sense of the immanence of enlightened beings), one can say correctly that Tibetans have become particularly spiritual among peoples. This is not to say that they are perfect. They are human, like all people, with many problems, and often put into practice their teachings and taming disciplines because they fear hell or other horrid evolutionary destinies. They are also egotistical, in fact grand individualists for the most part, people of mountainous and solitary terrains. But when they think "I," what they identify, even without much analysis, is their soul, not so much their body. For it is common lore that the subtle soul and body are what get reborn, not the coarse body that the vultures wait hungrily to eat. Therefore they have put the same kind of ingenuity into understanding those inner processes as materialistic peoples have put into understanding the environment.

9. Spiritual Renaissance

After Atisha's time and the founding of Radreng Monastery in 1062, for the next three centuries Tibetans turned their interests more and more toward Buddhist education, and monasteries were built all over the country. The vast work of translation was completed, and a voluminous indigenous literature was developed. No new royal dynasty emerged to control the whole country. Tibetan militarism was unable to return due to the power of Buddhism and its ethic of nonviolence. Local noble families still ruled regional areas, but more and more they shared even their social and political power with the rapidly developing monastic institutions. Important popular figures emerged, such as Marpa and his famous disciple Milarepa.

During the thirteenth and fourteenth centuries, the Mongolian Empire unified most of Eurasia, and Tibet also was a part of it. In reality Tibet was very little changed, divided into thirteen main administrative regions, each run by a combination of a local ruling family and a local monastic hierarchy. The Sakya hierarchy was formally put in charge of all by Khubilai Khan, but the Sakya hierarch was more of a spiritual figurehead than an active administrator. Toward the end of the fourteenth century, the Mongol Empire fell apart, and the native Tibetan dynasty of Pagmodru asserted control over Tibet.

Around 1400 a spiritual renaissance was ushered in by the life work of Lama Jey Tsong Khapa (1357–1419), who came to be known as the *Precious Master*. Tsong Khapa shared with Padma Sambhava and Atisha a special recognition by Tibetans, seen as a child prodigy, a reincarnation of Manjushri, from an early age. He is generally accepted as having attained full enlightenment in 1398, at the end of an arduous six-year retreat. For the last twenty-one years of his life after that, his popular impact increased exponentially, and the example he lived, teachings he gave, books he wrote, temples he refurbished, and institutions he founded all set the tone for the subsequent five hundred years of Tibetan civilization. While assisted in his development by the pioneering work of his many predecessors, he considered himself particularly inspired by Atisha to renew the movement the latter had begun three and a half centuries earlier.

This renaissance was based on a new level of national dedication to the practice of Buddhism and the realization of Buddhahood as the main aim of Tibetan life. It was sealed by Tsong Khapa's founding the Great Prayer Festival in Lhasa in 1409, commemorating an apocalyptic moment in Shakyamuni's biography as known to the Tibetans, the two weeks of miracles performed near the great Indian city of Shravasti toward the end of his teaching career. During these miracles, Shakyamuni demonstrated to his whole civilization that the power of the compassion released by enlightenment is greater than the power of gods and kings, and he let it be known that enlightened beings could manifest whatever any individual needs to further his or her evolution and understanding. Tsong Khapa offered gold and bejeweled celestial ornaments to the Jowo Rinpoche image of Shakyamuni Buddha enshrined in the Jokhang cathedral to symbolize the nation's recognition of the Buddha's eternal presence, that the Buddha miracles are always accessible. The festival celebrated the distinctively Tibetan Buddhist sense of the immediacy of enlightened and compassionate beings. A tradition thus began for the whole nation to come together for two weeks of prayer and celebration every lunar new year. The keys of the city were turned over to the monastic abbots, and all ordinary business was suspended. This festival was a core event for all Tibet from 1409 until 1960, when the Chinese occupation stopped it by force in Lhasa.

After the renaissance led by Tsong Khapa, the spiritual synthesis of Tibetan Buddhism was complete. Tsong Khapa himself refused to reincarnate in an official manner, giving the reason that he had established a curriculum in the philosophical and apocalyptic monasteries that should produce plenty of Buddhas, and one of those should rightfully occupy the Ganden throne of the head of the order. The following centuries saw the rippling outward of this spiritual synthesis in a gradual process of transformation of the social, political, and physical landscape of Tibet. Monasteries were built on an unprecedented scale, with three major monasteries constructed in the Lhasa area alone, housing over twenty thousand monks (Lhasa's own lay population was no more than thirty-five thousand). Many people become intensely determined to devote their "infinitely precious human lives endowed with freedom and opportunity" to fulfill their evolutionary purpose and attain the perfect freedom and happiness of enlightenment. The social climate became more peaceful, as fewer individuals were available for the armies of the aristocratic warlords.

Although Tibetan warlords shared the general preference of military rulers for soldiers and productive housewives over monks and nuns, they seemed at first to feel relatively unthreatened by this immense wave of monasticism; in fact they joined in competition with one another to see who could sponsor more monasteries.

One of Tsong Khapa's disciples, the master Gendun Drubpa (1391–1474), had attained great awakenings in his lifetime and had performed great deeds, founding the huge Tashi Lhunpo Monastic University in southern Tibet and teaching hosts of disciples. After his death he turned up reincarnated as the son of a yogin and yogini couple of central Tibet. When he began to talk, he revealed he was the reincarnation of Gendun Drubpa and expressed his wish to be reunited with his disciples at his home monastery at Tashi Lhunpo. Named Gendun Gyatso (1475–1542), he spent long years in retreat, gave great teachings, built more important monasteries, and made daring inner voyages as an Adept or "psychonaut," as I like to call them. He remembered during his samadhis that he had been previously born as Dromtonpa, the disciple of Atisha, remembering as well many other former lives.

His next reincarnation was called Sonam Gyatso (1543–1588), who continued the universal spiritual education program, the building of monasteries, the taming of individuals, and his inner voyages as a psychonaut. He was invited to the court of the Mongol king Altan Khan. Somehow he tamed this formidable warlord, taught him it was better not to throw prisoners of war into the Yellow River for sport, better not to sacrifice captives or animals to the ancestors and the war gods, and, instead of such fierce shamanism, to take refuge in the Three Jewels of Buddha, Dharma, and Sangha and practice renunciation, compassion, and wisdom to evolve to become a Buddha. Altan Khan was so impressed by his encounter with a person he obviously perceived to be a superior being, a more evolved life-form, that he gave him the name Dalai Lama, *dalai* a Mongol word for "ocean." Counting his two predecessors retroactively, Sonam Gyatso became known as His Holiness the Third Dalai Lama.

Toward the end of Sonam Gyatso's life, the social situation in Tibet was unstable due to the resistance of the Tibetan warlords, who began to fear the ascendancy of the fully monasticized civilization coming from the Tibetan renaissance of 1400. The fourth reincarnation was discovered among the Mongols, in the family of Altan Khan, which led to closer relations between the Mongols and the Tibetans.

By the end of the sixteenth century, the warlord rulers of Tibet felt overwhelmed by the popular dedication to enlightenment education, monastic vocations, and monastery building. A period of violent persecution of monasteries ensued around the turn of the seventeenth century, with the fate of the country in the balance. Even the Monlam Chenmo New Year Festival in Lhasa was suspended by the southern Tibetan warlord for several years. Basically, the secular forces of the militaristic, aristocratic warlords tried to assert themselves to eclipse the rise of the monastery-centered, spiritual lifestyle, in parallel with what was happening simultaneously in the Reformation in northern Europe, at the end of the Ming Dynasty in China, and with the consolidation of the shogunate in Japan. The monastic leaders resisted this effort, and the warlords relentlessly tried to turn the different orders against one another. The Dalai Lama, by now the beloved spiritual leader of a huge population, called for help from the Mongolian warlord Gushri Khan, who had become his disciple. The Mongolian swept into Tibet and crushed the coalition of warlords that had resolved to reverse the monasticization of the land. These warlords were disarmed, and a peace was made that elevated the main monastic leader to head of the nation.

10. *Inner Modernity: The Monastic Nation*

In 1642, almost exactly a thousand years after the building of the Jokhang cathedral, His Holiness the Fifth Dalai Lama (1617–1682) accepted responsibility for the whole society and was crowned king of Tibet. He concentrated within himself the roles of the abbot Shantarakshita, the king Trisong Detsen, and the psychonaut Adept Padma Sambhava. He founded the Ganden Palace Victory Government that Tibetans still consider their legitimate government today. The Great Fifth, as he is known, created a unique form of government eminently well suited to Tibet's special society. It was almost completely demilitarized, acknowledging the centrality of the monastic institutions in the national life and the priority given to nonviolence. He rebuilt the Potala Palace on the Red Mountain at Lhasa, where Emperor Songzen Gambo had lived. His palace was three buildings in one: a monastery for the abbot, a fortress for the king, and a Buddha-realm mandala for the Adept, both a monument to Lokeshvara's paradise Potalaka in south India and an axial pedestal for the mandala of the Kalachakra Buddha, the Buddha of Shambhala, the hidden country of the north and land of the future apocalypse.

The nobility was virtually expropriated, retaining the use and income from parts of their hereditary estates only as salary for service to the

Ganden Government. They were completely deprived of their private armies and lost their feudal power of life and death over their peasants, who up to then had closely resembled the medieval serfs of Russia and Europe. And, with thanks to the Mongolian supporter, the Great Fifth asked him and his army to return to Mongolia, and the Land of Snows became the first postmodern nation, postmodern in the sense of unilaterally disarmed. As the Protestant princes of northern Europe and the shoguns of Japan had seen, a nation could not afford a universal military and a universal monastery at the same time, which caused them to terminate the monastery. In Tibet alone at this time did the monastery terminate the military and create a bureaucratic government to maintain a principled peace. International security was to be attained by diplomacy and moral force, not by military prowess.

The Great Fifth soon entered into an agreement with the new pan-Asian emperors of the era, the Manchus, to guarantee Tibetan independence and national integrity. The Manchus were a Tungusic people from the forest lands north of Korea. They had conquered northern China in 1644 and wished to conquer the rest of East Asia. Due to his authority over the fearsome Mongols, the Dalai Lama was seen as a potent ally by the new Manchu emperor. In 1652 an alliance was formed between the Manchu Shun Chih emperor and the Great Fifth. The Manchus recognized the Dalai Lama's secular authority over Tibet and his spiritual authority over the world as they knew it. The Dalai Lama recognized the Manchus as legitimate rulers of Manchuria and China and as international protectors of the Buddhist Dharma, its practitioners and institutions in Tibet and Mongolia. The bottom line was that the Dalai Lama agreed to encourage the Mongols to practice Buddhism, and the Manchus agreed to protect the peace for the demilitarized Buddhist societies. The Tibetan pacification of the Mongols, the demilitarization of that most militarily powerful society, is one of the remarkable social transformations in history, though it is no more astonishing than Tibet's self-transformation over the previous millennium.

In the 309 years of the Dalai Lamas' uninterrupted rule over Tibet, a remarkable society was developed. It was completely demilitarized and "educationalized," in that the monastic vocation was thriving at the highest rate it ever achieved in any society anywhere. There is no space here to describe this society in detail. It was not Shangrila, in that Tibetans themselves believe that Shambhala (Shangrila's model) exists in the north polar region of the planet, and Tibetans were highly aware of the all-too-human faults of their Land of Snows. But it was still a land blessed by the presidency of Lokeshvara, the messiah figure believed in by the vast majority of the people. It was the land of his sacred mantra, OM MANI PADME HUM! "Come! Jewel in the Lotus! In my heart!" It was therefore a place of unprecedented opportunity for the individual intent on enlightenment: maximum low-cost lifelong educational opportunities, minimum taxes, no military services, no mortgages, no factories of material products, no lack of teachers and realized beings, and even the opportunity to develop the ability to take rebirth in the womb, home, town, region, or class of one's choosing and then to return to one's favorite retreat cave, monastery, or retreat villa.

The table here sums up the process of development of Tibet's Buddhist civilization.

SUMMARY OF THE STAGES OF THE "CIVILIZING" OF TIBET

1. Militaristic, dynastic Tibet—ca. 540 to 840. Conquering dynasty comes to its pragmatically viable limits, meets Buddhism, and imports it as a preferable matrix of its civilization, creating legitimacy for itself and the internalizable ethic of a peaceful Tibetan society; suffers apparent nativistic reverse ca. 840.

2. Nationalistic but regionalized Tibet—ca. 840 to 978. Atavistic movement assaults Buddhism as weakener of militaristic fiber of nation, suppresses it and its countermilitary institution, monasticism. But the Buddhist program continues counterculturally through the ministries of lay Adepts descending from Padma Sambhava's teachings. Buddhist masters retreat to eastern Tibet and neighboring countries and preserve traditions there.

3. Medieval, regionalized, dualistic Tibet—ca. 978 to 1244. Regional princes sponsor the revival of Buddhism. Lumey (950–1025) returns from Khams; Rinchen Zangpo is sent to Kashmir; Atisha (982–1054) comes to Ngari in 1040; Drom founds Radreng in 1056; Marpa (1012–1096) establishes the Kagyu order; the Khon family founds Sakya in 1073. Regional nobles legitimize their authority by aligning themselves with charismatic monastic leaders.

4. Feudal, centralized Tibet, still dualistic, but protomillennial—ca. 1244 to 1640. Thanks to the Mongol Empire, a central state reemerges beginning with the Sakya regency, later with three nationalistic, secular regimes, the Pagmodru, the Rinpung, and the Tsangpa. The spiritual power of the Sakya hierarch merges with the secular power. After the fragmentation of the Mongol Empire in the fourteenth century, charismatic lamas fail to assume political power, which is controlled by aristocratic regimes. Reincarnations start, begun by the Karmapas. In 1409, with Tsong Khapa's founding of the Monlam Chenmo Festival, the renaissance, energized by the visionary millennialism at the heart of the festival, comes to Tibet, with a new burst of energy for monastic education.

5. Modern nationalistic Tibet, founded on inner modernity—ca. 1642 to 1951. This stage begins with the Great Fifth Dalai Lama's coronation in 1642, which resolves a century of conflict between lamas and warlords who feared the vast growth of monasticism. The Dalai Lama proceeded to build a monastic, modern nation-state, unique on the planet. This Ganden Palace Government was founded on popular millennialism, combining myths of the future Buddha Maitreya, the reincarnations of Lokeshvara, and the prophecy of Shambhala. For the first time in Buddhist history, a monastic took the throne of a nation. Warlords were expropriated, disarmed, and bureaucratized with monastic official counterparts and received the income from their hereditary estates as salary for government service. The annual budget was devoted to the support of monastic education. The military was gradually phased out, with three centuries of relative peace, a unique, mass-monastic, unilaterally disarmed society. This was an "interior industrial revolution," wherein enlightened people were fabricated on a monastic assembly line, with a technology of life, death, and reincarnation. All was rationalized to support the individual's attainment of enlightenment.

11. The Present Day

Tibetan interior modernity has adapted quite well to the rest of the world's industrial modernity, where the encounter was not violently forced. The Chinese communists, however, have attempted to impose on Tibetans their Marxist materialism, communistic egalitarianism, and an industrial focus on the productions of this life through an all-out assault on Tibetan Buddhism. It has included the destruction of monastic institutions, monks and nuns, Scriptures, outdoor monuments, Mani stones, prayer flags, personal rosaries and prayer wheels, icons, paintings, photographs of the Dalai Lama, even knowledge of the Tibetan language. Intensive communist thought-reform sessions were held year in and year out for decades. The Chinese have killed members of the upper classes, forced the redistribution of whatever forms of wealth were not extracted for the economy of China, imposed Chinese language education and indoctrination in Maoist writings, and enlisted all able-bodied persons in labor brigades, work gangs, production units, and so forth. All of these measures caused the deaths of approximately 1.3 million people, destroyed all the architectural and artistic treasures of the nation, and eradicated the intelligentsia entirely except for a few people who survived the prison camps or who escaped into exile.

These efforts have nonetheless been dismal failures. The minute the Chinese occupation administration was distracted by the post-Mao disturbances in the early 1980s, the Tibetans rose up as one and began to rebuild monasteries, to become monks and nuns, to restore their previous social order based on occupation and talent, to travel to India on pilgrimage, and to receive initiations and teachings from the Dalai Lama and other teachers. The Chinese were astounded that such "primitive" thinking could have survived their "revolutionary" onslaught; but they rather uneasily acquiesced in the Tibetan choices because they hoped to make Tibet an attractive tourist destination and so needed colorful monasteries and quaint monks and ceremonies. By the late 1980s, the monks and especially nuns began to make peaceful protests against Chinese occupation, and the government cracked down on the monasteries with a heavy hand.

Meanwhile, in exile in India, Nepal, and Bhutan, as well as in North America, Europe, and Australia, the Dalai Lama and about 150,000 Tibetan refugees have succeeded in keeping their unique civilization somewhat alive. They have their own school system within the Indian education system, so young Tibetans can learn Tibetan language, history, and some basic religious teachings. They have also maintained a high rate of monasticism, with more than twenty thousand monks and nuns, about one sixth of the population in exile. The curricula of the monasteries and nunneries continue with very little alteration in the spiritual studies and practices, though a modicum of modern, secular learning is added to orient the religious in the contemporary world. Tibetan spiritual teachers have attracted large followings in Europe, the Americas, Australia, Japan, Taiwan, and Southeast Asia, and some have written spiritual best-sellers. The Dalai Lama has received the Nobel Peace Prize and has met and is respected by most of the world's major religious and secular leaders. The communist Chinese regime has still refused to recognize him or his people's right to self-determination, and it still succeeds in getting other governments to ignore the reality of Tibet as the price of trade relations with China.

Tibetans are a success story as refugee communities go, with little history of violence, crime, or persisting poverty, and they take very easily to the professions of the modern economy. The further chapter of the amazing social experiment of Tibetan Buddhist civilization cannot yet be written, as it involves the coming experience of the political freedom Tibet will inevitably gain, as the restructuring of big-power, twentieth-century colonialism that began with the U.S.S.R. becomes global. Then we will see if a society touched by living Buddhas, with a different popular sense of the purpose and value of human life, with a determined spiritual orientation, will adopt some elements of a materialistic modernity. Which elements will it adopt, and which will it reject? Will Tibetans use computers to aid them in their quest of evolutionary perfection in Buddhahood? Will they militarize, never again to taste the bitterness of conquest and occupation by an outside power? Will they exploit and ruin their own environment? Will they industrialize in an external manner? The world will get a chance to see if a culture oriented to the possibility of becoming a perfect Buddha can persist in a materially modern setting.

12. Are There Several Essential Tibetan Buddhisms?

More than half a dozen important Tibetan Buddhist orders have existed, and any given order has various levels and layers of doctrine, method, practice, and result. In modern times there are said to be four main orders, the Nyingma, the Sakya, the Kagyu, and the Geluk. The Geluk are by far the most numerous; the Nyingma is second, the Kagyu third, and the Sakya the smallest. Like the Benedictines, the Franciscans, the Dominicans, and so on in the West, these orders have different histories, with emphasis on different texts and practices. They have held heated debates over points of doctrine and interpretation over the centuries. But do they have essential differences in philosophy and religious practice?

My answer is that they do not. I must avow that my personal background is a long association with the majority order, even though I have received teachings and initiations from teachers of all four. It is the tendency of a majority to emphasize its essential sameness with the corresponding minority, while the minority tends to emphasize its distinctiveness. Still, correcting for any bias these factors of personal history and general tendency might prompt, the essence of the way that all these orders present Buddhism seems the same.

All consider Shakyamuni the main Buddha of this world-epoch. All consider that a Buddha is a superhuman, superdivine being who has transformed from a human state to a perfect omniscience and a perfect evolutionary ability to manifest whatever compassion requires to interact with whomsoever. All consider that many such Buddhas after Shakyamuni have graced this planet and that many have lived in Tibet. They are credited with having created Tibetan civilization. Many Tibetans have become Buddhas, many still reincarnate life after life to continue to teach their disciples, and many more will become Buddhas. They want to be Buddhas because that for them is the pursuit of happiness. Buddhas are happier, more peaceful, more beautiful, more powerful. They have achieved real freedom from internal compulsions as well as external obstructions, such as any suffering or even death. All the teachings of all the orders of Tibetan Buddhism agree on this basic vision of life as an opportunity to join the Buddhas. It is rational to take advantage of that opportunity, because not doing so does not guarantee any status quo, and, as life has been and will continue to be infinite in its permutations, it is dangerous to meet death without having attained the ability to stay conscious, cool, and on course through its transitions.

Given the broad area of agreement, individual masters, scholars, and writers within the same order or within different orders have of course given different prescriptions about exactly what are the best methods for attaining Buddhahood—which are faster for a certain type of practitioner, which are less practical, what is the order in which they should be employed, what are the preparations, and so forth. There is a tremendous amount of debate on all of these subjects. In fact, since it is finally a fully developed understanding—insight become transcendent wisdom—that makes possible the attainment of Buddhahood, and since understanding comes about through a relentless process of critiquing prejudice, erroneous views, and ignorant preconceptions, critical debate itself is an important vehicle of liberation and enlightenment. Tibetan Buddhists cultivate a heightened ability to think critically, to doubt everything in a systematic way, in order to break through prejudice and to experience reality nakedly as it is. Therefore it is natural that great practitioners and scholars should use their critical acumen to debate every conceivable matter.

13. The Essential Readings

One of the amazing things about Tibetan civilization is the vastness of its literature. The current written form of its language was established in the seventh century C.E., four hundred years before Chaucer and almost a thousand years before Shakespeare. Woodblock printing was begun in earnest from the fourteenth century, a century before Gutenberg. Up to 20 percent of the people were monastics, more than half of whom were educated and literate. Thus a nation that probably never numbered more than ten million—nowadays six or seven million—has two different canons of Indian texts translated from Sanskrit, numbering over three hundred volumes, each volume of which would translate into a roughly two-thousand-page English text. Radiating out from that canon are collected works in Tibetan of hundreds of eminent scholars, saints, and sages, some of which number in the hundreds of volumes. These include many works of history, cosmology, astronomy-astrology, grammar, linguistics, poetics, medicine—veterinary as well as human—epistemology, psychologies of various kinds, philosophy, and immense numbers of ritual and liturgical texts. Then there are monastic catalogs, training manuals, disciplinary records, ceremonial manuals, and numerous historical documents. In addition to this huge Buddhistic literature, there is an entire mirror version, still huge although considerably smaller, of the Bon religion, which has its own canon, supposedly translated from the Persian, and Tibetan extracanonical collections in the same categories as the Buddhist. In the secular sphere there are plays, poems, decrees, law codes, land records, titles, architectural and craft manuals of all kinds. In short, for a contemplative culture, Tibetans were incredibly verbal and literary, not to say wordy!

The selection of key texts, therefore, is no small feat; inevitably so much has to be left out. In this book I have focused first on the essence of the essence, "The Quintessence." I present this as the key to the distinctive attainment of Tibetan Buddhist civilization, the vivid sense of the immediate presence of Buddhas in ordinary, daily reality, the personal immanence of the enlightenment reality in the Lama, or Mentor, figure. The first Panchen Lama, Panchen Losang Chökyi Gyaltsen, mentor of the Great Fifth Dalai Lama, wrote the *Lama Chöpa* (*Mentor Worship*) by collecting and quintessentializing all the traditions of "Buddha-Mentor Yoga," which is the key practice of using the personal mentor as a living icon of the present Buddha. The *Mentor Worship* also collects all of the central teachings of the path shared by all the orders of Tibetan Buddhism, running from recognition of the Buddha in the mentor through refuge in the Three Jewels, appreciation of the evolutionary opportunity in human life, renunciation of mundane preoccupations, development of the loving mind of the spirit of enlightenment, the messianic determination to accomplish the happiness of all beings, and the liberative realization of selfless wisdom, right up to the practice of the creation stage and perfection stages of the Tantras at the very doorway of perfect Buddhahood.

In chapter 2 we look at the Tibetan vision of the life of Shakyamuni, abridging a biography written by a famous Tibetan lama of the nineteenth century. In chapter 3 we look at how the Buddha was found in the mentor as Tibet developed, and we present various rationales and structures of the path. Chapters 4 through 6 present the three stages of the exoteric path for the evolutionary development of a human individual from ordinary egocentric living to the perfect enlightenment and boundless lifestyle of a Buddha.

Chapters 7 and 8 offer abridged forms of esoteric materials from the *Esoteric Communion* (*Guhyasamaja*) *Tantra*, its creation stage as arranged for practice by Tsong Khapa and its perfection stage as received from the Indian Adepts Shakyamitra and Nagarjuna. These materials are usually not for presentation to an uninitiated audience. I have nevertheless decided to present them in this case, following the green light given by my personal mentor, His Holiness the Dalai Lama, who has himself published initiation ceremonies, considering it now necessary to present at least the general outlines of these sublime visions and yogas in order to disarm those who, for various propaganda reasons, have misrepresented Tibetan Buddhism as corrupt. I have also left out enough detail so that a person who wanted to go beyond reading to actual meditation on the *Esoteric Communion* would have to seek a teacher, accomplish the prerequisites, and receive initiation to do so.

In chapter 9 I present a few typical Scriptures and prayers of broad popularity among Tibetans to illustrate how full their universe is of the Buddha-presence. Throughout the text, I have let the Tibetan texts speak for themselves, although terms and ideas requiring special explanation are elucidated in the Notes section at the back of the book.

CHAPTER I

The Quintessence: The Mentor Worship

by Panchen Lama I,
Losang Chökyi Gyaltsen

INITIAL SELF-CREATION

Through the great bliss state,
I myself become the Mentor Deity!
From my luminous body
Light-rays shine all around,
Massively blessing beings and things,
Making the universe pure and fabulous,
Perfection in its every quality!

REFUGE

I and all space full of mother beings
From now until enlightenment
Take refuge in the Mentor and the Three Jewels!

NAMO GURUBHYOH
NAMO BUDDHAYA
NAMO DHARMAYA
NAMO SANGHAYA

(3x)

For the sake of all mother beings,
I will become a Mentor Deity,
To install all beings in the supreme
Exaltation of being Mentor Deities!

(3x)

For the sake of all mother beings, in this very life I will very swiftly realize the exaltation of the primal Buddha Mentor Deity; I will free all
mother beings from suffering and install them in the great bliss Buddha
state. For that purpose I will undertake the profound path of Mentor
Deity Yoga!

(3x)

OFFERINGS

OM AH HUM
Primal wisdom in reality appears as inner offering and individual offerings and works to create the distinctive bliss-void wisdom in the fields
of the six senses, outer, inner, and secret clouds of offerings totally fill-

ing earth, sky, and all of space with inconceivable visions and sacred
substances.

In the middle of all-good offering clouds
arranged in the vast heavens of bliss-void indivisible,
in the crown of a miraculous wish-granting gem tree,
radiantly beautiful with leaves, flowers, and fruits,
on a sparkling jewel lion-throne,
on cushions of spreading lotus, sun, and moon,
sits my thrice-kind Root Mentor,
the actuality of all Buddhas!

His form is of a fulfilled mendicant,
with one face, two arms, smiling radiantly,
right hand in the Dharma-teaching gesture,
left hand flat in meditation, holding a bowl of elixir.
He wears the three robes glowing saffron color,
head beautiful with the yellow scholar's hat.

At his heart sits the omnipresent Lord Vajradhara,
with one face, two arms, sapphire blue in color,
holding vajra and bell, embracing Lady Vajradhatvishvari,
both ecstatic in the play of bliss and void.
Resplendent with many-faceted jewel ornaments,
draped with divinely wrought silken clothes.

Adorned with the signs and marks, shining like the sun,
surrounded by halos of five-colored rainbows,
my Mentor sits in the vajra posture.
His five aggregates are really the five Bliss Lords,
his four elements the four Ladies, his sense-media, nerves,
muscles, and joints really the live Bodhisattvas,
his body hairs the twenty-one thousand arhats,
his limbs the Lords of Ferocity.
His light-rays are protectors and fierce spirits,
and the world gods lie beneath his feet.
Around him sit in rows an ocean of live and ancestral Mentors,
archetype deities, and divine mandala hosts,
Buddhas, Bodhisattvas, angels,
and defenders of the Dharma.

Each of their three doors of body speech and mind
is marked by the three vajras, OM AH HUM,

the iron hooks of light-rays from their heart HUMS
draw spiritual duplicates from their natural abodes.
Wisdom heroes and icon heroes become indivisible
and substantially present.

SUMMONING

O source of success, happiness, and goodness,
all-time live and ancestral Mentors, archetypes, Three Jewels,
along with heroes, angels, protectors, and defenders,
out of compassion, come hither and stay here!

Though all things are really free of coming and going,
you accord with the natures of various disciples
and perform appropriate miracles of love and wisdom;
Holy Savior with your retinue, please come here now!

OM GURU BUDDHA BODHISATTVADHARMAPALASAPARIVARA
    EHYEHI/
JAH HUM BAM HOH

Wisdom heroes and symbol heroes become inseparable!

SALUTATIONS

Mentor like a gem embodied, diamond bolt,
Live compassion from the great bliss element
You bestow in the fraction of a second
The supreme exaltation of the three bodies—
I bow to the lotus of your foot!

Primal wisdom of all Victors of the buddhaverses,
Supreme artist to create whatever tames each being,
Performer in the dance of upholding the monastic form,
I bow to the feet of the Holy Savior!

Eradicating all evil along with instincts,
Treasure of a measureless jewel mass of good,
Sole door to the source of all joy and benefit—
I bow to the feet of the Holy Mentor!

Teacher of humans and gods, reality of all Buddhas,
Origin of the eighty-four thousand holy teachings,

Shining axis of the entire host of noble beings—
I bow to all kind Mentors!

To the Mentors in all times and places,
And all worthy forms of the Three Jewels,
With faith and devotion and oceans of praise,
I bow with bodies as many as atoms in the universe!

OFFERINGS

To the Holy Mentor Savior with his retinue,
I offer an ocean of various offering clouds;
From well-arranged, bright, broad, jewel vessels
Four streams of purifying nectars flow.

Earth and sky are filled with graceful goddesses,
With beautiful flowers, garlands, and showering petals,
Delicious incense smoke adorns the heavens
With summer rainclouds of sapphire blue.

Masses of lamps lit by suns, moons, and radiant gems
Shine ecstatic light-rays to illumine the billion worlds;
Boundless oceans of fragrant waters swirl around,
Scented with camphor, sandalwood, and saffron.

Himalayas of human and divine food heap up,
Wholesome food and drink with a hundred savors;
The three realms resound with sweet melodies
From infinite specific varieties of music.

The outer and inner sensual goddesses
Pervade all quarters and present the glorious beauty
Of form and color, sounds, scents, tastes, and textures.

MANDALA OFFERING

These hundred trillion four-continent, planet-mountain worlds,
With the seven major and seven minor jewel ornaments,
Perfect realms of beings and things that create great joy,
Great treasures of delight enjoyed by gods and humans—
O Savior, mercy treasure, supreme field of offering,
My heart full of faith, I offer it all to you!

Here on the shore of the wish-granting ocean
Of actually arranged and carefully visualized offerings,
This is a garden where the mind is captivated by the blooming
  lotuses
Of offering substances which are all perfections of life and
  liberation,
Where one is delighted by the scents of all-good offerings
Which are beautiful flowers of the mundane and transcendent,
Physical, verbal, and mental virtues of myself and others,
And where one is satiated with the rich fruits
Of the three educations, the five paths, and the two stages—
I offer it all to please you, Holy Mentor!

This delicate tea, rich with a hundred tastes
Saffron-colored, finely scented,
And the five hooks and the five lamps,
Purified, transmuted, and magnified
Into an ocean of elixirs—
I offer it to you!

A host of attractive, slender, youthful beauties,
Highly skilled in the sixty-four arts of love,
The heavenly, contemplative, and orgasmic heralds,
Exquisite, magic consorts—
I offer them all to you!

Great primal wisdom of unblocked orgasmic bliss,
Inseparable from the unfabricated natural realm,
Spontaneous, beyond theory, thought, and expression,
This supreme ultimate spirit of enlightenment—
I offer it to you!

I offer these various specific medicines of goodness
Which conquer four hundred four addiction sicknesses,
And to please you I offer myself as servant—
Please keep me in your service while space lasts!

CONFESSION

From beginningless time, whatever sinful acts
I did, had done, or rejoiced at others' doing,

I repent before you, O Compassionate Ones,
Confess and solemnly swear never to do again!

Though things are naturally free from signs
I heartily rejoice in all the dreamlike
Perfect virtues of ordinary and noble beings
That bring them all their happiness and joy!

Clouds of perfect wisdom and love mass together
In order to grow, sustain, and prosper
The garden of help and happiness for infinite beings,
Let the rain of profound and magnificent Dharma fall!

Though your diamond body knows no birth or death,
You treasure chest of Buddhas self-controlled in union,
Fulfill my prayers until the end of time—
Please stay forever without entering Nirvana!

The mass of perfect virtue thus created,
I dedicate to stay with you, my Mentor, life after life,
To be cultivated by your threefold kindness,
To attain supreme communion of Vajradhara!

PRAYERS

Source of excellence, vast ocean of justice,
Endowed with many jewels of spiritual learning,
Saffron-robed, living Shakyamuni Lord,
Patriarch, Discipline-holder,
I pray to you!

Possessor of the ten excellent qualities,
Worthy to teach the path of the blissful lords,
Dharma master, Regent of all victors—
Universal Vehicle Spiritual Guide,
I pray to you!

Your body, speech, and mind well controlled,
You are a genius, tolerant and honest.
Without pretense or deception,
You know mantras and Tantras.
Having the ten outer and ten inner abilities,

Skilled in the arts and the instructions,
Chief of vajra masters,
I pray to you!

You precisely teach the good path of the blissful
To the savage, hard-to-tame beings of these dark times,
Who were not tamed by the visits of countless Buddhas,
Compassionate Savior,
I pray to you!

The sun of Shakyamuni now sunken over time,
You perform the deeds of a victorious Buddha
For beings who have no spiritual Savior,
Compassionate Savior,
I pray to you!

But a single of your body's pores
Is better recommended as our field of merit
Than the Victors of all times and places—
Compassionate Savior,
I pray to you!

The beauty wheels of your Bliss Lord Three Bodies
Ecstatically unfold the net of miracles of your liberative art,
Leading beings by participating in ordinariness—
Compassionate Savior,
I pray to you!

Your aggregates, elements, media, and limbs
Are the five blissful clans' Fathers and Mothers
The Bodhisattvas male and female, and the Ferocious Lords,
Supreme Three Jewel Mentor,
I pray to you!

Your nature is the million wheels of mandalas
Arising from the play of omniscient primal wisdom,
Chief Vajra Master, Lord of the Hundred Clans,
Communion Primal Savior,
I pray to you!

Inseparable from the play of unblocked orgasmic joy,
Universal Lord, you pervade all moving and unmoving,
You are actual, ultimate, all-good spirit of enlightenment,

Beginningless and endless,
I pray to you!

SOLEMN PRAYER

You are Mentor!
You are Archetype Deity!
You are Angel and Protector!
From now until enlightenment,
I seek no other Savior!
With compassion's iron hook
Please look after me,
In this life, the between, and future lives!
Save me from the terrors
Of both life and liberation!
Bestow on me all powers!
Be my eternal friend!
Defend me from attack!

INITIATION AND BLESSING

By the power of thus praying three times,
The vital points of the Mentor's body, speech, and mind
Emit white, red, and blue elixir light-rays,
First one by one and then all together,
Which dissolve into my own three vital points,
Purify the four blocks, and grant the four initiations.
I attain the Four Bodies, and a duplicate of the Mentor
Melts in delight and blesses me completely.

USING THE BLESSINGS IN THE PATH

By the power of offering, respecting, and praying
To the Holy Mentor, supreme field of benefit,
Bless me, Savior, root of help and happiness,
That you can happily look after me!

This liberty and opportunity found just this once,
Understanding how hard to get and how quickly lost,
Bless me not to waste it in the pointless business of this life,
But to take its essence and make it count!

Fearing the blazing fires of suffering in the hellish states,
Heartily taking refuge in the Three Jewels,
Bless me to intensify my efforts
To cease sins and achieve a mass of virtue!

Tossed by fierce waves of evolution and addiction,
Crushed by the many monsters of the three sufferings,
Bless me to intensify my will to liberation
From this terrifying boundless ocean of existence!

As for this egoistic life-cycle unbearable as a prison,
Ceasing the delusion that it's a garden of delight,
Bless me to hold high the victory banner of liberation,
And enjoy the treasure of noble gems, the three educations!

Thinking how these pathetic beings were all my mothers
How over and over they kindly cared for me,
Bless me to conceive the genuine compassion
That a loving mother feels for her precious babe!

Not accepting even their slightest suffering,
Never satisfied with whatever happiness,
Making no distinction between self and other,
Bless me to find joy in others' happiness!

This chronic disease of cherishing myself,
Seeing it the cause creating unwanted suffering,
Resenting it and holding it responsible,
Bless me to conquer this great devil of self-addiction!

Knowing the cherishing of my mothers as the bliss-creating mind,
Door for developing infinite abilities,
Though these beings should rise up as bitter enemies,
Bless me to hold them dearer than my life!

In short, the fool works only in self-interest,
The Buddha works only to realize others' aims,
With the mind that understands these costs and benefits,
Bless me that I can exchange self and other!

Self-cherishing the door of all frustration,
Mother-cherishing the ground of all excellence,
Bless me to put into essential practice
The yoga of exchanging self and other!

Therefore, O compassionate Holy Mentor,
Bless all beings to obtain happiness,
Letting my mothers' sins, blocks, sufferings
Entirely take effect upon me now,
Giving them all my joy and virtue!

Though the whole world be full of the fruits of sin,
And unwanted sufferings fall down like rain,
Seeing this as exhausting past negative evolution,
Bless me to use bad conditions in the path!

In short, whatever happens, good and bad,
By practice of the five forces, essence of all Dharma,
Becomes a path to increase the two enlightenment spirits,
Bless me to contemplate indomitable cheer!

Bless me to make my liberty and opportunity meaningful,
By practice of the precepts and vows of mind development,
Applying contemplation at once to whatever happens
By the artistry employing the four techniques!

Bless me to cultivate the spirit of enlightenment,
To save beings from the great ocean of existence,
Through the universal responsibility of love and compassion,
And the magic of mounting give and take upon the breath!

Bless me to intensify my efforts
On the sole path of the all-time victors,
Binding my process with pure messianic vows,
And practicing the three ethics of the supreme Vehicle!

Bless me to perfect the generosity transcendence,
The precept increasing giving without attachment,
Transforming my body, possessions, and all-time virtues
Into just the things each being wants!

Bless me to perfect the justice transcendence,
Not surrendering, even to save my life, my vows
Of individual liberation, bodhisattva, and secret mantra,
Collecting virtue, and realizing beings' aims!

Bless me to perfect the tolerance transcendence,
So that, even if every being in the world were furious,
Cut me, accused, threatened, even killed me,
Without strain, I could repay their harm with benefit!

Bless me to perfect the enterprise transcendence,
So that even if I had to spend oceans of eons
In the fires of hell for the sake of each and every being,
My compassion would never tire of striving for enlightenment!

Bless me to perfect the meditation transcendence,
Through the one-pointed samadhi that transcends all flaws
Of distraction, depression, and excitement,
Focused on the truth-free reality of all things!

Bless me to perfect the wisdom transcendence,
Through the yoga of ultimate-reality-spacelike equipoise,
Connected with the intense bliss of the special fluency
Derived from wisdom of discrimination of reality!

Bless me to complete the magical samadhi,
Understanding the procedure of truthless appearance
Of outer and inner things, like illusions, dreams,
Or the reflection of the moon in water!

Bless me to understand Nagarjuna's intended meaning,
Where life and liberation have no iota of intrinsic reality,
Cause and effect and relativity are still inexorable,
And these two do not contradict but mutually complement!

Then bless me to embark in the boat to cross the ocean of the
     Tantras,
Through the kindness of the captain vajra-master,
Holding vows and pledges, root of all powers,
More dearly than life itself!

Bless me to perceive all things as the deity body,
Cleansing the taints of ordinary perception and conception
Through the yoga of the creation stage of Unexcelled Tantra,
Changing birth, death, and between into the three Buddha bodies!

Bless me to realize here in this life
The path of clear light/magic body communion,
Coming from you, Savior, when you put your toe
In my eight-petaled heart-center Dhuti-nerve!

If the path is not complete and death arrives,
Bless me to go to a pure buddhaverse
By the instruction for implementing the five forces
Of mentor-soul-ejection, the forceful art of Buddhahood!

In short, life after life forever,
You, Savior, please care for me never apart,
Bless me to become your foremost child,
Upholding all the secrets of body, speech, and mind!

You, Savior, at your perfect Buddhahood,
May I be foremost in your retinue—
Grant me good luck for easy spontaneous achievement
Of all my goals, temporary and ultimate!

Thus having prayed, may you, Supreme Mentor,
Joyously come to my crown to bless me,
Sit surely, your toenails glistening,
In the pistil of my heart-center lotus!

CHAPTER 2

Seeing the Buddha

Quintessence Segment

REFUGE

I and all space full of mother beings
From now until enlightenment
Take refuge in the Mentor
And in the Three Jewels!

NAMO GURUBHYOH
NAMO BUDDHAYA
NAMO DHARMAYA
NAMO SANGHAYA

Shakyamuni Buddha Through Tibetan Eyes

by Tse Chokling Yongdzin Yeshe Gyaltsen

For a Buddha to visit earth is as extremely rare as for an udumvara flower to bloom from earth to heaven. Why? To become a Buddha in the world, one must conceive the supreme spirit of enlightenment and accumulate massive stores of merit and knowledge for an immeasurably long time over three incalculable eons. Innumerable relativities must be arranged, such as purifying the buddhaverse, fulfilling the vows, and developing the continua of the disciples. It is very difficult to arrange so many relativities. Therefore this world is usually sunken in ages of darkness, and the illuminated eon of a Buddha's advent is barely a possibility.

It is very hard for beings caught in this world's life-cycle to develop even a tiny virtuous mind. Whatever virtue they do develop relies only on the Buddha's power. If it is so very rare to have a tiny good feeling such as faith in the Buddha, why mention how rare it is for one to develop ethical discernment about evolutionary actions through finding faith in the Three Jewels or to be moved by transcendent renunciation to abandon longing for mundane successes and learn the path of liberation? If it is so very rare to be moved by transcendence to learn the path of liberation, why mention how rare it is to be moved by the precious spirit of enlightenment that cherishes others over self to learn and constantly practice for many incalculable eons the ocean of Bodhisattva deeds?

How did our compassionate Teacher first conceive the spirit of enlightenment? Innumerable eons ago, when he happened to be born as a bull in one of the hells, pulling a cart in a team, he felt compassion for a weaker fellow bull. He told the Yama-demon Alang that he would pull the load alone. Alang was so angry with this moment of compassion, he killed him with his trident, and the Bodhisattva was born at once in the Thirty-three heaven.

Then he began to accumulate merit during three incalculable eons. He served seventy-five thousand Buddhas during the first incalculable eon, from Mahashakyamuni to Rashtrapala, seventy-six thousand in the second incalculable, from Bhadrakara to Indradhvaja, and seventy-seven thousand in the third incalculable eon, from Dipamkara to Kashyapa.

This way of describing the three incalculable eons of gathering the stores of merit and wisdom is in terms of general Buddhism. The Mahayana Sutras describe this in another way. Long ago the Teacher, when he was in the learner's path, served and honored Buddhas as countless as grains of sand in the river Ganges. He consummated his deeds of development, and purification, and manifested the Beatific Body with its five certainties in the Akanishta heaven world called "Flower Ornament Essence." Without ever leaving that body, he accomplished beings' aims by manifesting emanations according to the faculties of each disciple in worlds throughout space. Then, as the time approached when, as the fruition of his ancient spiritual conceptions and vows, he was to manifest a Supreme Emanation Body in this Saha universe, our compassionate Teacher incarnated as the Brahmin boy Anuttara during the time of the Buddha Kashyapa. He became a monk in the company of that Lord Victor and received the prophecy from him; "You, Brahmin boy Anuttara, after my Nirvana, when human beings in this Saha world live only a hundred years, will become a Realized Lord, a Saint, a Perfected Buddha, Wise and Ethical, Blissful, World-knowing, Unexcelled Human-Taming Charioteer, Teacher of Humans and Gods, a Buddha called Shakyamuni. After turning the Dharma wheel until you are eighty, your teaching will last a long time after your Nirvana." This prophecy became well known all over the world. After the Brahmin boy Anuttara died, he went to Tushita, manifesting as the divine, last-life Bodhisattva Shvetaketu. The Bodhisattva Shvetaketu dwelt in the Tushita heaven, living happily in thirty-two thousand mansions endowed with millions of perfections and divine ornaments, listening to the eighty-four thousand varieties of music and song. From that music, empowered by his own merits and the blessings of the Buddhas, emerged the message "You have a magnificent mass of merits, infinite consciousness, understanding, intelligence. Your wisdom is luminous, your power is matchless, your magic power is extensive. You must remember the prophecy of Dipamkara. Supreme Eminence, by the glory of your merit, the Tushita Palace is very beautiful, but since you have the heart of compassion, descend to raise the golden banner in the world." The music exhorted him again and again to visit our world of Jambudvipa.

The Bodhisattva went out of the great mansion and entered into the palace Dharmottana and sat on the lion throne Sudharma. He taught the Dharma extensively to the Bodhisattva Maitreya, the god-king Samtushita, and the whole assembly of Bodhisattvas. Then, wishing to manifest the Buddha deeds on earth, he performed the five searches; for the time, the place, the lineage, the bone, and the woman able to serve as mother.

As for the search of time, he remembered the prophecies of all previous Buddhas and renewed his resolve to descend to earth to help the beings in this dark age of the hundred-year life span.

As for the search of country, a Buddha's visit to earth is only for the sake of disciples, and humans and gods are the main disciples. If he manifested a Supreme Emanation in heaven, humans could not attend him. Teaching the gods has only slight benefit, since they are distracted by desires and it is hard for them to generate transcendent renunciation, so they are not fit for individual liberation vows. And the gods can go to earth to hear the Dharma. So the deed of manifesting a Supreme Emanation Body is only done among humans. Among humans, Jambudvipa humans are poor, short-lived, but often very intelligent. It is easy for them to feel intense renunciation, and it is possible for evolutionary impetus accumulated early in life to ripen later in the same life. Thus, intending to teach the teaching of both Sutra and Tantra here in Jambudvipa, the Bodhisattva Shvetaketu decided to manifest the Buddha deeds here.

As for the search of lineage, Buddhas can perform the Buddha deeds by incarnating either in the royal class or the priest class, but they always pick the one that is highest in status at the time, and in this world the royal caste has been highest since the beginning. At that, he saw that the Shakya King Shuddhodhana had the most taintless royal lineage. As for the search of the clan: He saw that the families of both Shuddhodhana and Mayadevi were flawless for seven generations, and so decided to be born as their son. As for the search of the mother, Mayadevi had already vowed to give birth to Buddhas many lives previously. So he decided to be conceived in her womb.

Having concluded the five searches, he went to the Sudharma throne and gave 108 teachings to the assembled gods and Bodhisattvas. He crowned Maitreya as his successor and then proclaimed his intention to manifest supreme Buddhahood on earth.

Then the Bodhisattva, in full sight of all the gods, entered into a multi-storied pagoda produced as a miniature jewel womb, a glorious mansion of bliss, duplicate of the Ucchadhvaja Teaching Palace. This jewel pagoda was circumambulated by all the gods and Bodhisattvas and began to shake and vibrate. Then the Bodhisattva emitted the countless ninefold light-rays such as "bliss ornament," dispelling all gloom from the billion-world galaxy and overwhelming suns and moons with its luminosity, eradicating the suffering of the lower states in a second, insulating all beings against their addictions, and accomplishing all activities such as manifesting the appropriate visions to whomsoever needed taming.

Then a light specially designed for his mother emitted from all his pores, a light called "illumination born of the element of all mothers' excellence." Mayadevi, then taking her monthly purification retreat, felt this light enter her body, giving her great bliss, distinguishing her body as outstanding from the bodies of all beings, her womb becoming vast as space yet not expanding beyond the size of a human body. In her right side appeared a lovely pagoda made of serpentine sandalwood called "Jewel Array of the Bodhisattva Sphere," square, four pillared, adorned with upper stories, of the size to accommodate a six-month-old child. Within it was a second pagoda, and within that a third, each not touching the other, indestructibly solid and firm yet pleasant to the touch, with a supreme blue color, like an abode of the desire-realm gods. A half-ounce of its substance was so precious the entire billion-world galaxy filled with jewels could not equal its value. Its environs were filled with flowers surpassing the flowers of the gods, redolent with the five sense-attractions. Within the third pagoda was a round throne fitting for a six-month-old child, with a child's robe upon it made of an exquisite fabric, whose light made Brahma's robe seem dull. Indra strove to enhance the luster of the mother and make the womb pure.

Then the Bodhisattva Shvetaketu, with his inconceivable divine retinue and offerings, gradually descended from Tushita, and, appearing as a young snow-white elephant with six tusks, entered the mother's right side in the first watch after midnight. He assumed the appearance of a six-month-old child, wearing the robe and seated cross-legged on the throne in the pagoda in the mother's right side, accompanied by a retinue of Bodhisattvas as numerous as atoms in ten universes, each dwelling within sandalwood pagodas all around him.

On the night when the Bodhisattva entered his mother's womb, a great udumvara flower born of the merit of feeding holy persons in previous lives covered the ocean and great earth, reaching up to the Brahma heaven. All the nurture of the billion-world galaxy congealed in the form of a drop of nectar on that flower. It was seen only by Brahma, who collected it in a sapphire vessel and offered it. The Bodhisattva drank it and his body flourished; no other living being could have digested it. Light-rays like a mass of flames shone from his body in the womb, extending for five leagues around.

As the Mother reported: "To hear the Dharma from the Bodhisattva, the four great kings and the giant lords come in the morning, and the Bodhisattva teaches them, raising the finger of his right hand. They sit in seats and hear the Dharma. Then he sends them away when they are satisfied. Likewise in midday the gods Indra and company come. In the afternoon Brahma comes and offers the drop of nectar. In the first watch of the evening the Bodhisattva host attends, and light-rays emit from his body to create lion thrones for them, and he gestures and makes the great symbols of the Dharma."

Thus for ten months he dwelt in the womb like that, developing and liberating countless disciples, innumerable Bodhisattvas, Brahma and Indra and the Four World Guards and so on, and the dragons and the giants and so on. As the time approached for the birth, the following thirty-two signs emerged in the gardens of King Shuddhodhana: Everything blossomed, eight jewel trees grew spontaneously, twenty thousand treasure troves opened of their own accord, jewel sprouts grew in the house, delicious scented oils and perfumes oozed forth, and young lions from the Himalayas surrounded the palace without harming anyone. Five hundred young white elephants came down and touched the king's foot with their trunks. Divine children came and played in the laps of the wives of the king and chased away any evil spirits. Dragon princesses carrying offerings appeared half-bodied in the sky. Ten thousand full vases surrounded Kapilavastu. Divine princesses carried vessels of scented water on their heads. Ten thousand goddesses appeared carrying umbrellas, banners, drums, and horns. Winds did not blow and raise the dust. Water did not agitate or flow. Sun, moon, and stars stood still. Jewel nets festooned Shuddhodhana's palace. Fire would not burn. Upper stories, parapets, and porticoes were hung with jewels and wishing gems. Treasuries were filled with jewels and precious brocades and their doors burst open. There was no hooting of owls. Sweet sounds sounded. Beings' actions ceased. All directions were equal. Crossroads and marketplaces were adorned with cool flowers. Pregnant women delivered themselves easily.

Mayadevi wished to go to the Lumbini Garden, and King Shuddhodhana and King Viprabuddha cleaned the garden, adorned it, and filled it with offerings. A great light filled the garden, illuminating all the earth. Jeweled flowers bloomed, and their petals radiated sounds "Is he born?" Then King Shuddhodhana commanded his subjects to clean all the paths from the palace to Lumbini, moisten them with scented waters, adorn them with various flowers, make offerings with inconceivable music and songs, array innumerable jewel chariots, and set tens of thousands of warriors as guardians. Having adorned all the chariots with jewels, he escorted Queen

Mayadevi. She entered the jeweled chariot and was drawn by the Four Guardian Kings. As they went, the king of gods Indra cleaned the road before her. Brahma fanned her from the side. Innumerable gods gazed unblinking at the Bodhisattva sitting in the pagoda in the womb and bowed and prayed.

Mayadevi arrived at Lumbini and descended from the chariot. She strolled from grove to grove, gazing at tree after tree. The ground was even, the green grass soft and pleasant. There was a luminous jewel tree relied on by the ancient queen Lumbini, worshiped by the pure-realm deities, its root, trunk, branches, and leaves adorned by jewels, blooming with human and divine flowers, with the scent of supreme incense, festooned with divine multicolored cloths, a royal tree called Plaksha. Mayadevi held on to a jewel tree branch with her right hand, and as she stretched and looked upward, from her right side he was born, emerging suddenly like a golden sacrificial post with a light like a million suns. Then the whole sky filled with divine offerings, and Brahma and Indra held him wound in a divine silken cloth. The dragon kings Nanda and Upananda offered him nectars. Countless gods and goddesses washed him, holding vases full of scented waters.

Then he said, "Look at me!" and placed his feet on the ground and walked seven steps in each direction. "I am the best in this world!" He emitted his great lion's roar. When the Bodhisattva was born from Mayadevi's right side, his body's light was more bright than a thousand suns rising at one time. It illuminated all universes at once, even penetrating underground depths. Any being touched by that light felt filled with happiness; emotional addictions and sufferings suddenly ceased. The sandalwood pagoda in which the Bodhisattva had lived in the womb was carried away by Brahma and set up in the Brahma deity heaven as a holy shrine. At that time all flowers bloomed, fruits ripened. Flowers rained down from heaven. The three lower states were ceased. The earth moved six ways.

At the second the Bodhisattva was born, sons were born to the four great kings in the four great cities. In Shravasti, Brahmadatta had a son, illuminating the whole country like a mirror, so his name was Prasenajit. In Rajagrha, a son was born to Mahapadma like a rising sun, so he was called Bimbisara. In Kaushambi, Senashataka had a son also like a sun rising over the world, so he was called Udayi. In Ujjain, King Ananta had a son who seemed to illuminate the world like a lamp, so he was called Pradyota. Each of them was proud of his son's excellent qualities.

At the same time in Kapilavastu, many other princes, princesses, commoner boys and girls, warriors, brahmins, and merchants were born. Foals, baby elephants, and calves were born by the thousands. There were many miraculous happenings.

Since the birth of his son accomplished all his wishes, King Shuddho-dhana named him Siddhartha, "Accomplisher of Aims." Father and mother asked the augurers for the fate of their son and were told that if he stayed in the home he would become a world-conquering monarch and if he donned the robes of a monk and went from home to homelessness he would become a transcendent lord, a saint, a truly perfect Buddha. They stayed seven days in Lumbini. Since the light from his birth had gone out all over the world, the Himalayan sage called Asita and his clairvoyant companions saw it and heard the gods rejoicing and proclaiming how soon there would be a perfect Buddha in the world. They decided to go pay homage to the Bodhisattva.

The Bodhisattva was escorted back to Kapilavastu. According to the local religious custom, when a child is born, one must take him to pay homage to the local and world deities. The king took the prince to the temple in a jeweled elephant chariot. The proud Shakya warriors were unable to bear the majestic radiance of the Bodhisattva and bowed low. So he was called Shakyamuni, "Sage of the Shakyas."

When the Bodhisattva was about to enter the temple, the idol of the tribal deity Shakyavardhana came to life and escorted him in, touching the child's feet with his head. When the right foot of the Bodhisattva was placed on the threshold, the idols of Chandra, Surya, Indra, Vishnu, Maheshvara, Brahma and so on arose from their shrines and bowed to the Bodhisattva's feet. The earth shook. When Shuddhodhana saw this, he gave him the name Devatideva, "God of Gods," since the gods had touched his feet.

Then the rishi Asita with his retinue came to look upon the face of the Bodhisattva. Shuddhodhana honored them and let them see the prince. The rishis saw the thirty-two signs and eighty marks on the prince's body and felt intense faith. They knew by clairvoyance that it would take thirty-five years for the prince to turn the wheel of Dharma. They realized they would not be alive that long and taste the elixir of the Dharma; they felt deep sorrow and wept. Shuddhodhana asked them if they saw some evil portents. They replied, "No evil portents; the prince will certainly become a Buddha and turn the wheel of Dharma. We are weeping since we know we will die and will miss his teaching; so we feel our loss." The rishis made earnest prayers over the Bodhisattva and then returned to their abode.

When Siddhartha reached seven, they tried to adorn him, but ornaments lost their lustre on his lustrous body. He was educated in letters, mathematics, archery, jumping, wrestling. In each case, he knew inconceivably more than his teachers and used the opportunity to teach them, his mates, and thousands of attending gods new lessons in these arts, especially as connected to the Dharma. Then Yashodhara and sixty thousand princesses came to amuse the Bodhisattva, and, though the Bodhisattva was not naturally lustful, he enjoyed himself. He even multiplied himself so that each girl thought she was with him alone. He passed some time in such a round of amusements, but his former vows soon ripened, and the songs and music of the dancing girls began to emit verses reminding him of the real nature of life and his vow to renounce the world and attain enlightenment.

"Seeing beings beset by a hundred sufferings, become their savior, refuge, and resort, their benefactor and their ally. Your own former vow was just this. Remember your vow, 'To help beings, do the virtuous deeds of former heroes.' Now is your time and this your measure. Supreme sage, it is time for you to leave your home." His former life stories emerged from the music. "The three worlds blaze with suffering of sickness and old age. They blaze with death and birth without savior. Beings always ignore the way to renounce this helpless existence, and cycle through their lives like bees in a bottle. The three worlds are unstable like autumn clouds. Birth and death of beings are like watching a play. Beings' life span is like a flash of lightning. It goes more swiftly than a mountain waterfall." Thus exhorted, the Bodhisattva thought that the time had come for his transcendent renunciation.

The Bodhisattva began to go out with his charioteer Chanda, and he saw the four sights: an old man, a sick man, a corpse, and a mendicant seeker of truth. The Bodhisattva was shocked, since he had been carefully shielded from such realities since he was very little. He decided that life was too precious and fragile to waste on mundane pursuits and that he should become a mendicant to seek a full understanding of reality, in order to benefit his subjects and all other beings, to help them discover a way out of the endless suffering of the ignorant life.

He was then twenty-nine. He went up on the roof of his palace and bowed to all the Buddhas and vowed to attain enlightenment quickly for the sake of all beings. The whole sky was full of Bodhisattvas, Brahma, Indra, the Four World Guardians, and all good deities, as well as demons, fairies, and dragons, all carrying various offerings. Vajrapani and Vaishravana overcame all the guards around the palace and set up divine ladders to the roof. The prince came down the ladders and mounted his horse Kanthaka, and Indra opened the lucky gate at the east. Thus led by the gods, he covered over a hundred miles and saw the dawn at the bank of a beautiful river, where the three pure monuments commemorated the spot where three past Buddhas had cut their hair. The Bodhisattva commanded Chanda to take his ornaments and Kanthaka back home to the family. Chanda obeyed his command while letting fall a rain of tears.

The Bodhisattva cut off his long princely hair and flung it into the sky, where it was borne aloft by Indra. He thought his expensive silk robe unsuitable for a renunciant and wished for a mendicant's orange robe; so Indra brought him a monk's robe. He felt he should get still further away from his homeland, so he crossed the Ganga and entered the kingdom of Magadha. Thus the Teacher threw away the glories of a world conqueror like so much spittle, giving up his ornaments and clothing, renounced the world and became a mendicant, vowing, "This is what disciples must do!" So later those who seek the stages of the path of enlightenment should think over this example of the teacher again and again.

Joining the ascetic wanderers, the Bodhisattva was so intense in his austerities, making four times the efforts of others, the other shramanas called him Mahashramana, the "Great Wanderer." When Shuddhodhana heard that the Bodhisattva had no servants, he sent five hundred attendants to take care of him. The Bodhisattva sent them back but kept five young brahmins, led by his old companion Kaundinya, to join him in his austerities.

Then the Bodhisattva set himself with his companions to practice the most severe austerities on the bank of the river Nairanjana, living on one grain of rice a day and sitting cross-legged in samadhi for six years. By those six years of ascetic discipline, he developed billions of gods and humans for entry into the three Vehicles, all the while being surrounded by the worship, prayers, and offerings of all classes of beings, from gods to serpents. Those gods and humans with a propensity for the magnificent vision of evolution saw the Bodhisattva as residing in a jewel tower, living in bliss, teaching the Dharma all the time to develop gods and humans. But beings in general agreed that they saw him engaged in the terrible ordeals of ascetic practice, thereby earning the respect of and evolving toward enlightenment four million two hundred thousand fanatically religious ascetics.

The Bodhisattva thought to himself, "One cannot attain Buddhahood through austerities alone. I should rely on a middle way between the two extremes and I should attain Buddhahood now." The limitless Buddhas also urged him again and again to leave his austerities and manifest the deed of attaining Buddhahood beneath the tree of enlightenment. So he quit his ascetic ordeals and let himself breathe more freely, partaking of ordinary food. He washed in the Nairanjana river, then wore a clean cloth. He went to beg alms food from the two village maidens, Sujata and Balarama, who had ancient vows to assist him in this way. On the fourteenth day of the spring month of Vaishakha, the two maidens took the essence of milk of a thousand cows and offered it in a golden urn, and the Bodhisattva drank it completely that evening. His body immediately was restored to its former health and radiance; the thirty-two major marks and eighty minor signs of enlightenment appeared on it, along with exquisite halos of light-rays. All kinds of beings, from gods to serpents, brought their own best food to nourish him, and, using his magical power to make them invisible to each other, the Bodhisattva consumed all of their offerings. In this way, they all felt they participated in his enlightenment, and all of them developed their own aspiration for evolutionary fulfillment.

The Bodhisattva thought about where he should perform the deed of final enlightenment, and all the deities and beings of all kinds showed him the Vajrasana under the Bodhi tree across the Nairanjana to the west where all Buddhas have always gone for the final achievement of Buddhahood. The gods cleaned his path and flowers rained from the heavens. The World Guardians hung golden nets, and Indra made the victory tower adorned with nets. The Yama gods brought sapphire nets, and the Tushita gods brought pearl nets, and the Nirmanarati gods brought rose-apple gold bell nets, and the Vashavarti gods brought nets of divine jewels. There were jewel thrones, jewel nets, jewel towers, incense powders, jeweled staircases, jewel cloths draped in the trees, and so on, along with hosts of worshiping gods and goddesses, as well as innumerable other kinds of beings reverently in attendance. Brahma, the king of gods, told them all to revere the Bodhisattva with all their hearts, as he was going to fulfill his ancient vow. The whole world was filled with divine golden lotuses and jewel substances and fragrances, as if it was a heavenly paradise, like a hundred thousand pure buddhaverses revealed in this world.

In the evening, as the sun sank lower in the sky, the Bodhisattva went to the tree of awakening, which had been adorned by the four goddesses of the tree. From the soles of his feet shone light-rays which terminated the lower states of existence, cooling the sufferings and addictions of beings and making them happy, revealing to them all the lands of the Buddhas. Whenever a great being went to the enlightenment tree, the whole great earth resonated like a brass gong being struck. When the Bodhisattva went there, he remembered that previous Buddhas had sat upon a grass mat, and he wished for one from the gods of the pure abodes. Indra read his thoughts and emanated himself as the grass-seller Svasti and gave a load of kusha grass to the Bodhisattva, excellent grass, blue as a peacock's throat, rightward curving, fragrant, soft to touch. "By this grass may you attain the path of former Buddhas, enlightenment, the deathless! Please accept it, O ocean of virtues; may I also finally become a Buddha!"

Then the Bodhisattva circumambulated the enlightenment tree seven times and bowed to it, to follow the example of previous Victors. He then placed the grass blades in a circle, their tips pointed inward, arranging them evenly. He sat down on the grass mat, balanced his body in cross-legged posture, and focused his awareness. He faced the east and vowed, "Until I truly attain the end of the contamination of all kinds of sufferings, even though my life will end, I will not move from this posture."

Innumerable Bodhisattvas gathered from the buddhaverses of the ten directions and manifested various magical displays; creating flower palaces, radiating thousands of colors from their bodies, radiating sunlike rays, shaking the earth, carrying four oceans on their heads and sprinkling the ground with fragrant waters, offering jewel-offering trees, flying in the sky, dissolving their bodies and turning into garlands filling the universe, pronouncing millions of discourses from the pores of their bodies, making their bodies huge, bringing trees with Bodhisattva bodies emerging halfway from each leaf, bringing axial mountains, stimulating masses of water with their feet, making great sounds like great drum rolls filling a billion universes.

Then the great devil Mara began to marshal his armies and obstruct the Bodhisattva to distract him from enlightenment by raining down weapons upon him. The Bodhisattva, seeing all things as like magic illusions, had no fear of those devil armies. To tame them, he showed his magic power by appearing to swallow all their hosts within his mouth, causing them to flee in terror. But they remembered themselves and turned again against him, flinging various weapons, which only turned into a flower canopy and palace. They sent fierce flames fanned by their poison breath, which only turned into a hundred-petaled lotus of pure light. The Bodhisattva rubbed his head with his right hand and the devils saw a great flaming sword in his hand and ran away to the southern direction. Again they overcame their fright and threw even more powerful missiles, which only turned into garlands that decorated the Bodhi tree.

Seeing the powers of the Bodhisattva, the devil Mara was stirred by jealousy and hate and addressed him thus: "You, why do you sit at the circle of enlightenment?" The Bodhisattva replied, "In order to attain the unexcelled intuitive wisdom!" Mara said: "Hey, royal prince! Get up! Manage your kingdom! What makes you think you have the merit to achieve liberation!" Then he threw his mighty discus, which only turned into a giant flower; and the mountain thrown by his soldiers became a flower pond. The Bodhisattva said: "Evil one! You, by means of one extraordinary offering, attained the lordship of the desire realm. I made many different a hundred thousand ten million trillion extraordinary offerings during three incalculable eons, underwent ordeals of total letting go for the sake of beings, and thereby I attain the unexcelled intuition of reality—there is no hope that I will not attain that unexcelled intuition." Then Mara replied, shouting in a loud voice, "Well then, you are my witness of having attained desire-realm lordship by a single act of offering! But who is your witness of having performed offerings for three incalculable eons in order to attain the unexcelled intuition?" The Bodhisattva was unafraid, with his mind of great compassion, and gently rubbed his whole body with his right hand adorned with wheel and svastika, manifesting all Buddhas of all worlds; then he touched the great earth in the good luck gesture, saying, "This earth is my witness! This earth is the abode of all beings, it has no partiality, being equal toward the moving and the unmoving. This is my witness that I do not lie! You must accept this as my witness!" As soon as he had touched the earth with his right hand, the great earth quaked in six ways and the eighteen great signs occurred.

Then the earth goddess Prithivi, with her host of attendants, emerged from the earth from the navel up, beautiful with her ornaments, bowed in the direction of the Bodhisattva, joined her hands in reverence, and said, "Yes! It is so, O holy being! It is as you say! I have directly beheld it! It is like that! I along with the gods am your witness!" And she addressed the devil, "Evil one, it is as the divine Transcendent Lord has spoken!" And then she instantly disappeared.

In that way Mara was overwhelmed and silenced, and he inclined his crown and stood still. At that time the other devils heard the sound made by the Bodhisattva's hand striking on the ground as a sound of conquest, of roaring, of terrifying danger. Millions of those devils heard a command from the sky "Take refuge in this one!" They flung themselves down on their faces and cried out, "We request refuge with this holy person!" Mara the evil one with his armies was afraid and wanted to escape but was unable to move. The Bodhisattva radiated light and gave him refuge from his terror. At that time, in the devil's retinue a hundred million eight thousand demons and a hundred thousand million trillion ninety-six thousand animals conceived the spirit of enlightenment. Eighty-four thousand gods with previous practice attained the tolerance of birthlessness. The great earth quaked in six ways. The Lord's body radiated light, which flooded the world with great illumination, eradicated the agonies of the three hellish states, terminated the bondages, and rendered all beings free of harm from cruelty, pride, and hate.

Then as the Lord was about to attain unexcelled enlightenment, Vajrapani entered his heart and praised him with the 108 names, and the Lord gave his approval to Vajrapani.

Then the gods wanted to throw flowers, but the more experienced gods told them to wait for a sign. Then the ten-direction Buddhas shouted their approval of the perfect Buddhahood of the Transcendent Lord. The

Bodhisattvas created a giant jewel umbrella that covered this whole universe with a great net of light-rays. They bowed to Lord Shakyamuni and offered it to him in the proper manner. Then the Lord, staying cross-legged, rose up into the sky seven palm-tree heights and a great shout arose: "The path is broken. Suffering is terminated. The taints are dried up." Then all the gods scattered flowers.

The various gods all brought various kinds of offerings and adorned the entire circle of enlightenment. The Bodhisattvas in the sky all made offerings and sang praises. And the Lord himself proclaimed, "Merits have ripened, happiness is given, all sufferings are dispelled. The wishes of all meritorious humans are fulfilled. The devil is conquered, and enlightenment is quickly reached. Sorrow is extinguished, attained is the cool reality of peace."

Such a manifestation of the deed of awakening is a deed of the Supreme Emanation Body for the sake of disciples. This very teacher has been stated to have already attained enlightenment countless eons earlier. Thus the above manner of attaining Buddhahood is that taught in terms of ordinary reality.

The way of enlightenment in terms of the Mantric path is as follows: On the eighth day of the Vaishakha month, he left his evolutionary body on the bank of the Nairanjana and went with his mental body into the Akanishta heaven. Then, according to the Yoga Tantra version, he entered the great mandala of the diamond realm and manifested the deed of awakening through the door of the five enlightenments. According to the Unexcelled Yoga Tantra version, he entered the mandala of the *Esoteric Communion* and received from Bodhichittavajra the initiation characterized by the great natural intuitive wisdom, purifying even the subtlest dualism and arising in the Union Body. In the *Yamantaka Tantra*, it is said he conquered the devil by arising in the bodies of the red-and-black Yamantakas. In short, there are infinite inconceivable accounts of his attainment of enlightenment taught in the esoteric Tantras.

Thus, in his thirty-fifth year in the predawn of the fifteenth day of the Vaishakha month of the male wood horse year called Jaya, he manifested the deed of perfectly accomplished Buddhahood. He spent the first seven days at the enlightenment tree. He traveled far and wide throughout the billion-world galaxy in the second week. He spent the third week looking at the enlightenment tree without blinking. He spent the fourth week wandering east and west in the four continents surrounded by the four oceans. He spent the fifth week in the dragon Muchilinda's kingdom. He spent the sixth week at the Nyagrodha tree and ripened many naked ascetics for enlightenment. He spent the seventh week in the serpentine sandalwood grove entertaining the merchants Trapusha and Bhallika, receiving their offerings of food and magically creating one begging bowl out of the four stone bowls offered by the four great kings. He composed good-luck verses for the sake of the two merchants and predicted their eventual enlightenments.

Then the Lord thought, "I have understood this profound truth, profound illumination, hard to realize, not the sphere of the intellectuals, knowable only by the wise; if I expound it to others, they will not understand. I should abide in the yoga of staying happy by myself." And also, "Profound, peaceful, uncomplicated, clear light, uncreated, I have attained this elixir of truth. Though I teach it, others will not understand. Better stay silent, in the midst of the forest." And so he remained averse to teaching. Innumerable Bodhisattvas of all directions and countless deities requested him to teach, especially the king of the billion-world universe, great Brahma, yet the Buddha remained silent and focused intently within. Then Brahma returned to the Brahma heavens.

The Lord remained thus withdrawn in order to intensify others' reverence for the Dharma, to increase Brahma's virtue in having to ask him again and again, and to show how very profound the truth is. Knowing this, Brahma exhorted Indra, "Take Maheshvara and many other gods of the desire and form realms and go to the Lord and urge him to teach the Dharma." Still, the Buddha was difficult about teaching, and Brahma, knowing this, brought sixty-eight thousand Brahmas with him one evening into the presence of the Lord. They all folded their hands in supplication and made their request. "The Dharma previously taught in Magadha was impure and tainted, we understand. Please open the door of the taintless elixir of Dharma, please teach us how to understand it. May the Muni dispel the darkness with the lamp of Dharma! May you raise the victory banner of the Transcendent Lords! It is time for you to express the sweetest speech. May you sound your lion's roar!" The Lord replied: "Brahma, I, with great difficulty, have conquered my faults and have understood. Those enveloped in existence and attachments will not understand this Dharma well." Brahma insisted: "In the world there are the intelligent, the mediocre, and the dull. Some beings are easy to tame. If they do not hear the Dharma, they will be lost. Please teach the Dharma!" and, "Previously to seek the Dharma you gave away even a thousand heads."

Finally, the Lord agreed and said, "Open up the gates of the elixir of immortality! Who wants to listen, set aside your doubts. O Brahma, the expansive Dharma is for humans; don't be contentious, and I will explain it briefly." Thus he gave his commitment to teach the Dharma.

Then the gods rejoiced and proclaimed that "the Lord will turn the wheel of Dharma, to bring benefit and happiness." The four goddesses of the Bodhi tree asked the Lord, "Where will you turn the wheel of Dharma?" The Teacher replied that Varanasi is the holy place of former sages, where many thousands of millions of sacrifices had been held, and therefore it is the place to turn the wheel of Dharma.

Then the Lord went to the land of Kashi, the city of Varanasi, accepting alms, staying at the deer park in Rishipatana. The five companions saw him coming from afar. "The greedy ascetic Gautama who has lost his renunciation is coming over here. Let's not speak to him, nor rise up for him, nor salute him nor offer him a seat!" Though they made such a plan to humiliate him, Kaundinya did not agree to it in his heart. The moment the Lord arrived at the abode of the five at the bank of the waterfall, his glory and energy overwhelmed them and they began to tremble on their seats. They all gave up their plan and rose from their seats. "Venerable Gautama, how good you have come! Please sit down on this seat we prepared!"

Then the Lord sat on the seat and the five eagerly addressed him, calling him by name and clan name and "venerable." The Lord spoke, "You should not address a Transcendent Lord in such a manner. You will suffer for a long time if you do." They then responded crudely, "But Gautama, by your former regime and ascetic disciplines you did not attain the unexcelled goal of the religious path. Then have you been able to attain your goal by this new code of conduct?" He spoke, "A renunciant should not rely on two extremes. Which two? The inferior code of bad persons who persist in the destructive regime of indulgence in desires, and the striving for self-mortification—these two damage the noble path. You should not rely on these two extremisms, should open your eyes and wisdom to the middle path, and you will achieve peace, superknowledge, perfect enlightenment, and Nirvana. What is the middle way? It is the noble eightfold path."

Then the Lord remembered that this very place of Rishipatana was where he was to turn the wheel of Dharma, in that place where former victors had turned the wheel of Dharma seated on a thousand seven-jewel thrones. And Brahma erected his lion throne, which was forty-two thousand leagues high. Likewise, other Brahmas and Indra and a hundred million Bodhisattvas also erected similar thrones. The gods of earth and heaven magically set up a vast arena for turning the wheel of Dharma, adorned, beautiful, magnificent, with pools seven hundred leagues in breadth. There were umbrellas and pavilions in the sky and the desire-realm gods offered eight thousand thrones, asking him to sit there and turn the wheel of Dharma.

Then the Lord, to venerate the ancient victors, circumambulated three of the thrones, and fearless as a lion sat cross-legged on the fourth throne.

Brahma, Indra, and the Bodhisattvas all turned to him sitting on the lion throne. The five mendicants, having bowed to the Lord, also sat in a disciplined manner. At that time the Lord's body shone forth light-rays terminating the suffering of the six kinds of beings. The eighteen great omens occurred. The Saha world became level, all beings became loving. That light exhorted, "The Victor practiced for a hundred thousand eons. Who wants to hear his Dharma, for the long-term sure result, come here to hear the Dharma." Then gods, dragons, ogres, fairies, titans, garudas, eaglemen, kinnaras, and great serpents, all these eight species understood and gathered round. Countless ten-directions Bodhisattvas also came there; this entire billion-world galaxy was pervaded by beings not leaving empty even the space of a hair-tip.

Then the ten-directions Bodhisattvas and the Brahma and Indra of this Saha world and other powerful beings bowed to the Lord's feet and asked him to turn the wheel of Dharma in order to heal many beings. Brahma in particular said, "For these beings oppressed by the hundred sicknesses of the mass of addictions, O Victorious Doctor, please turn the holy wheel and make them free. Share the seven treasures, O Leader, please turn the wheel! Fulfill your intent, destroy the plague, please turn the supreme wheel!" And he offered to the Lord the thousand-spoked wheel made of rose-apple gold shining with a thousand light-rays, used by the ancient Victors, while he requested him to turn the wheel of Dharma.

Then the sky full of Bodhisattvas, the eighty thousand main deities, the dragons, ogres, fairies, snakes, kinnaras, great serpents, Kaundinya and his four companions, and the whole assembly gathered to hear the Dharma, without a single sound. They all sat silently looking only at the Victor. Then the Lord, in the later part of the night, turned the wheel of Dharma, promulgating the twelvefold repetition of the middle path abandoning the two extremes, including the names of the four truths, the choices they involve, their recognition, abandonment, realization, and meditation, and the eightfold path that follows. And from that melodious speech, all the various disciples heard the words they needed to hear to be tamed, receiving the teachings of all three Vehicles according to their inclinations. The venerable Kaundinya and Jvalatejas and so on, all the eighty thousand gods, developed the taintless eye of Dharma.

Then the Lord spoke again to Kaundinya. "Do you fully understand this Dharma?" He replied, "The Lord has fully bestowed it." Then the venerable Kaundinya became known as "Full-understanding Kaundinya," and the Three Jewels were established in this world. And the gods again said, "Friends! The Lord at Varanasi has turned, repeating three times in twelve modes, the Dharma wheel, endowed with a truth that no one has ever turned thus appropriately in this world. The gods are increased thereby, and the titans are decreased."

Then the Lord twice again taught the four truths to the five ascetics, and Full-understanding Kaundinya's mind was liberated from contamination, free of grasping, and he became a perfect saint. Then in the world there was another saint, the Lord being the first. The other four ascetics also saw the truth. Then the fivefold group just realized intuitive wisdom, and their marks and symbols as fanatics disappeared. Their hair flew off, they instantly possessed the three Dharma robes and the begging bowl, and they became fully graduated mendicants. And the Lord praised them, saying, "This Full-understanding Kaundinya is the supreme of those holding the standards of renunciants." Then the Lord taught the other four extensively, that form was not self, about suffering and impermanence, and the other four also realized sainthood; there were then five saints in the world and the Lord was the sixth.

Having thus been taught, four thousand million gods and eighty-four thousand humans saw the truth. Thereby a hundred million beings conceived the spirit of enlightenment.

Thus the Teacher attained perfect enlightenment and yet still made it hard to get him to teach the Dharma, making it necessary to request him again and again. When he began to teach the Dharma, he did not teach first about profound voidness and so forth but taught the precepts of discipline, such as keeping the roundness of the Dharma robe, the abstention from afternoon food, and the need not to lapse into extremisms about food and clothing, then teaching the four noble truths. Then among the four truths, he taught the truth of suffering. From among its four aspects, he first taught impermanence. By this pattern of deeds, when the discerning person understands how to think it over, she can gain firm certainty in the practice of the stages of the enlightenment path. First, one must rely on a spiritual friend, the root of the whole mass of goodness. Then, not being content with whoever happens by, the disciple must examine whether the spiritual teacher has the right qualifications; one needs to rely on a qualified teacher. The teacher also must not just teach anyone whether or not they are fit but examine whether the disciple is a fit vessel or not. When the disciple is to be taught, then, like a brave mother healing a child or a doctor curing a patient, the teacher must cultivate the personality of the disciple by examining her scope. Since the foundation of all positive qualities is pure ethics, it must first be developed. Since it is the method to develop first an aversion to the preoccupations of this life and then an aversion to the life-cycle in general, one must teach the impermanence of all created things, especially this contaminated body. In this way the disciple can diminish attachment to this life and create ambition for the future life, and then lose attachment to the whole life-cycle and create firm aspiration aiming for liberation. When such an intention has been created, then the root of the life-cycle, the truth of origin, is introduced. In this way, by understanding the way to lead gradually to the higher paths, one will know how to turn even the biography of the teacher into a practice.

Gradually the Teacher taught the limitless other discourses included in the first wheel of Dharma in other places and at other times. Having attained perfect enlightenment, the Teacher took care of the first five disciples such as Kaundinya, the second five such as Yashas, the five hundred that came along with Shariputra and Maudgalyayana in Rajagrha, and countless great beings such as Mahakashyapa. His fame spread throughout the whole country.

When King Shuddhodhana heard about it, he was delighted. He wanted to meet the Buddha, sending messengers again and again to invite him to Kapilavastu. Then the Lord saw the need to tame countless Shakyas such as his father Shuddhodhana, his foster mother Prajapati, and so on. So during the rains one year he told a messenger, "Tell the king I will come, but the Transcendent Lord and the Community of mendicants will stay not in the royal palace but in the academy of holy persons of the city."

The Lord said to Maudgalyayana, "Tell the mendicants that the Lord will go to Kapilavastu to meet his father; whoever among them wishes to witness the father-son meeting should take up their Dharma robe." Then the Lord traveled to the bank of the waterfall Rohika, nearby Kapilavastu, along with a great community of twelve hundred fifty mendicants. When King Shuddhodhana heard he had arrived, he had well-adorned seats set up in broad and open spaces. He had the crossroads, streets, and squares of Kapilavastu cleaned and sprinkled with sandalwood water, setting up bowls of sweet incense, festooned with many silken streamers. He ordered the Shakyas, "Let your best carriages be prepared. Why? Because today we will have an audience with the Lord Buddha." "Yes, God!" they said and prepared their best vehicles. Then the king adorned the way between the city and the banyan grove as a royal way, spreading fresh sand, adorning it with flowers, draping it with streamers, staffing it with dancers, singers, musicians, and drummers. The king mounted his chariot and departed with great royal glory and power, attended by eighty thousand Shakya princes. Some of the Shakyas were mounted on blue chariots drawn by blue horses, with blue ornaments and nets of bells, blue-robed attendants, blue parasols, swords, coiffures, jeweled yak-tail whisks, and boots, with blue robes, ornamented greeting scarves, with charioteers with blue reins and whips, with blue banners and blue ornamented cohorts; others had all their equipment in yellow, others in red, others pure white, and others multicolored.

Seeing King Shuddhodhana thus attended like a crescent moon emerge from the city, the Lord, attended by the twelve hundred fifty mendicants such as the First Five, Yashas, Mahakashyapa, Gaya Kashyapa, Shariputra, and Mahamaudgalyayana and so forth, intentionally gathered the most powerful gods, such as the four great kings, Vemachitra of the titans, and all the gods of the desire and form realms. The Lord knew how great was the pride of Shuddhodhana and knew that the Shakyas would not respect him if he touched the ground of Kapilavastu. So he rose up in the air the height of seven palm trees and performed miracles of radiating fire and light in all directions and releasing streams of water from his body. All the mendicant saints rose up six palm trees' height in the air, ranging themselves around to greet the king. Then the god Brahma appeared on the Lord's right, a bit larger than human size, and the god Indra on the left, and around them were the four kinds of desire-realm gods holding up royal parasols and fanning him with cooling yak-tail fans. The four great kings stood in the east and west with hands cupped together in reverence. The gods filled the sky with jewel towers, making offerings with flowers and incense powders, offering heavenly music and songs, with a fine gentle spray of incense rain descending from the clouds.

Seeing such a host of mendicants and such miraculous displays, the father king did not recognize the Lord; he became confused, and asked his attendant, Kalodayin, "Among the many orange-robed mendicants, where is the prince?" Then Kalodayin pointed out the Lord to the king, saying, "This one is the Lord, O King of Men, behold him!" Then, by the power of the Lord, those gods and humans could see each other; and the king saw the Lord, the gods who were making offerings to the Lord, and the sky full of divine jeweled towers, and he was greatly amazed. "When he was a youth, I said he would be a lord of the Dharma. And that is what this is. I only have a human following, but the Lord, he has a following of both gods and humans!" The Shakyas all came out of the city and gathered together, wondering, "Will the father pay homage to the son or the son pay homage to the father?" Then the great king Shuddhodhana bared one shoulder of his priceless robe, placed his right knee on the ground, and paid homage to the foot of the Lord with his jeweled coif and diadem, and said: "O thou of vast intelligence, I bow thrice to your universal feet! When you were born, the earth quaked, and the shadow of the rose-apple tree did not leave your body." But when the father had thus revered the son, the Shakyas felt suspicious, wondering, "How can this be? What does it mean?" King

Shuddhodhana addressed them: "Wise ones, it is not the young prince that I salute; I have bowed three times to this Lord of gods and humans."

Then the Lord withdrew his magical manifestation, and, in the midst of the community of mendicants, sat on a lion throne adorned with various divine fabrics by the desire-realm gods. The desire gods held a divine canopy above him. Then King Shuddhodhana's voice felt choked, his heart felt heavy, and his eyes filled with tears, as he spoke: "When you dwelt in the spacious mansion in your father's palace, why did you go alone into the wilderness filled with dangers?" The Lord spoke: "Lord of men! Freeing themselves from the bonds of the household, the sages live happily in the ten abodes of the noble ones." Along these lines, father and son had a lengthy conversation. Finally the king was happy, and he bowed again to the Lord, fully recognizing him as a blissful Buddha. Then the king thought: "My son has attained such excellence! It is my great fortune!" Then the Lord gave an appropriate teaching there in the banyan garden, and seventy-seven thousand Shakya princes saw the truth. The next day he taught at the Brahma garden, and seventy-six thousand Shakyas saw the truth.

The Shakya Amrtodhana had a six-year-old son named Ananda who had been predicted to become an attendant of the Lord; so the father wanted to keep him away from the Lord by all means possible. But the Lord thought, "I should go to Kapilavastu for the sake of Ananda." When Amrtodhana hid Ananda in his room, the Lord opened the door with magical power, and Ananda came out, picked up a yak-tail fan and came to fan the Lord. When the Lord left, Ananda followed in his footsteps, and no one could turn him back. Amrtodhana realized the prophesied time had come, so he sent Ananda on an elephant to the banyan garden. When he reached there, the Lord had Dashabala Kashyapa confer the renunciation vows. From that time Ananda fulfilled the prophecy by happily serving the Lord. The next day the Lord taught the Dharma at the Rohatika garden, and Amrtodhana and seventy-five thousand Shakyas attained the fruit. But Devadatta did not respect the Lord and slandered him.

King Shuddhodhana invited the Lord to the midday meal; having offered the meal, the king took the sacrificial vase and formally offered the Nyagrodha garden. The Lord dedicated the merit of the gift and went there to spend the summer rains retreat, with the king and the Shakya people visiting him often to listen to the Dharma. At that time, King Shuddhodhana experienced strong mental swings between extreme depression and intense delight, and so did not attain the fruit. Then the Lord, to rid the king of the gleeful mood when he thought "My son is the only one with the greatest magical powers!" sent Maudgalyayana to visit him. When he asked the saint, "Do other disciples have great powers?" Maudgalyayana replied, "There are many others with great magical powers." Then the king was free of his exulting mind, realizing that others besides his son had great magical powers. Next, to free the king from his depression, which had arisen when he had thought that the gods, humans, and titans used to make offerings to the Lord but now only the humans were doing it, the Lord taught the Dharma to the host of gods. Indra, knowing the problem, told Vishvakarma to build a pagoda of four jewel substances in the Nyagrodha garden with various thrones in it. The four great kings sat in the four door-ways. The Buddha was invited there, and the desire and form gods, the dragons, the ogres, the fairies, the titans, the bird-men, the kinnaras all gathered around, along with the Great Disciples. Outside sixty thousand spirits gathered. At that time the Lord sat on the throne adorned with various jewels and taught the Discourse called *The Demonstration of Reality: The Bodhisattva Samadhi of the Meeting of Father and Son.* Maudgalyayana brought King Shuddhodhana out of Kapilavastu to the divine pagoda. When Maudgalyayana entered and began to bring Shuddhodhana with him through the eastern door, he was stopped by King Rashtrapala, who said, "Don't go in." "Why not?" "The Lord is explaining the Dharma to the divine audience. Humans are not allowed in." "Who may your honor be?" "Great King! I am Rashtrapala." Then King Shuddhodhana went into the south, west, and north doors and had similar encounters with the other three great kings. Then King Shuddhodhana was free of his depression and felt an ambition: "Hey! I would like to see the Lord teaching that pure audience of gods." Then the Lord had the intuition that King Shuddhodhana would die of frustration if he could not see the Buddha teaching, and so he magically made the jewel palace transparent, and the king could see the Buddha's body without obstruction. Seeing it, he felt joy and reverence and bowed to the Lord's two feet and sat down to one side. Then the Lord made a sign to the titan king Vemachitra to make offerings. Then Vemachitra mounted his seven-jewel chariot and put many titan women in the jewel chariots drawn by jewel horses, carrying various offerings, erecting jewel palaces in offering, praising and offering to the Lord with intense reverence. Likewise the titan king Bali and Rahu and so on and the bird king Supaksha also worshiped. Then the dragon princesses offered jewel umbrellas, and the dragon kings Nanda and Upananda filled garlands with red pearls and purified everything with blazing and dripping fire and water from various wish-granting gems within the seven-jewel mansions. Then the serpent spirits and the host of the four great kings offered jewel canopies and the fairies offered pools filled with lotuses upon the earth-guarding pillar deities. And the kinnara king offered a seven-jewel house adorned with jewel umbrellas, and Indra offered a jewel mansion. All the gods made offerings and sang praises, and the Lord smiled.

Then King Shuddhodhana was totally enveloped with love for his son, and so the Lord taught the *Father-Son Meeting Sutra,* the samadhi to tame that attachment. King Shuddhodhana attained the fruit of stream-entry in the Mahayana, finally attaining the tolerance of the uncreated along with the seventy thousand Shakyas. The Lord smiled, and when Ashvathama asked the reason, he predicted the enlightenments of Shuddhodhana and the Shakyas and told Shariputra to promulgate the Sutra.

If you can reflect properly about this story of what happened when father and son met, you can understand the need not to be attached to your relatives and dear ones of this life when you try to practice a pure Dharma. If you really want to help your relatives, dear ones, and friends, you will transcend the home and enter homelessness, abandoning concern for greatness in this life and even the perfect successes of the life-cycle. Abiding in pure ethical conduct, you must apply yourself to practice the path in solitary places, and you will feel a firm certitude about the keys of the preparations, practices, and applications of the stages of the path to enlightenment.

Then the Lord reached the age of forty-one in the iron male mouse year and spent the rains retreat in the Thirty-three heaven. The Lord wished to take care of his mother, Mayadevi, who had taken rebirth in the Thirty-three heaven and also wished to develop the roots of virtue of innumerable deities there. Sitting before the Sudharma palace, the mantra of Ushnishasitatapattra emerged from his crown-dome. He then went to the gods' pleasure park together with Brahma and Indra and the eight classes of gods and also Mahamati and the other many Bodhisattvas. At that moment light-rays radiated, and all the tormented beings from the three wretched states were liberated from their sufferings and set upon jewels in the presence of the Lord, where they began to sing his praises.

Then the Lord sat upon a flat stone like a white blanket, under the divine tree Kalpadruma, spending the rains retreat with eight thousand saints such as Shariputra, Mahakashyapa, Mahakatyayana, Purna, Potala, Ashvatama, Kapina, Mahodara, and Subhuti, and also Ananda. Many Bodhisattvas also gathered, and the great mother Mayadevi was immensely delighted. For the Bodhisattvas to live comfortably she taught the spell of Shankara.

At that time, the Lord was dwelling only with tenth-stage Bodhisattvas. Maitreya requested the teaching to alleviate the sufferings of the humans of Jambudvipa. The Lord touched his foot to the ground, emanating a magical fierce deity, who subdued the evil beings, and then he taught the Achala Tantra. A god became aware that he would die and be born as a pig and began to beat his breast in terror. The Lord went there and told him to go for refuge to the Three Jewels. When he did so, he was reborn instead as the son of a merchant in Vaishali, given the name Prajna.

While the Lord was staying in the Thirty-three heaven, Mahamaud-galyayana remained on earth to tend the teaching. When any ordinary person was wondering where the Lord was staying, King Bimbisara and King Prasenajit and the four assemblies would ask Mahamaudgalyayana, who was spending the rains retreat in Shravasti. "Where is the Lord staying?" "He is staying in the heavens." Then they were happy. They returned to him again after the three months of the rains retreat and said, "Now it has been a long time since we saw the Lord, please invite the Lord to return with our word of request." Maudgalyayana went to the heaven in an instant and made the request of the four assemblies to the Lord. Then the Lord, knowing that humans could not climb to the heavens and that the gods could descend to Jambudvipa, acknowledged their request and sent Maudgalyayana back to say that he would descend in seven days to the city of Sankhasya. Maudgalyayana went back in an instant and informed the humans and then returned to the Thirty-three. Aniruddha told King Udayana about it, who was very happy and had the city cleaned, set out offerings everywhere, and made that whole place into a divine pleasure garden.

Then on the twenty-second day of the middle autumn month, the Lord set out for the earth, and Indra commanded Vishvakarma to magically create three stairways. On the central sapphire staircase, Shakyamuni descended with his attendants. On the right one of gold, Brahma with the form-realm gods descended, fanning the Lord with jeweled yak-tail fans. On the left one made of crystal, Indra with the desire gods came carrying royal umbrellas. The Lord came half the way down by foot, to create merit for Vishvakarma, and half the way by magic, in order to prevent loss of faith in people. Once below the altitude of twelve leagues, the gods could not bear to descend due to the rising human smell, so he caused a sandal-wood smell to spread everywhere. Since if human men could see divine women or if human women could see divine men, they would die, he magically caused men to see all the gods as male and women to see them all as female. And so he entered the city of Sankhasya and sat down on a lion throne erected by Indra.

When the Lord was fifty-seven, in the male fire dragon year, he performed the great miracles in Shravasti. Now since the Teacher had attained perfect Buddhahood, he had developed and liberated countless gods and humans. All the nine great kings of the Jambudvipa continent made offerings to the Teacher along with his Community of great disciples. The six religious teachers such as Purana were disturbed by jealousy and wished to rival the Teacher. The evil Mara also stirred up their minds, intensifying their competitiveness. The six teachers went to King Bimbisara. "O king! We and Gautama are said to be wise, so it is right for us to hold a contest of miracles." The king said, "You all are being foolish. How can you compete with the Buddha's great miraculous power?" The six teachers replied, "In seven days we will compete in miracles, and you will see." The king said, "I will prepare this contest, though I fear you will be shamed." The king then communicated with the Lord, who said, "I myself know the time." Then the king prepared the place for the miracle competition; but on the seventh day, the Lord left for Vaishali with his Community.

The six teachers rejoiced and became arrogant: "Gautama's miracles were not on our level! You didn't believe in us, but he fled when he had to compete!" Then they and King Bimbisara all followed the Buddha to Vaishali. The people of Vaishali welcomed the Lord. The six teachers set up a miracle competition again after seven days. The Lord was requested and again said, "I myself know the time." But on the sixth day he departed for Kosambi and King Udayana.

Again they followed and requested a competition, and this time the Lord left for Anga of King Shunchidala. There again they followed, requested the competition, and the Buddha left for Champa and King Indravarma. Again they followed, and this time the Lord went to King Brahmadatta's Varanasi. Again they followed, and this time the Buddha went to Kapilavastu of the Shakyas. All this time the six teachers were becoming more and more arrogant and urged King Bimbisara again and again to make the Lord compete with them in miracles. The king said to them, "If you repeat this again three more times, I will banish you and send you away." They then thought, "This king is the partisan of Gautama. But King Prasenajit is said to be completely impartial. So let's ask him to make it happen," and they followed the Lord to Shravasti, where he was staying in the Jetavana Monastery. At that time, King Bimbisara had five hundred horsemen and an assembly of four hundred and ten thousand followers, the Licchavis had five hundred horsemen and seventy thousand followers, Udrayana had eighty-one thousand followers, Shunchidala had fifty thousand followers, Indravarma had sixty thousand, Brahmadatta had eight hundred thousand, and the Shakyas had nine million followers. The whole forest of Shravasti was filled with this great multitude.

Then the six teachers spoke to Prasenajit. "The ascetic Gautama has made appointments with us for miracle competitions; whenever the time comes, he flees. Now, a great audience has assembled in your country. You, King, are like the earth, without partiality; it is fitting for you to be the judge. If Gautama wins, we will become his disciples; if we win, we will rule." The king said, "Why do such lowly persons as you, who know next to nothing, want to compete in miracles with the great King of Dharma? I fear you will lose." They replied, "You may have been deceived by Gautama. If we compete, it will be clear." The king said, "In that case, I will request the Lord." Then King Prasenajit asked the Lord three times. The Lord knew that here in Shravasti the previous Buddhas had manifested their great miracles after gathering a great host of people, and he said, "Great King! Please prepare things after seven days, find an open place outside the city, and erect a stadium."

Then King Prasenajit draped the stadium for the great miracle contest in hundreds of thousands of cloths and swept down the road from Shravasti out to it with sandalwood-scented water. Banners and victory standards were erected. Pennants were hung. He made it like a divine pleasure garden. He erected there a golden lion throne for the Lord, adorned with jewels. The followers of the six teachers erected six stadiums adorned with cloths and thrones for the six teachers, according to their own means. The six teachers arrived first and sent a messenger to the king, "Divine One! We are here! Please send someone to bring the ascetic Gautama." The king and his retinue went to the stadium and sent a brahmin boy to invite the Lord.

On the first day of the last month of winter, the Lord, like a king of geese, flew through the sky to the stadium of great miracles. Seeing him, Prasenajit said to the six teachers, "The Lord has just shown a miracle. Now it is your turn to do so!" They replied, "Lord! Since such a great multitude is here assembled, what sort of miracle is this? Who knows whether it is ours or Gautama's?"

When the Lord entered within the great miracle pavilion, the assembled humans, animals, and deities all saw a great fire consume the pavilion and a great light was emitted. The six teachers said, "Good! Now the ascetic Gautama has burned the stadium. If he is capable of that, then here he might be peaceful." The many faithful, such as King Prasenajit, Queen Malavati, the merchant Anathapindada, and their attendants and so on, all sat silently with understanding in their hearts, while the six teachers and their disciples rejoiced. What had really happened was that the Buddha's power had made the fire to cleanse the impurities of the stadium. When the fire died down, the stadium appeared even more beautiful. The king was delighted and said to the teachers, "The Lord has shown his miracles! Now you show yours!" They lost their eloquence and fell silent.

Then King Prasenajit made bounteous offerings of food and equipment to the Lord in the stadium. The Lord took his toothpick and stuck it in the ground, and he manifested a seven-jewel tree, five hundred leagues high, with flowers the size of chariot wheels, and with fruits the size of a five-quart vase, with aromatic breezes, emitting the sound of the Dharma, more brilliant than sunlight. Beginning with this, for a whole fortnight, each day the vast multitude beheld astounding miracles, became faithful and attentive to the Dharma, and were individually established on the three paths.

On the second day, King Udrayana made offerings, and two jewel mountains shining with rainbow colors appeared on the Lord's right and left sides, the right one upholding various flowering trees producing delicious fruits that satisfied many people. On the left-hand mountain sweet grass grew which satisfied the grazing animals. On the third day, King Shunchidala made offerings, and when the Lord threw the water used to rinse his mouth on the earth, it made a two-hundred-league jewel pond adorned with the seven precious gems filled with lotuses of many colors, which radiated light-rays that filled earth and sky and amazed and delighted the entire assembly. On the fourth day, when King Indravarma made offerings, the Lord created eight great canals on each of the four sides of that jewel pond, from which water tumbled into the pond, emitting the sounds of the Dharma. On the fifth day, when King Brahmadatta made offerings, the Lord emitted from his smile a dazzling golden light which illuminated the entire billion-world universe, filling the bodies and minds of all beings it touched with intense bliss, relieving them of the three sufferings and the five obstructions.

On the sixth day, when the Licchavis made offerings, the Lord made it possible for each member of all assemblies to read the thoughts of each other member and to know the good and bad evolutionary actions of the other; and all were delighted and praised the Lord. On the seventh day, when the Shakyas made offerings, each member of the assembly saw himself or herself as a world emperor, with the seven precious ornaments and the thousand sons, receiving the homage of the princes and ministers, and all felt great joy.

On the eighth day Indra invited the Lord, and when he placed his right foot within the sweet-scented mansion, the earth quaked and the five hundred Rishis whom the six teachers had asked to help them thought it was the sign to come. When they arrived, the Lord emitted a ray from his body, and they saw the Lord become as beautiful as the sun; they felt great faith, and they all attained sainthood. The Lord returned again to the great miracle stadium with the five hundred saints and sat on the lion throne erected by Indra in the midst of the vast multitude.

Then the Lord made himself invisible on his throne and performed the four actions in the four directions, going, standing, sitting, and lying down, emitting various light-rays. Flames roared from the lower part of his body, and water streamed from the upper part, and vice versa. Then the Lord touched the earth with his hand and the dragons offered a chariot-wheel-size lotus with a thousand golden petals and diamond anthers that sprouted up from the ground, and the Lord sat in the calyx of the lotus. Then many lotuses just like it sprouted forth, and many emanated Buddhas sat in them, filling the world up to the Akanishta heaven. Some of those Buddhas blazed with flames, some became luminous, some streamed with rain, some emitted lightning, some prophesied beings' omniscience, some asked questions, some answered them, some walked, some ate, some stood, some sat, some lay down. Even all the children could see these Buddhas without obstruction, and thus all were blessed. All the kings and their retinues from all the countries, and the many hundreds of thousands of humans and gods beheld the miracle without blinking and bowed to it unceasingly. They were delighted and scattered flowers and incense powders. And the emanated Buddhas uttered many verses of teaching. The Lord said, "O mendicants, the great miracle will disappear, don't cling to its sign," and he disappeared.

King Prasenajit said to the six teachers, "Hey! The Lord has shown the great miracle. Your turn has come—now you show something!" Then Purana Kassapa was silent and elbowed Makkhali Gosala, who did the same to Sanjaya Belatthiputta, who did the same to Ajita Kesakambala, who did the same to Pakhuda Kaccayana, who did the same to Nigantha Nataputta, who did the same once again to Purana. The king repeated his request three times, and still they were speechless and elbowed each other and became paralyzed and discouraged and hung their heads and were speechless, their minds withdrawn and bodies shaken. Then the Lord touched his lion throne and a great bellow like a bull's sounded, and five great ogres emerged and destroyed the thrones of the six teachers. And Vajrapani, holding a vajra with fires blazing from its tip, brandished it over the heads of the six teachers, emitting a red wind and a fierce rain, and the six teachers were terrified and fled. But their followers, ninety thousand strong, felt faith in the Buddha, renounced the home life, and attained sainthood. Then the Lord emitted light-rays from his eighty thousand pores and manifested a Buddha on a lotus on the tip of each ray. Each Buddha sat and taught them the Dharma.

On the ninth day, when Brahma made offerings, the Lord made his body tall enough to reach the Brahma heaven, illuminating heaven and earth with light-rays, and taught the Dharma. On the tenth day, the four great kings made offerings, and light-rays blazed from the body that reached up to the summit of existence. On the eleventh day, the householder Anathapindada made offerings, and the Buddha became invisible on his throne, emitted rainbow light-rays, and taught the Dharma. On the twelfth day, when the householder Chitra made offerings, the Lord entered the trance of love and radiated golden light-rays that enfolded whomever they touched into the abode of universal love. On the thirteenth day, King Shunchidala made offerings, and two light-rays emerged from the navel of the teacher seated on the lion throne, extended seven arm spans into space on either side, and created giant lotuses on the tip of each, with an emanated Buddha seated on each. From their navels two light-rays were emitted with lotuses and Buddhas on their tips and so forth until the entire billion-world universe was filled with emanated Buddhas. On the fourteenth day, when King Udrayana made offerings and scattered flowers, the flowers were transformed into twelve hundred fifty jewel chariots of blazing gold, tall enough to reach the Brahma heavens, adorned with precious wishing gems, with an emanated Buddha seated in each, radiating a light that enabled all to see the entire billion-world galactic universe.

On the fifteenth day, when King Bimbisara made offerings, each dish had food of a hundred tastes, satisfying the entire multitude. The Lord touched the earth with his hand, and the assembly saw all the beings in the eighteen hells suffering various miseries, burned by blazing flames and so on, crying, "How we suffer these terrible torments!" All were terrified and felt intense compassion. The hell beings themselves could see the Buddha. Rays of light like liquid gold flowed from his five fingertips, and that golden light touched the bodies of the hell beings and relieved their suffering. The instant they heard the Dharma, they passed away from there and were reborn in a higher state.

Thus when the Teacher had performed such great miracles in Shravasti, the faithful humans and gods erected there a Great Miracle Monument, square, with four stages, with niches on each side.

Subsequently the Lord turned the wheel of Dharma infinitely in various lands of gods and humans. On the Vulture Heap Mountain, to a countless assembly of Bodhisattvas from the heavenly pure lands, of disciples, gods, and dragons and so on, he taught the precious *Transcendent Wisdom Sutras.* That was called the central teaching, the signless Dharma wheel. Then in other countries he taught the *King of Trances Sutra,* the *Buddha Garland Sutra,* the *Jewel Heap Sutra* and so on, immeasurable Sutras of the central teaching. Thereafter he taught the final teaching Sutras such as the *Elucidation of the Intention,* in Vaishali and so on.

On another level, he taught the Dharma wheel of mantra at the very same time. While he was teaching the *Transcendent Wisdom Sutra* on the Vulture Heap Mountain, in other embodiments he taught infinite Unexcelled Yoga Tantras such as the *Wheel of Time* at the Glorious Dhanyakataka Monument. Likewise he taught infinite teachings of the four

Esoteric Mantra Tantras in many heavens, such as the summit of Mount Meru, the Thirty-three heaven, the Tushita heaven, the Brahma heavens, and in many special places on earth, such as the realms of dragons and of ogres and the kingdom of Oddiyana and so on. Nowadays there are some confused people who think that the Teacher Shakyamuni may have taught the Sutras but not the Mantric Tantras. But such thoughts and positions are irrational chatter. When the Teacher spent a rains retreat at the Sudharma center in the Thirty-three heaven, the Arya Ushnishasitatapattra emerged from his crown-dome and taught the supreme Aparajita mantra. From then on, the initiation and instruction of the *Arya Sitatapattra Action Tantra* of the Transcendent Buddha clan has continued without interruption until today. Again, when the Lord went to the Potala Mountain, he taught many Action Tantras, such as the *Dharani of the Great Compassion Lord Simhanada* and the *Dharani of the Thousand-Armed Thousand-Eyed Compassion Lord* and so on; and these initiations and instructions of the Lotus clan Action Tantras have continued uninterruptedly until the present day. Again the Teacher, in order to purify the sins of King Ajatashatru, taught the *Vajravidarana,* vajra class, Action Tantra, and we have its instructions in unbroken descent. Further, he taught the well-known measureless Action Tantras, such as the *Trisamayavyuha* and so on; the Performance Tantras, such as the *Vairochana-abhisambodhi* and the *Vajrapanyabhisheka;* and the Yoga Tantras, such as the *Vajradhatumandala* and the *Tattvasamgraha* and so on—all taught at the time of enlightenment in Akanishta heaven.

Then there is the well-known story about when the Lord spent the rains retreat in the Thirty-three heaven, and Indra saw the godling Vimalamani die and take rebirth in hell and so asked the Lord for a method to release him from that horrid state. The Lord taught the *Durgatiparishodhana Tantra* and gave its personal instruction to Indra, who then performed the hell-cleansing rites. That godling was immediately released and born in a higher heaven, and so Indra was filled with great faith and reverence and gratitude and bowed to the Lord and made offerings to him: "Wonder! The blessing of the mantras of the Buddhas is astounding, whereby a being who has fallen into the unredeemable hell is quickly reborn in heaven."

The Teacher also taught the Unexcelled Yoga Tantras. On the full moon of the Chitra month at the glorious Dhanyakataka Great Monument, at the request of King Suchandra of Shambhala, to an assembly of many millions, he taught the *Kalachakra Tantra,* at the same time teaching most of the other Unexcelled Yoga Tantras, such as the *Mahavajrabhairava Mulatantra* and so on, entrusting those Tantras to the Lord of Secrets, Vajrapani. Furthermore, the ultimate, consummate, and peak of all Unexcelled Yoga

Tantras is stated in unison by all Great Adepts to be the *Glorious Esoteric Communion Tantra,* and that Tantra is said in its preface to have been stated by the Lord when dwelling in a measureless mansion within a triangle having the shape of the vulva of the vajra goddess, to an assembled host filling the entire realm of space. And in the seventeenth chapter, when requested by His Holiness the Savior Maitreya and Vajrapani and so on, the Lord himself said that incalculable, innumerable eons ago from the Nirvana of the Realized Lord Dipamkara up to the Transcendent Lord Kashyapa the Buddhas had not taught any Unexcelled Yoga Tantras. And finally, in order to care for King Indrabhuti of the land of Oddiyana, the Lord again taught the *Esoteric Communion* and entrusted the Tantra to Vajrapani. And all the Great Adepts agree that then King Indrabhuti meditated on it and attained communion in his single lifetime.

Here some may think that, since most of the Unexcelled Yoga Tantras are said to be taught by Vajradhara and not by Lord Shakyamuni, he did not in fact teach them. This shows lack of discernment. How can one say that the Lord did not teach Tantras that he taught while creating himself as the Lord of the mandala with the accoutrements of the Beatific Body? The Lord is seen to change his outfit to teach the Dharma even in the monastic literature.

For example, look at the story of the barbarian king Kapina. He sent a messenger to the kings of the six great cities, especially King Prasenajit. "You all should come to visit me within seven days! If you don't come, it will be war! I will destroy your countries." That messenger delivered his message to the kings of five of the cities and they all were terrified and went to Shravasti and told King Prasenajit. Then they all went together to the presence of the Lord and told him about it. The Lord said, "Send that messenger to me!" King Prasenajit said to the messenger, "There is a magical king greater than me—go to him!" When the messenger went to the Jetavana Monastery, he gave the message to the Lord, seated in state as a world emperor. The magical king crushed it under his foot and commanded the messenger, "I am a great emperor, master of the four continents. Why does your stupid king not behave obediently toward me? You go to him and tell him this for me! 'You come to my presence within seven days! If you don't come, I will punish you according to my law.'" When King Kapina came to Shravasti, all the kings under the sun escorted him. They went to the Jetavana Monastery, transformed into a divine city like Indra's Sudarshana on top of Mount Meru, and the Lord sat in state with the outfit of a world emperor. Maudgalyayana was transformed into his chief minister. When the great king Kapina saw this, he thought, "His image is greater than mine, but how is his power?" Then Indra, in the guise of a charioteer, brought the rainbow bow of the gods and presented it to the chief minister. The minister gave it to the barbarian king, but the latter could not even lift it. Then the magical king took the bow and tapped it with his little finger, which literally petrified King Kapina, making him unable to move. Then when the Lord as a magic king bent the bow, the earth quaked. He shot one arrow and it pierced in succession seven great iron drums, splitting into five arrows, from whose tips countless light-rays emitted, each of them with a world emperor on its tip. Those light-rays accomplished the aims of beings, and they sounded verses of praise and teaching. Then the pride of power of King Kapina was quieted, and he thought, "Ema! What is this?" The Lord then taught him the Dharma and he saw the truth. Then the Lord reverted to his usual form, and King Kapina, along with his eighteen thousand ministers, renounced the home life and attained sainthood; he was called the Venerable Mahakapina.

In this case, who in his right mind would say, "King Kapina was tamed by a world emperor, not by the Lord!"

Further, many Unexcelled Yoga Tantras often say, "stated by the Lord Shakyamuni." It is well known in the *Kalachakra Tantra.* Further, the *Manjushri Namasamgiti,* well known as the root of many Unexcelled Yoga Tantras, states: "Thereupon the Lord Shakyamuni saw all the great clans of secret mantra, the three clans, the secret mantra clan, the mantra-holding clan. The mundane and the transcendent clan, the great clan that illuminates the world, the supreme clan of the Great Seal, seeing the great crown-dome clan, the Lord of the Word made this verse. Having the six kings of secret mantra, nonduality emerged and he stated this qualified by nonproduction." And also, there is the colophon, "The true expression of the ultimate names of the Holy Manjushri, spoken by Lord Shakyamuni, is completed."

Further, as for the *Samvaratantra* being taught by Shakyamuni, the *Dakarnava Tantra* clearly says, "This was stated by the Shakya Lion in this time of contention."

Therefore, those who wish from their hearts to practice the stages of the path of enlightenment should not entrust their minds to any false tales of foolish people and must develop a certitude from the depths of their being that the compassionate Teacher Shakyamuni taught everything from the root of the path, the way of reliance on the spiritual friend, up to the attainment of communion, the ultimate fruit of the culminating path of mantra. Having understood that there is no instruction beyond the teachings of the Victor, they should place their trust in the actual teaching of the Buddha as the supreme of personal instructions.

Thus, the compassionate Teacher, King of the Shakyas, limitlessly taught the Three Baskets and Four Tantra Divisions, according to the vow of Samantabhadra, "In god language, the languages of dragons and ogres, serpent and human languages, according to all the sounds of all beings, I will teach the Dharma in every language." He taught according to the languages of all beings such as gods and dragons, a single statement of his being understood by each being in their own language. And so infinite teachings emerged according to the faculties and inclinations of each being. Infinite teachings ceaselessly emerged from each pore of his body, and all of the teachings of the Buddha could only have been taught by him. We only summarize this infinite profusion of teachings according to the antidotes needed by the individual disciple's addictions, as "eighty-four thousand groups of teachings."

Thus that compassionate Teacher turned measureless wheels of Dharma of Individual and Universal Vehicles, developing and liberating countless humans and gods. The Teacher spoke to his followers: "The fourfold community should read the twelve branches of Scripture that confer benefit and happiness. Apply yourselves to the individual liberation practice. The elders should support the younger with equipment. The younger should not summon the elder by name. To the faithful, you should show the Teacher's birth, Buddhahood, Dharma teaching, and Nirvana. O mendicants, if you have any doubts about the three jewels and the four truths, you should ask about them." And the Lord took off his upper robe. "Mendicants! It is rare to see a Transcendent Lord! Behold the body of the Transcendent Lord!" The mendicants were silent for a moment. "All created things have the nature of destruction. This is the last statement of the Transcendent Lord." Then, next to a pair of Sala trees, he placed his head to the north to show that "in the future, in the northern Land of Snows, my complete teaching will vastly spread," during the male iron dragon year, which was his eighty-first year, on the full moon day of the month of Vaishakha. Though in ultimate reality there was no interruption of his Form Body manifestations and miraculous activities, in order to give incentive to those disciples still holding on to permanence, to instruct them that Transcendent Lords are very rare and hard to meet, by the power of previous spiritual conceptions and vows, he manifested the way of ultimate Nirvana. Though the Victor himself attained Nirvana, by the power of his ancient spiritual conception and solemn vows he blessed the teaching to remain for five thousand years, and he increased profusely his heritage and relics, blessing the whole of Jambudvipa to be filled with monuments.

Those who have the essential concern to practice the stages of the path of enlightenment must understand that all the Victor's teachings of Sutra and Mantra are exclusively methods for their own attainment of enlightenment, thinking, "That compassionate Teacher taught this Dharma for the sake of liberating me personally from the suffering of the hellish states and the life-cycle in general and to establish me in the exaltation of Buddhahood." They should make effort to remember the Teacher's excellence, kindness, and compassion, and worship and invoke him with faith and reverence. At the start of the Teacher's teaching of the Dharma, he taught the group of five the four aspects of the noble truth of suffering, beginning with impermanence. At the end, with his statement about how all created things have the nature of destruction, again he taught impermanence. If intelligent people know how to examine this fact, they can understand this as a great key for energizing their practice of the path to enlightenment.

At the beginning, thinking over the fact that one will not live long, being perishable by nature, energizes the urgency of entering the Dharma. At the medium level, thinking over the process of impermanence leads one to lose appetite by knowing the unreliability of even the successes of the life-cycle, which energizes one's meditation of the path. At the level of the great being, thinking over impermanence, how all beings have been careening from life to life unceasingly, helps one cultivate the spirit of enlightenment through the seven causal precepts, such as mother recognition, and helps one to practice the Bodhisattva deeds. Even when one contemplates the view of the central way, it proceeds according to the saying "from impermanence, suffering, from suffering, he taught selflessness." First one meditates impermanence and eliminates the mentality habituated to the permanent, unique, independent self. Then one can engage in meditating the central view free of the extremist fabrications. Then, having cultivated character by means of the ordinary path, when one enters the Mantric path, remembering impermanence energizes one with the urgency of needing to learn the Tantric Vehicle.

One should understand the biography of the Teacher in this way, bringing its message into one's practice of the path.

CHAPTER 3

བཤེས་གཉེན།

Meeting the Buddha in the Mentor

Quintessence Segment

You precisely teach the good path of the Blissful
To the savage, hard-to-tame beings of these dark times,
Who were not tamed by the visits of countless Buddhas,
Compassionate Savior,
I pray to you!

The sun of Shakyamuni now sunken over time,
You perform the deeds of a Victorious Buddha
For beings who have no spiritual Savior,
Compassionate Savior,
I pray to you!

But a single of your body's pores
Is better recommended as our field of merit
Than the Victors of all times and places—
Compassionate Savior,
I pray to you!

The beauty wheels of your Bliss-Lord Three Bodies
Ecstatically unfold the net of miracles of your liberative art,
Leading beings by participating in ordinariness—
Compassionate Savior,
I pray to you!

Your aggregates, elements, media, and limbs
Are the five Blissful Clans' Fathers and Mothers
The Bodhisattvas male and female, and the Ferocious Lords,
Supreme Three Jewel Mentor,
I pray to you!

Your nature is the million wheels of Mandalas
Arising from the play of omniscient primal wisdom,
Chief Vajra-master, Lord of the Hundred Clans,
Communion Primal Savior,
I pray to you!

Inseparable from the play of unblocked orgasmic joy,
Universal Lord, you pervade all moving and unmoving,
You are actual, ultimate, all-good spirit of enlightenment,
Beginningless and endless,
I pray to you!

SOLEMN PRAYER

You are Mentor!
You are Archetype Deity!
You are Angel and Protector!
From now until enlightenment,
I seek no other Savior!
With compassion's iron hook
Please look after me,
In this life, the between, and future lives!
Save me from the terrors
Of both life and liberation!
Bestow on me all powers!
Be my eternal friend!
Defend me from attack!

INITIATION AND BLESSING

By the power of thus praying three times,
The vital points of the Mentor's body, speech, and mind
Emit white, red, and blue elixir light-rays,
First one by one and then all together,
Which dissolve into my own three vital points,
Purify the four blocks, and grant the four initiations.
I attain the Four Bodies, and a duplicate of the Mentor
Melts in delight and blesses me completely.

The Three Body Mentor Yoga, The Natural Liberation Not Ceasing the Three Poisons

by Padma Sambhava

OM—AV KAA AAH!
To the unborn, nondeveloping Truth Body Mentor,
In the palace of the perfect, all-pervading Realm of Truth,
With reverent devotion, ardently I pray!
Naturally free without abandoning misknowing delusion,
I freely accept the perfect Truth Body blessing,
As effortless, nonartificial, primal wisdom!

To the deathless, great bliss Beatific Body Lama
In the palace of bright, pure wisdom's universal bliss,
With reverent devotion, ardently I pray!
Naturally free without abandoning lust and longing,
I freely accept the effortless Beatific Body blessing,
As the instant liberation of inner wisdom's universal bliss!

To the ineffable, self-created Emanation Body Mentor,
In the palace of the flawless perfect lotus,
With reverent devotion, ardently I pray!
Naturally liberated without abandoning misconceiving hatred,
I freely accept the effortless Emanation Body blessing
As self-evident wisdom's introspective self-illumination!

To the impartial great bliss Trinite Body Mentor,
In the palace of authentic clear light introspection,
With reverent devotion, ardently I pray!
Naturally free without abandoning subject-object dualism,
I freely accept the great bliss Triple Body blessing
As original wisdom's Triple Body spontaneity!

O compassion on these suffering conscious beings
Who wander in the life-cycle, darkened with delusions,
Not knowing their own minds as the infinite Truth Body—
May all of them attain the Body of Truth!

O compassion on these conscious beings, misguided in desires,
Who wander in the life-cycle, identifying with lust and clinging,
Not knowing their self-awareness as great bliss Beatific Body—
May all of them attain the Body of Beatitude!

O compassion on these misconceiving beings
Who wander in the life-cycle, with the dualistic mind of hate,
Not knowing their own minds as the born-free Emanation Body—
May they all attain the Body of Emanation!

O compassion on all beings who are not yet Buddhas,
Trapped by the presence-habit of addictive and objective veils,
Not knowing their own minds as the indivisible Three Bodies—
May they all attain the Three Bodies of Buddhahood!

Atisha's Pith Saying

When Atisha arrived in Tibet, his three disciples, Ku, Ngog, and Brom, asked him, "To attain the high state of liberation and omniscience, which is more important to follow, the precept of the lama, or the scriptures and commentaries?"

Atisha replied, "The precept of the lama is more important than the scriptures and commentaries."

"Why?" they asked.

"If you know that emptiness is the prime characteristic of all things, and even if you can recite the entire canon by heart, if, at the time of practice you do not apply to yourself the precept of the lama, you and the Dharma will go your separate ways."

They asked, "Please define the practice of the precept of the lama. Is it simply striving to practice mental, verbal, and physical virtuous deeds, acting in accordance with the three vows of individual liberation, Bodhisattvahood, and Tantra?"

"Both of these will be insufficient," replied Atisha.

"Why?"

"Although you keep the three vows, if you do not renounce the three realms of cyclic life, your deeds will only increase your worldliness. Although you strive day and night to commit physical, verbal, and mental virtuous acts, if you do not dedicate your efforts to universal enlightenment, you will end up with numerous wrong attitudes. Even though you meditate and come to be considered holy and a wise teacher, if you do not abandon your interest in the eight worldly concerns, whatever you do will only be for the purpose of this life, and in the future you will miss the right path."

Again they asked, "What is the highest teaching of the path?"

Atisha replied, "The highest skill lies in the realization of selflessness. The highest nobility lies in taming your own mind. The highest excellence lies in having the attitude that seeks to help others. The highest precept is continual mindfulness. The highest remedy lies in understanding the intrinsic transcendence of everything. The highest activity lies in not conforming with worldly concerns. The highest mystic realization lies in lessening and transmuting the passions. The highest charity lies in nonattachment. The highest morality lies in having a peaceful mind. The highest tolerance lies in humility. The highest effort lies in abandoning attachment to works. The highest meditation lies in the mind without claims. The highest wisdom lies in not grasping anything as being what it appears to be."

"And what is the ultimate goal of the teaching?"

"The ultimate goal of the teaching is that emptiness whose essence is compassion."

Milarepa's Meeting with Peldar Boom from
The Hundred Thousand Songs

Homage to the Mentor!

One autumn, the holy Milarepa was on his way to the northern Horse Gate Mountain to practice meditation, and he came to Gebha Lesum in Chung. The villagers were busy harvesting. In a particular large field, many people were laboring under the direction of a very beautiful girl, about fifteen years of age, who showed the signs of being a wisdom Dakini-angel.

Milarepa approached her and said, "May the patrons please give alms to me, a yogin."

The girl replied, "O yogin, please go rest at that house over there. I will come soon."

Accordingly Milarepa went to her house, pushed the door open with his staff, and entered. At once an ugly old woman with a handful of ashes came forward, cursing, "You yogin beggars! I never see you stay put! In summer you come begging for milk and butter! In the winter you come for grain! I'll wager you wanted to sneak in with no one home to steal the jewels of my daughter and daughter-in-law!" Fuming and trembling with rage, she was about to throw the ashes at Milarepa.

He stopped her, saying, "Wait, Grandma! Listen a minute to Milarepa's song!"

He then sang a song with nine meanings:

One, above is the happiness of high birth and freedom.
Two, below are the sufferings of the three horrid states.
Three, between are those not free to choose where to be born.
These three have come together for you now,
Grandma, you burn with anger,
And even hate the Dharma!
Look at your thoughts and see your mind!
You should practice a spiritual teaching,
And rely on a reputable mentor!

When you were first sent to this house,
Could you imagine yourself becoming such a hag?
In the morning you get up from bed,

In the evening you go to sleep,
Between you do the endless housework;
You are engrossed in these three things.
Grandma, you are the unpaid maid.
Watch your thoughts and see your mind!
You should practice a spiritual teaching,
And rely on a reputable mentor!
Then think how things might be better.

The head of the family is the most important,
Otherwise, income and wealth are next,
And children are indispensable.
Now these three are before you.
Grandma, you're unimportant, with no share.
Watch your thoughts and see your mind!
You should practice a spiritual teaching,
And rely on a reputable mentor!
Then think how things might be better.

You get, and the thief will rob you,
You don't get, and bandits attack,
You struggle to avoid injury and death.
Now you are subjected to these three things.
Grandma, you burn with fury at crowds of foes!
Watch your thoughts and see your mind!
You should practice a spiritual teaching,
And rely on a reputable mentor!
Then think how things might be better.

Identifying the girlfriends of men,
Gossiping about your children,
Chattering of widows and relatives!
Now you are obsessed with these three things!
Grandma, are you tolerant when you gossip?
Watch your thoughts and see your mind!
You should practice a spiritual teaching,
And rely on a reputable mentor!
Then think how things might be better.

You get up like pulling a stake from the ground,
You walk like a waddling bird,
You sit like a stone drops to ground,
These three now have become your lot!

Grandma, your mind is done in by your body's illusions.
Watch your thoughts and see your mind!
You should practice a spiritual teaching,
And rely on a reputable mentor!
Then think how things might be better.

Outside your skin is creased with wrinkles;
Inside your bones stick out from your withered flesh;
Between you are deaf, dumb, blind, and confused;
Now these three have become your lot!
Grandma, wizened show of ugliness!
Watch your thoughts and see your mind!
You should practice a spiritual teaching,
And rely on a reputable mentor!
Then think how things might be better.

Your food and drink are cold and foul,
Your coat is heavy and torn,
Your bed is a heap of coarse hides;
Now these three have become your lot.
Grandma, you are half woman and half bitch!
Watch your thoughts and see your mind!
You should practice a spiritual teaching,
And rely on a reputable mentor!
Then think how things have come to this.

Upward, to gain high birth and freedom
Is rarer than a star in daytime;
Downward, the life-cycle and horrid states
Happen easily as flesh is pierced;
Now, discouraged, paralyzed by death,
Grandma, remorseful, you have no heart for death?
Watch your thoughts and see your mind!
You should practice a spiritual teaching,
And rely on a reputable mentor!

Due to the compassion and the melodious speech of the holy man, the
old woman could not help but feel deep faith. The ashes in her hand were
released and fell to the floor. She regretted her previous behavior and broke
into tears.

Meantime the girl from the field came back to the house. Seeing the old
woman in tears she turned to Milarepa and cried, "O yogin, you don't

seem very religious! Did you hit this poor old woman?" The grandmother quickly intervened: "No, no, please don't wrongly accuse him! He never said anything unkind to me. It was I who treated him wrongly. He gave me such true teachings as I had never heard, I was deeply moved to faith. I only cried because I realized how far from the Dharma I have gotten. Now you are not like me. You are young, and have wealth and faith. This is the great Mentor called Milarepa. You should serve him and make offerings and ask him for teachings and instructions."

The girl replied, "If that's it, then you both are amazing! Are you the powerful Milarepa? Just meeting you brings great merit! If you would tell us the history of your lineage, it will inspire your disciples. It will instruct us in how to transform our perceptions. So please tell your lineage."

The reverend Milarepa thought, "This girl is destined to become a disciple," and so he sang this song of his lineage:

The Truth Body is pervasive All-Good Samantabhadra.
The majestic Beatific Body is great Vajradhara;
The Emanation Body, saving beings, is Shakyamuni.
I am the yogin who descends from these three;
Daughter, do you have faith in this lineage?

"Your lineage is a great wonder," said Peldar Boom, "it is like the glacier at the head of all rivers. I have heard that you Dharma practitioners rely outwardly on a mentor who marks your process of consciousness, so that you can inwardly realize the unborn Body of Truth. Please tell me what kind of root mentor do you rely upon?"

Milarepa replied, "I have the following kind of root mentor," and he sang a song on how to rely on a qualified mentor:

The outer mentor shows you wisdom from without,
The inner mentor teaches awareness from within,
The reality mentor teaches reality in your mind.
I am a yogin who has all three mentors,
Daughter, do you have faith in these three?

"These mentors are outstanding," exclaimed the girl, "like turquoises strung on a woven gold chain! But before we ask for their teachings, what sort of empowerments do we request?"

Milarepa then sang:

Touching the vase on your crown is the outer empowerment;
Showing your body to be divine is the inner empowerment;

Identifying the intrinsic nature of the mind is the real empowerment;
I am a yogin who has all three empowerments;
Are you the daughter who wants to receive them?

Peldar Boom exclaimed, "These empowerments are indeed profound! Like the lion, king of beasts, overwhelming all other animals. I have heard that after empowerment, awareness is introduced to the path by means of reality instruction. What is that instruction?"

In answer to her question, Milarepa sang:

Outer instruction is learning, thinking, and meditating;
Inner instruction is stone-to-bone identification of intuition;
Real instruction is realization free of uniting and dividing;
I am a yogin who has all three instructions;
Are you the daughter who wants to receive them?

Peldar Boom declared, "These instructions are like reflections in a clear mirror! But after instructions, I have heard that one must retire to a hermitage and practice sacrifice! How do you perform such sacrifice!"

Milarepa sang in answer:

Retiring to a solitary hermitage is outer sacrifice;
Turning the body into food is inner sacrifice;
Absolute, radical sacrifice is reality sacrifice;
I am a yogin with all three sacrifices;
Are you the daughter who wants to receive them?

The girl said, "This sacrifice is an extremely great wonder, like a great eagle flying in the sky, overawing all lesser birds! But I have heard that some yogins who perform sacrifice transform negative circumstances into the path by using the mantra 'PHAT.' Please tell me the meaning of PHAT."

Milarepa then sang:

Outer PHAT collects scattered thoughts;
Inner PHAT rouses depressed intelligence;
Real PHAT focuses on experience of reality;
I am the yogin who has all three;
Are you the daughter who sounds them?

She exclaimed, "This PHAT is extremely wonderful! It assures swift and massive accomplishment, like the war drum and command of a king! But if one puts it into practice, what will arise?"

Milarepa sang in reply:

Base experience is the uncontrived vast immersion;
Path experience is the uncontrived great straight way;
Fruit experience is the uncontrived Universal Seal;
I am the yogin who has all three experiences,
Are you the daughter who achieves them?

Peldar Boom then said, "These experiences are like the bright sun dawning in a cloudless sky, illuminating all things. They are extremely wonderful! But realizing them gives you what sort of assurance?"
Milarepa sang again:

Free from gods and devils is view assurance;
Free from focus and distraction is meditation assurance;
Free of hope and fear is goal assurance;
I am a yogin with these three assurances.
Are you the daughter who wants them?

Thereupon the girl felt great faith in the holy man and bowed at his feet. With full devotion she invited him in and attended him respectfully. Then she said, "O mentor, I have been blocked by ignorance and have not thought of the Dharma! Now, O mentor, I will be your attendant; through your great compassion, please teach me the Dharma." Thus owning her past faults, she offered this song of formal request:

Ankay! Precious mentor!
Supreme person, Buddha emanation!
How dull, ignorant, and confused was I!
How great is evil in this world!
Southern clouds shaded me in summer heat,
But I never felt the cool!
Winter cold was so intense,
I never noticed flowers blooming!
My bad instincts were so strong,
I could not recognize you as an Adept!
I'll tell you the story of this woman child:
Lowly in evolution, I took this lowly body.
Trapped and blocked in lowly life-forms,
I never noticed I was a Buddha.
Lacking courage, I thought not of Dharma.

Though I aspired to practice Dharma,
I was overcome by laziness.
For a woman, the good life is safe bondage,
A bad life is losing all companions.
We lose touch with our kind parents.
With our husbands we think of suicide.
We have high ambitions but small determination,
Quick to scold, skilled in accusation,
Knowing all the gossip in the land,
Families must keep us away with dogs!
Though generous in public with food and wealth,
We are privately stingy and ill-tempered!
Seldom do we think of transience and death.
Hindrances always follow us like shadows.
Now, from my heart I want to practice Dharma.
Please give me a teaching simple to understand
And easy to put into practice!

Pleased, Milarepa sang in reply:

Ankay! Daughter Peldar Boom,
This your tale of a woman's life,
If I praise it, you will be self-conscious.
If I disparage it, you will be angry.
If I speak reality, it will reveal faults.
Now, listen to me, this wise old man!
If you wish from the heart to practice Dharma,
Rather than cleaning up your face,
It is better to clean your heart.
More than quitting fantasies and pretensions,
It is better to embrace a humble status.
More than quitting serving children and husband,
It is better to rely on a qualified Mentor.
More than giving up this life's business,
It is better to attain the future's great goal.
More than quitting greed and stinginess,
It is better still to give impartially.
Clever it is to know these things.
You, girl, fool around like a playful mouse;
Dharma is scarce for smooth-tongued women.
You, girl, are like a wild peahen;
Dharma is scarce for a sultry beauty.

You, girl, are like a merchant at market;
Dharma is scarce for the wily-minded.
If you want to practice Dharma rightly,
Follow me and do as I do.
Meditate in mountains without distraction.

Peldar Boom then sang this request to the holy man:

Ankay! Precious holy man,
Yogin whose friendship benefits.
In the days I am busy with endless work.
At night, stupefied I fall asleep.
All day long food and clothing make me slave.
I have no time to practice Dharma.

Milarepa replied, "If you want to practice the Dharma, you must recognize mundane business as your enemy and renounce it." And he sang a song called "The Four Renunciations":

Ankay, daughter Peldar Boom,
Faithful girl, alive and rich!
Future lives' journey is longer than this life's—
Do you know how to prepare provisions?
If you don't know how to prepare provisions,
Since generosity creates them, get into giving.
The enemy watchdog called avarice
You think helps you but causes you harm.
Do you know stinginess as your enemy?
If you do, see that you renounce it!

Ankay, daughter Peldar Boom!
Future life is more obscured than this one.
Do you know how to light your lamp?
If you don't know how to light it,
Since it's clear light, get into meditation.
The enemy "delusion" lies in unconsciousness,
Though you think it helps, it causes harm.
Do you know delusion as your enemy?
If you do, see that you renounce it!

Ankay, daughter Peldar Boom!
Future lives are more dangerous than this life—
Do you know how to prepare your escort?
If you don't know how to prepare a guide,

Since it's the holy Dharma, get into its practice.
All-absorbing are the enemies called "relatives,"
You think they help but they cause great harm.
Do you know relatives as your enemy?
If you do, see that you renounce them!

Ankay, daughter Peldar Boom!
The path of future life is longer and narrower;
Do you know how to train your stallion?
If you don't know how to train your mount,
Since it's enterprise, get into diligence!
The enemy "laziness" will lead you astray.
You think it helps, but it causes harm.
Do you know laziness as your enemy?
If you do, see that you renounce it!

Peldar Boom then said, with great determination, "Sir Mentor! I do not know how to train to prepare for future lives; but now I will try to do so. Please have compassion for me and give me instruction in meditation."

The holy man was quite delighted and replied, "If you practice the Dharma with such determination, in my tradition, it is not necessary to change your name. Since you can achieve enlightenment whether monk or layperson, you don't need to shave your head or change your clothes." Then he sang her a song of meditation instruction called "The Four Examples and Five Meanings":

Ankay, daughter Peldar Boom,
You rich and pious girl!
Use the sky as example,
Meditate without limit and center!
Use sun and moon as example,
Meditate without clarity and obscurity!
Use this mountain as example,
Meditate without movement or change!
Use the great ocean as example,
Meditate without surface or depth!
Create the meanings within your mind,
Meditate without contempt or yearning!

In this way he taught her the vital points of body and mind and set her to meditate. After the girl had developed a good realization, she offered the following recital to dispel doubts and obstructions:

Ankay! precious holy one!
Ona! supreme Buddha emanation!
I was happy meditating like the sky,
But uncomfortable meditating the clouds.
Please instruct me to meditate the clouds.
I was happy meditating sun and moon,
But a bit uncomfortable meditating all the stars.
Please instruct me to meditate planets and stars.
I was happy meditating the mountain,
But uncomfortable meditating the trees.
Please instruct me to meditate the trees.
I was happy meditating the great ocean,
But uncomfortable meditating the waves.
Please instruct me to meditate the waves.
I was happy meditating my own deep mind,
A bit uncomfortable meditating the many thoughts.
Please instruct me to meditate my thoughts.

The holy man was very pleased with this expression of her contemplation. So he sang her this song to dispel obstructions and intensify the impact of her realization:

Ankay, daughter Peldar Boom,
Listen, you rich and faithful girl!
If you were happy meditating the sky,
Clouds are but miracles of the sky;
So see them as the sky itself!
If you were happy meditating sun and moon,
Planets and stars are but miracles of sun and moon;
So see them the same as sun and moon!
If you were happy meditating this mountain,
Trees are but miracles of the mountain;
So see them as the actuality of the mountain!
If you were happy meditating the ocean,
Waves are but miracles of the ocean;
So see them as the actuality of the ocean!
If you were happy meditating your natural mind,
Thoughts are but miracles of the mind;
So set them in the actuality of the mind!

From then on Peldar Boom meditated and understood the reality of the nature of the mind. Eventually she achieved perfect realization and then ascended with her human body to the pure land of the angelic Dakinis, accompanied by the sound of heavenly drums.

This is the story of Milarepa meeting his spiritual daughter, Peldar Boom, one of his four main female heirs, at Geba Lesum of Jung.

Dromtonpa's Outline of the Path

After Atisha passed into final liberation, Drom the Teacher became his successor. On one occasion his three main disciples, the brothers Potowa, Chengawa, and Puchungwa, asked him, "Please tell us the way of practice that includes the essence of all paths to omniscient Buddhahood."

The spiritual friend Drom answered, "Though there is an incalculable number of precepts, each of which gives entry to the path of enlightenment, if one has the necessary ground for practice, there is only one thing to attain."

"What is that one thing?" asked the three brothers.

"That which has the essence of voidness and compassion. To explain: Voidness is the absolute spirit of enlightenment; the realization that all things are naturally and truly unborn. Compassion is the relative spirit of enlightenment; it is universal compassion reaching out to all beings who have not yet realized their fundamental birthlessness. Thus those who practice the path of the Universal Vehicle should first strive to develop these two forms of the spirit of enlightenment. Once the spirit of enlightenment has been conceived, it should be diligently cultivated. By doing so, one is sure to realize Buddhahood with its Form Body and Truth Body, the ultimate fruition of attaining the two kinds of spirit of enlightenment.

"There are many methods to conceive the two kinds of spirit of enlightenment. Condensing them into a way of practice, there are only three root methods and nine branch methods growing from them. The three root methods are mind development, the accumulation of merit and wisdom, and the quest of samadhi. Each root method has three principal branches.

"The three principal branch methods of mind development are the meditations on impermanence, love and compassion, and the selflessness of all persons and things. Among the various methods of mind development, these three are the most important, incorporating all the others.

"The principal branch methods for the accumulation of merit and wisdom are to honor the Mentor, to venerate the Three Jewels, and to honor the Sangha. These three are the only important methods, incorporating all others.

"The principal branch methods of the quest of samadhi are to maintain impeccable ethical conduct, to pray to the mentors of the lineage, and to keep constant solitude. In seeking the supreme samadhi of quiescence and insight, these are the only important methods, incorporating all the others.

"By practicing these nine methods, you will naturally develop the two kinds of spirit of enlightenment. When you develop the absolute spirit, you will effortlessly realize that all outer and inner things are empty of reality status, originally lacking true creation, and utterly free from proliferation. This realization will bring you boundless joy. When you develop the relative spirit of enlightenment, you will feel a profound love and compassion for those beings who have not realized the absolute spirit of enlightenment. From then on, whatever you do will only be for the benefit of those many beings, and, since you have attained the spirit of enlightenment, all you have already done will benefit them also.

"There are two ways to integrate absolute and relative spirits of enlightenment. When you develop the absolute spirit, you experience the voidness of all existence; at that very moment of experience of voidness, you will develop intense compassion for all beings, since they are not negated by the experience of voidness. When you develop this relative spirit of enlightenment, this profound compassion for all beings, you will simultaneously feel the nonseparation of self and others. Appearances are like a magician's illusions; they are actually devoid of intrinsic reality.

"When you have successfully developed this integrated realization of the two kinds of spirit of enlightenment, you have correctly entered the path of the Universal Vehicle. By cultivating that realization, you will perfect your meditation and will naturally obtain the Form and Truth Bodies of Buddhahood. The Truth Body arises from voidness, the absolute spirit of enlightenment. The Form Body arises from compassion, the relative spirit of enlightenment. From the cultivation of the indivisible two kinds of spirit of enlightenment, you will reach the indivisible Truth and Form Bodies of Buddhahood."

GAMPOPA'S FOUR THEMES

1. Turning the Mind to the Dharma
2. Practicing the Dharma as a Path
3. Removing Confusion While on the Path
4. Purifying Confusion into Primal Wisdom

Manjushri's Revelation to Sachen Kunga Nyingpo
(1092–1156)

If you have attachment to this life,
You are not a religious person.
If you have attachment to existence,
You do not have transcendent renunciation.
If you have attachment to your self-interest,
You do not have the spirit of enlightenment.
If grasping arises,
You do not have the authentic view.

The Three Principles of the Path

by Tsong Khapa

Reverence to all the holy mentors!
I will explain as best I can
The key import of all the Victor's teachings,
Path praised by all the holy Bodhisattvas,
Best entry for those fortunates who seek freedom!

Listen with clear minds, you lucky people
Who aspire to the path that pleases Buddhas,
Strive to give meaning to liberty and opportunity,
And are not addicted to the pleasures of cyclic living.

Lust for existence chains all bodied beings,
Addiction to cyclic pleasures is only cured
By transcendent renunciation.
So first of all seek transcendence.

Liberty and opportunity are hard to get,
And there is no time to life; keep thinking on this,
And you will turn off your interest in this life.
Contemplate the inexorability of evolutionary effects
And the sufferings of life—over and over again—
And you will turn off interest in future lives.

By constant meditation, your mind will not entertain
A moment's wish even for the successes of this life,
And you will aim for freedom day and night—
Then you experience transcendent renunciation.

Transcendence without the spirit of enlightenment
Cannot generate the supreme bliss
Of unexcelled enlightenment—therefore,
The Bodhisattva conceives the supreme spirit of enlightenment.

Carried away on the currents of four mighty streams,
Tightly bound by the near inescapable chains of evolution,
Trapped and imprisoned in the iron cage of self-concern,
Totally enveloped in the dark of misknowledge,
Born and born again and again in endless cyclic lives,
Uninterruptedly tortured by the three sufferings—
Such is the state of all beings, all just your mothers—
From your natural feelings, conceive the highest spirit!

Though you experience transcendence,
And cultivate the spirit of enlightenment,
Without wisdom from realizing voidness
You cannot cut off the root of cyclic life—
So you should strive to realize relativity.

Who sees the inexorable causality of things,
Of both cyclic life and liberation,
And destroys any objectivity-conviction,
Thus finds the path that pleases victors.
Appearance inevitably relative
And voidness free from all assertions—
As long as these are understood apart,
The victor's intent is not yet known.
But when they coincide not alternating,
Mere sight of inevitable relativity
Secures knowledge beyond objectivisms,
And investigation of the view is perfect.
More, as experience dispels absolutism
And voidness clears away nihilism,

You know voidness dawn as cause and effect—
Then you will never be deprived by extremist views.

When you realize the essentials
Of the three principles of the path,
Rely on solitude and powerful efforts
And swiftly achieve the eternal goal, my son!

CHAPTER 4

Practicing Transcendent Renunciation

This liberty and opportunity found just this once,
Understanding how hard to get and how quickly lost,
Bless me not waste it in the pointless business of this life,
But take its essence and make it count!

Fearing the blazing fires of suffering in the hellish states,
Heartily taking refuge in the Three Jewels,
Bless me to intensify my efforts
To cease sins and achieve a mass of virtue!

Tossed by fierce waves of evolution and addiction,
Crushed by the many 'gators of three sufferings,
Bless me to intensify my will to liberation
From this terrifying boundless ocean of existence!

As for this egoistic life-cycle unbearable as a prison,
Ceasing the delusion that it's a garden of delight,
Bless me to hold high the victory banner of liberation,
And enjoy the treasure of noble gems, the three educations!

Treasury of Wish-Fulfilling Gems:
A Textbook of Universal Vehicle Precepts

by Kunkyen Longchen Rabjam

Chapter Thirteen:

THE RARITY OF FINDING LIBERTY
AND OPPORTUNITY

Next, you who would study according to the Holy Ornaments
Should generate in mind the certain wisdom that reflects
On all the meanings appropriate to Individual Vehicle disciples,
And should especially contemplate in five ways.

First, you should contemplate the rarity of liberty and opportunity,
The misfortune of being born among a misguided people,
Of being born with imperfect faculties,
Of being deprived of the blessing of birth in a land with the doctrine,

Or of living in a wilderness of false teachings
Where it is very hard to meet many spiritual friends.

Foremost unfortunates who have lost this rare opportunity
Are hell beings, hungry ghosts, animals, long-lived gods and titans.
Then there are humans in wild lands untrod by Buddhas, with
    misguided views,
Humans unreceptive to teachings due to retardation or negative
    conditions,
Humans disturbed by the five poisons or possessed by the demon of
    self-deception,
The indolent and those immersed in a sea of negative evolution,
And the timid under the sway of others who pretend to be saviors.

Those deprived by these eight forms of misfortune,
Confused and unreceptive to the true path to freedom,
Suffer the ultimate bondage, since all they do is for ill.
Their human life-cycle is wasted in panic, with no hint of faith,
They engage in sin and vice with no thought of truth
And are notorious for breaking commitments and vows.
Divorced from any spiritual heritage, these eight types of
    unfortunates
Are estranged from truth, with no lamp to light their way to
    freedom.

We who have not been born in these circumstances
Should rejoice and strive to realize the holy doctrine.
Thus, considering the precise embodiments of living beings,
How a human body is evolved over countless life-cycles,
How, once in human form, well endowed, you are fit for truth,
And how this jewel makes you equal to the task of Buddhahood,
You should always carefully contemplate your liberty and
    opportunity.
Those born with imperfect faculties or in remote lands
Cannot grasp the truth, hold extreme views of evolution,
Have no faith in doctrine, no religion, and so befriend vice.

Through carefully reflecting numerous times
On having this body and the teaching, unlike such unfortunates,
You should contemplate in total certainty, day and night,
The full blessing of opportunity to practice the teaching,

Of having teachings to cultivate positive evolution,
Of being born as a human with perfect faculties,
With a perfect view of evolution undistorted by extremism,
Of having all that proceeds from these rare achievements.

Since perfect opportunity is hard to find, be diligent.
The Teacher came, spoke the truth, his teaching is preserved,
We enjoy the support of caring sympathetic guides.
Since this is so precious, apply yourself to practice.

This opportunity is as hard to win as the auspicious marks and signs.
If the yoke of an ox were adrift at sea,
How rare for a sea turtle to poke its head through the hole!
That is how rare it is to be born human.
As rare as corn attaching to the surface of a wall
Is precious birth in a central land.
As rare as a heavenly lotus growing in this world
Is a meeting with the true spiritual path.
As hard as threading raw cotton through the eye of a needle
Is precious success in the ways of the path once found.
As rarely as one finds a jewel on a desert island
Is how rarely one finds a true mentor.

So strive for success by diligence in these reflections.
Having abandoned meaningless activity for true success,
Whatever precludes the virtues that serve to ground freedom
Must be renounced as one strives toward the truth.

Misguided actions are senseless causes of misery,
Useless and of no help at the time of death; therefore,
Like painful thorns, work to finally get rid of them.
In this life, domestic relations, anxious cares,
And materialistic principles—the ills
That waste our opportunity—must be let go and renounced.
With constant mindfulness, awareness, and conscientiousness,
Contemplate your opportunity to reach enlightenment's freedom.

Whether on the move or at rest, even while eating and such,
You should eliminate the six faults such as indolence.
If you would achieve the great aims of ascendance and
    transcendence,
Be exemplary even in things like satisfying your appetites.
Day or night, you should strive to be wholly virtuous.

At every turn think how this life can serve that end.
Burn with flamelike zeal to provide for the future,
When by virtue you can transcend this unfortunate era
And quickly cross the ocean of cyclic life.

Chapter Fourteen:

LIFE'S IMPERMANENCE

Once acquired, this precious life with liberty and opportunity
Has the characteristics of instantaneity, impermanence, and decay.
The three realms are deceptive and illusory in nature.
Though beautified by the wealth of its four continents,
Our earthly environment is impermanent and exhibits decay.

Even this body should be recognized as a ball of foam,
Like those of all these beings now on earth.
In a hundred years, they will certainly not be,
Since everything born eventually dies.
Just as your own life span will come to an end,
In places like markets, crossroads, guest houses,
All these crowds of diverse beings will be scattered.

Contemplate the certainty from the heart that your relations
And the resources of your amassed possessions,
Like a city deserted, will come to nothing.
Since whatever wealth one has amassed
Is impermanent and without essence, you should be detached;
You ascend to the wealthy cities of paradise,
Even as you go beyond death and fall to miserable lives.

Be sure that pride in this life or wealth grants no equanimity,
Since one is separated in time from things outer and inner.
Since impermanence and death are certain,
Give up on the delusion of permanence.

Subatomic matter endures momentarily,
Being impermanent as a flash of lightning,
So you should realize ultimate truth just as quickly.
The variety of habitats and life-forms is transient,
Essenceless as an illusion or a banana tree,
Therefore this life-cycle is called impermanent,
And clinging to one's self or work is not acceptable.

Habitats and beings are made of four elements, subject to decay.
Embodied beings vanish like transient settlements.
Since compounds are everywhere, nothing at all is permanent.
Nothing in life is certain but that death is never partial.

So one must contemplate from the heart death's certainty.
Since, at the time when death comes, home and possessions,
Friends, the company of celebrated experts, and so forth
Are no company at all, you must realize ultimate truth.

One's perception of markets, riverbanks, miraculous trees,
Thunderheads, the movements of living beings, moon and sun,
Impermanent and transient, will likewise suddenly cease.
At the time of death, your best friends are your stores of virtue;
So rely on the ultimate, and strive to realize its essential meaning.

On the path of analysis, one must be ever mindful of death.
Measure your practice by watching the compounded decay.
With effort, abandon the fears and activities of this life,
Not resting in the ordinary even an instant.

Develop a renunciative, repentant mind of few diversions,
For the benefits and virtues of such a mind are infinite.
Eliminate worldly faults and naturally gather virtues.

Free from the permanence habit, stop enmity and kinship, desire and
    hate,
Be diligent in virtue, and know this life as deceptive.
Fully gather both stores, and the gods will see you as glorious,
You will ascend to the heavens, achieve lifetimes of bliss,
And quickly earn the state of enjoying the elixir of immortality.

Chapter Fifteen:

CONTEMPLATING THE NATURE OF FAITH

Following the natural realization of impermanence,
Devote yourself exclusively to building a store of faith.

With aspiring faith, work to choose wisely your path of evolution.
With confident faith, immerse your mind in the supreme objective.
With devoted faith, purify your mental qualities.
With sincere faith, eliminate doubt about the truth.
With certain faith, meditate on what you have learned.

Especially have faith in the excellencies of the teaching.
The nature of faith is like that of a good foundation,
As the groundwork of all spirituality,
It serves to foster the accumulation of virtues.

Like a ship, faith frees one from the waters of existence.
Like a convoy, it protects one from addictions and demons.
Like a ferry, it steers one to the island of liberation.
Like the king of gems, it accomplishes any wish.
Like a hero, it dims the glamour of vice.
The amassed holy stores are the ultimate wealth.

Since the unfortunate lack even the slightest faith,
Their faults will be truly limitless.
Like anchors at sea, they will not fathom freedom.
Like unready boats, they will never cross [the sea of] existence.
Like crippled hands, they will not earn their share of virtue.
Like burnt seeds, they will not sprout enlightenment.
Like the complacent, they will not manifest the form of truth.
Like those stuck in a rut, they roam in the egocentric life-cycle.

Generate pure faith in the doctrine with six objectives.
Generate aspiring faith for protection from existence.
Generate devoted faith for protection from sick relationships.
Generate devout faith for protection in this life.
Generate sincere faith from the purity of the ultimate realm.
Generate confident faith from learning about causality.
Generate certain faith from purely contemplating what you learn.

Relying on the ground of faith yields higher development.
Relying on the holy yields good relationships and insight into Sutra
    and Tantra.
Contemplating death builds confidence in evolutionary causality.
Contemplating learning yields diligence in the preliminary practices.
Thus higher development is achieved through faith.

Obscurations condition one to perceive a teacher's faults.
Ordinary relationships lead to lifestyles of self-centered hedonism.
Indulging indolence multiplies worldly activities.
Truthless actions such as these
Raise the high tide of evil obscurations.
Evolving through faith, in time one develops
Insight into life, death, and transference,

The ability to heal, bear the worst suffering, learn the teaching,
Understand the lives of superior beings, and remember your past
    lives.
Since these develop through faith and enhance life,
You should always meditate on the primacy of faith.

Measure faith by renunciation of cyclic life, devotion to the Three
    Jewels,
Attention to study and contemplation, devotion to the three
    educations,
Delight in virtue and dread of vice,
And by the aspiration to achieve higher virtues.

If you do not pursue the art of generating faith,
You will achieve no blessings but continually wander in cyclic life.
Therefore, whatever techniques you rely on,
You should exert yourself in methods of developing faith.

Recognize and abandon ambivalence about faith.
The most judicious never abandon faith,
For the slightest loss causes obscurations to grow;
Inviting negative conditions without the least care,
Even the most ingenious are unable to sustain any progress.
Those who are not completely sure, and so pursue pleasure,
Wander aimlessly and are stopped by the least circumstance.
So you must be continually mindful to avoid these six.

First, examine the objects of faith,
Then be as unchanging as the king of mountains.
Be unobstructed as a sunlit ocean sky.
Be like the bowstring, with neither tension nor laxity.
Be without sluggishness, like a steady ship.
Flow without interruption, like a great river.
Be pliant, like a young vine.
Be unperturbed by conditions, steadfast as space.

The benefits of faith are manifold and immeasurable.
As the ground of all things virtuous, it dispels misery.
As a guide on the path to enlightenment, it is the vessel of the
    profound.
As the tree of the holy intention, it is the consummate virtue.

Since it is the supreme way to virtue for living beings,
Be sure to apply yourself to the full, hundred-thousand-petaled lotus
   of faith.

Chapter Sixteen:

CONTEMPLATING EVOLUTIONARY CAUSALITY

Next, those endowed with faith should contemplate
How virtue and vice are to be adopted and abandoned
To accord with evolutionary causality.
Virtuous action is partly consistent with merit
And partly consistent with freedom, of which there are two kinds.

Virtues that have the evolutionary effect of pleasurable existence
Were defined by the Sage as being consistent with merit.
Many kinds are enumerated, but in essence such virtues are ten.
Three are physical, four verbal, three mental.
When these ten are unrelated to the formless contemplations,
They create the effect of human and divine happiness in the desire
   realm.
When related to the formless contemplations, there is another
   possibility.

Virtues create all kinds of pleasure in happy lives.
Avoiding killing leads to a long and healthy life.
Avoiding stealing leads to consummate wealth.
Avoiding sexual misconduct leads to freedom from marital strife.
Avoiding false speech leads to praise from others.
Avoiding abusive speech leads to the joy of pleasant conversation.
Avoiding slander leads to enjoying freedom from discord.
Avoiding gossip leads to one's word being honored.
Avoiding greed leads to attaining one's needs.
Avoiding malice leads to the delightful experience of peace.
Avoiding false views leads to a positive outlook.
Thus these ten virtues are the chariot of heaven.

Those who aspire to the bliss of transcendence must restrain
The ten sinful actions, since they cause the misery of bad migrations,
In long, medium, or short periods of descent into hellish, pretan,
Or animal lives, with their various sufferings;

And even cause suffering when heavenly life is attained.
Killing leads to short life spans with frequent illnesses.
Stealing leads to poverty and misfortune.
Sexual misconduct leads to marital strife.
Telling lies leads to much recrimination.
Slander leads to mutual discord among friends.
Abusive speech leads to quarrels and impotent speech.
Greed leads to lack of success in one's aspirations.
Malice leads to being fearful, and false views to a bleak outlook.

Thus the ten nonvirtues are like poisons,
Which knowledgeable persons strive to avoid.
The path to freedom achieves peace and enlightenment,
Helps one transcend existence and eliminate suffering.

Beings who enter the path of the three Vehicles to supreme
    attainment
Should develop their minds by contemplating the four
    immeasurables,
And reach the haven of enlightenment by practicing the six
    transcendences.

For those who strive day and night to develop virtues,
The Universal Vehicle especially is a great tide of good.
So prepare to conceive its spirit and incomprehensible actuality,
Then, by dedication, fully retain them.

These are the three principles leading to the path of freedom.
Whatever the practice, begin everything with altruistic intent.
View all things like space, through the eighteen voidnesses,
Meditate on clear light with the thirty-seven enlightenment
    accessories.
Practice the flawless six transcendences
Whose fruit is the achievement of unexcelled enlightenment.

Thus all things evident in cyclic existence
Evolve from virtuous and nonvirtuous instincts.
As evolution is not finished, this deceptive evidence is empty and
    unreal.
Therefore you must abandon nonvirtue
For the excellent path that pleases the Victors and their heirs.

The whole, consummate practice of a Victor's liberation
Is gathering the two stores to eliminate the two obstructions to their
    realm.
So knowing what comes of the store of virtue, be sure to be diligent.

Of virtues, the part conducive of merit is a cause of the life-cycle,
While the other part is conducive of achieving liberation.
In order to renounce the life-cycle, you must strive to abandon its
    cause.
While five of the transcendences are manifest as merit,
Guard what is taught as the second store, of intuitive wisdom.

Chapter Seventeen:

REALIZING THE SUFFERING OF THE LIFE-CYCLE AND THE BLISS OF TRANSCENDENCE

Next you should contemplate the sufferings of the life-cycle.
Since they lack essence and cannot endure,
The three levels and six forms of existence are a misery.
Hence you must work at the means to transcend them quickly.

In hellish lives, the misery is immeasurable.
As beings tear each other apart with their teeth,
In repetitive lives and deaths, the pain is impossible to bear.
Sawed along burn lines, you are repeatedly dismembered.
Your body is pulverized, crushed between mountains and boulders,
    or in chasms.
You are lured into buildings of red-hot iron,
Or onto a ground of burning embers smoldering with flames.
Your skin is flayed, you are impaled on a stake,
Consumed inside and out by searing flames,
Boiled in molten copper until your whole body dissolves into atoms,
Or roasted in iron traps in ceaseless torment, impossible to bear.
You are pounded, chopped, hacked, and ground into bits,
Baked, skewered, flattened between iron plates, and wound in
    burning wire.

Beyond these hot hells in all directions are the four surrounding
    hells,
Of putrid swamps, burning trenches,

And razor fields whose sword-leafed brush
Is entirely surrounded by forests of sword-leafed trees.
Hell dwellers experience a profusion of pains,
And their life span, in the biting and other seven hot hells,
Is equal to one day in the life of a desire-realm god.
Once one has earned life there by self-deceit, it is possible
To spend half an eon in the burning hells,
And then you may live one eon in the hell of ceaseless torment.

With glacial mountains and blizzards
Embodied beings suffer in eight ways in freezing hells.
From freezing blisters to bursting blisters,
Shivering moans to clenched teeth,
From cracking like a lotus, to shattering like a blue lotus,
Stricken with cold, one's misery is limitless.
The life span in the blister hell is the time it takes
To empty a hundred-bushel bin of sesame seeds, one seed every
    hundred years.
Life in each successive cold hell is twenty times longer than that of
    the previous one.

Pretan beings suffer violent hunger and thirst.
Those with outer obscurations burn for whatever goods they see.
Those with inner obscurations feel a blazing fire in their internal
    organs.
Those with general obscurations are obsessed with food and drink.
In twelve years, some may not even hear the sound of water.
For others, food and drink appear, but demon guards attack them.

The life span of pretans is from one hundred
To five hundred of our years, in which they suffer miserably.

As for animals, they devour one another.
Attacking, capturing, and killing each other,
They experience much pain,
In indeterminate life spans for as long as an eon.

Most humans also lack pleasant circumstances.
Through birth, old age, and death, they have many enemies and
    assailants.
Divorced from friends, they lose what they want
And often experience what they do not want.

Their desires unfulfilled, they suffer heat, cold, and exhaustion.
In return for help, they experience injury and ingratitude.
Their world is full of wrongdoing and pointless rivalry.
They experience no praise but countless untrue accusations.

As for titans, their endless hostility and fighting
Yield unbearable deaths by lightning bolts and so forth.
They have many and varied sufferings, with no pleasures.

Even the gods experience death transitions,
Eventual descent to lower rebirths and such.

The ocean of suffering is boundless and immeasurable.
All egocentric life-cycles resemble a burning abyss,
With no chance of true happiness, like a well
That trickles but never continually flows.

Hence those of sound mind should aspire to freedom
From such a heartless cycle of despair.
In the supreme liberation of transcendence,
Whose peaceful, luminous bliss is the peerless elixir,
Without permanence or change, free from fabrication,
A body of innate excellence, perfectly free from age and death,
A source of bliss and benefit.
Free from obscurations and without taints,
The rescuing force and refuge of all beings.
So you of fine mind should strive to attain it!

The Buddhist Layperson's Vow

"O reverend teacher, please attend to me! I, called so-and-so, from this time
for as long as I live, take refuge in the Buddha, supreme of gods and humans! I take refuge in the Dharma, supreme of things free from desire! I
take refuge in the Sangha, supreme of communities! May the reverend look
after me as a lay religious for as long as I live!"

(This is to be repeated after the mentor. On the third repetition, when
you say "look after me as a layperson," think that the vow has generated in
your continuum.)

The mentor says, "Excellent!"
The disciple says, "Excellent!"

"O mentor, please attend to me! As those holy saints abandoned killing as long as they lived, turning away from all taking of life, so I, called so and so, from this time forth for as long as I shall live shall abandon killing and turn away from taking of life! By this first branch I shall educate myself in the discipline of those holy saints! I shall practice it! I shall accomplish it! Furthermore, as those holy saints for as long as they lived abandoned taking the not-given, sexual misconduct driven by lust, pretentious lies, and the liquors of grain and distillation and all intoxicants and causes of recklessness; just like that, I, called so-and-so, from this time forth for as long as I shall live, shall abandon taking the not-given, sexual misconduct driven by lust, pretentious lies, and the liquors of grain and distillation and all intoxicants and causes of recklessness! By this five-branched vow, I will educate myself in the discipline of those holy saints! I shall practice it! I shall accomplish it!"

The mentor says, "Excellent!"
The disciple says, "Excellent!"

Monks' and Nuns' Vow: The Luminous Lamp of Powerful Rites, Early and Later Expressions of the Vows of Individual Liberation

by Purchok Jampa Rinpoche

Reverence to the Omniscient Lord!

From the *Manual of Renunciates,* there are two, the first giving the rite for achieving *Shramanera* (Wanderer) and the latter the rite for achieving Full Graduation. For whichever, one must first clean the place for the rite and set up a platform in the place of honor for an image of the Teacher, Lord of Sages, and a volume of Scriptures or of the monastic rites. Prepare the equipment necessary for the renunciate, and bring together mendicants worthy for assembly, performing the usual recitations and a dedication with a sacrificial cake. Then one should investigate that one's mind has not been infected by downfalls, or has been extensively repaired if infected, or at least one should perform recitation of general confession of downfalls. Then all are asked about their vows.

Then for the actual ceremony there are preliminaries, actuality, and conclusion.

First, one asks about problems that make the renunciant suitable or unsuitable. Then, in order to engage one in the gradual education in the teaching, one achieves the adjunct lay vow. Then, in order to promptly accept the discipline of Wanderer, one achieves the renunciation.

First, the man who wants to renounce comes before the mendicants who are oriented around the abbot. He kneels down on one knee. The abbot speaks:

"In order to allow you to take renunciation, you must be free of obstructing things. If an obstructed person renounces, either the vow is not born or, though it is born, it cannot stay and so on, and so it does not help your life. Furthermore, there is a transgression for me. So I must ask about obstructions; as the *Root Sutra* says, 'First the abbot asks about obstructions and then the occasion begins for the pure one.' Answer my questions without any side thoughts. You are not a fanatic? You are not younger than fifteen? Though at least fifteen, you are not incapable of scaring away crows? You have not been able to scare crows for less than seven years? You are not a slave? You are not a debtor? You are not proceeding without your parents' permission? You are not proceeding without your parents' permission from a country not far off? You are not an invalid? You are not an expelled female mendicant? You are not a thief? You are not an exile? You are not an outcast? You are not a hermaphrodite? You are not a neuter? You are not a serpent? You are not a beast? You are not a follower of the fanatics? You have not committed matricide? You have not committed patricide? You have not killed a saint? You have not divided the Community? You have not maliciously drawn blood from a Transcendent Lord? Of the four expulsionary transgressions, you have not committed any one of them? You are not living as a nihilist, disbelieving in cause and effect? You do not have a club hand and so on? You do not have albino hair? You do not have one fingernail and so on? You are not condemned by the king? You are not coming without the permission of the king? You are not coming without permission of the king from a not far-off country? You are not a famous bandit? You are not destitute? You are not a shoemaker? You are not an untouchable? You are not deformed? You are not a nonhuman being? You are not a person from the Northern Kuru continent? You have not changed your sex three times? You are not a mannish woman? You are not a habitual sinner? You are not an outlandish person born in another continent?

"When these have been asked and the answer has been 'I am not!' you are then determined as free of obstructions and suitable for renunciation. Now, since one must enter the Buddha's teaching methodically, you must achieve the adjunct lay vow upholding the five precepts along with the refuge vows. For that purpose, imagining this image of the Teacher to be the Teacher himself, bow three times. Say, 'I bow three times before you!' Then kneel down before him, join your palms together at your heart. The adjunct's vow is born by repeating the assertion three times, along with taking the refuges. Thus think along these lines:

"'Wherever one is born in the three realms of the egocentric life-cycle, it is a place of misery. My companions are companions in misery. What I enjoy is enjoyment of misery. In order to be liberated from the misery of the egocentric life-cycle, I must take refuge. Further, mundane gods cannot save me from the suffering of the life-cycle, as it is said, "Mundane gods, themselves bound in the prison of the life-cycle, who are they able to save?" Thus, since the Three Jewels have the power to save from the misery of the life-cycle, taking refuge in the Buddha, I receive a teacher of the path; taking refuge in the Dharma, I receive the actual refuge; and taking refuge in the Community, I find friends with which to practice the path. Thus, for the sake of all beings, I must achieve unlocated Nirvana, perfect Buddhahood! For that purpose, from this moment forth until I die, taking the complete adjunct vow, I must keep it. Please look after me as an adjunct layperson upholding the five precepts.'

"Thinking in that way, repeat after me. 'Venerable, please attend to me! I, named [say your name], from this time forth for as long as I shall live, as an adjunct, take refuge in the Buddha, supreme of two-footed beings! I take refuge in the Dharma, supreme of things free of desire! I take refuge in the Sangha, supreme of communities! For as long as I shall live, may the venerable look after me! I thus express the mantra of my own aim without excess or deficiency!' You must repeat this three times, again repeat after me for the second time. After the second repetition, since the words of the rite are in three parts, up to 'I take refuge in the Sangha!' expresses the refuge. 'For as long as I shall live, as an adjunct' expresses the self. 'The venerable please look after!' expresses the other. At the moment of saying 'as an adjunct' during the expression of self, the adjunct vow is born in your life. Since I have become your teacher, when I say in an emphatic voice 'as an adjunct' and you repeat 'as an adjunct,' that is the very moment you must generate the attitude of obtaining, thinking, 'This is the time I attain the adjunct vow!' This is very important.

"At that time, it is necessary to know you have attained the vow and to say that 'having become my teacher, may the teacher please look after me!' Put that in your mind, and again repeat after me the third time. When the third repetition is complete, I the master say, 'That is the method of attaining the adjunct vow. You have done well!' And you the disciple say, 'It is good!'

"Thereby you have attained the adjunct vow. Though you have attained it, if you do not keep it, it will not give much benefit and has great drawbacks; so you must keep it. As for the way of keeping it: thinking, 'as the saints mentally abandoned killing and so on, the five sins, and verbally and physically refrained from them, so I will learn!' Then repeat after me: 'Teacher, please attend to me. As the noble saints abandoned killing as long as they lived and refrained from killing, I [say your name], from this time forth for as long as I shall live shall abandon killing and refrain from taking life. By this first branch, I will educate myself in the precept of those saints. I will achieve it. I will accomplish it. Further, just as the noble saints for as long as they lived abandoned taking the not-given, wrong lustful sexuality, speaking falsehood, and refrained from grain alcohol, distilled liquor, and other intoxicants and drugs of recklessness, so I [say your name], from this time forth for as long as I shall live, I will abandon taking the not-given, wrong lustful sexuality, speaking falsehood, and refrain from grain alcohol, distilled liquor, and other intoxicants and drugs of recklessness. By these five branches, I will educate myself in the precepts of those saints. I will achieve them. I will accomplish them.'

"The teacher says, 'It is the method. It is good!'

"And the adjunct says, 'It is good!'"

The Renunciant Vow

There are three preliminaries: One requests to become renunciant because of conceiving an attitude of extreme ethical sensitivity and inner conscientiousness. To obtain the indispensable cause of renunciation, one must petition an abbot; the first activities are to transform oneself to bear the outfit of this Dharma.

First, the initiate's mat and medicine bag and various robes are folded on the left and right of the abbot, folded double with the multiple ends facing the abbot. His begging bowl should be there, not empty, but with a few white grains in it, along with his water filter. There must be an assistant for the abbot, a mendicant who is expert in the rite of renunciation. Then a mendicant spiritual teacher is ordered by the abbot.

"You, venerable, must be the sponsor to the Sangha for this request for renunciation."

That mendicant asks, "Is this destined one free of all obstructions?"

Then the abbot himself replies, "He is free and pure!"

Then that mendicant has the initiate bow three times to the Sangha and assume a kneeling position, with palms pressed together, wearing a white robe.

The mendicant then says, "Reverend Sangha members, please listen! This venerable one named so-an-so seeks renunciation from the Abbot so-and-so. A white-robed householder with hair and beard unshaven seeks renunciation into the discipline of the well-taught Dharma. This venerable so-and-so seeks renunciation, shaves his hair and beard, and wears the yellow robe. Through faith only in the real, he renounces the home life for homelessness under this Abbot so-and-so. He is pure of any of the obstructions, absolutely so. May he receive renunciation?"

Then the assisting mendicants say, "If he is absolutely pure!"

Second: One makes three bows to the abbot and then kneels before him with palms put together.

The abbot says, "You who want to receive renunciation must definitely have an abbot. And it is not enough to have any old kind, you need one who is both expert in the teaching and truly holy. And he must not be someone who resides elsewhere; so I must simulate being worthy to serve as abbot. So, thinking, 'Please serve as master, which really means "precious educator," and indirectly is the means for the proper achievement of the actuality of transcendence for the sake of gaining access to the exaltation of Nirvana, which has transcended all manifestations of the contaminated life-cycle!' then repeat as follows:

"'Preceptor, please attend to me. I, so-and-so, request that the preceptor please serve as master. Preceptor, please serve as my master! Preceptor, as master make me transcend!'"

Repeat this three times. At the third repetition, if the preceptor consents to serve as master, he becomes that. After that the master says, "It is the method. It is good!"

Third, one needs the three changes, the change of signs and outfit to those of a transcendent, a change of attitude, and a change of name, which helps to remind one not to forget those changes. First, the master orders a worthy mendicant to serve as assistant to shave the tuft of this venerable. That mendicant comes in front of the initiant and asks him, "Do you want your hair tuft shaved?"

The initiant replies, "I want it!"

A little water is poured on his head to wash it. From behind, the mendicant shaves the hair tuft and gives it to the master.

The master says, "Gods who delight in virtue, do you please rejoice!"

He combines the hair tuft with flowers and throws them in the direction of the Three Jewels. "I must give you your Dharma robe, upper and lower robes, begging bowl, mat, and water filter, while stating their need and meaning, and you must properly accept them; therefore, bow three times!"

The mat and the upper robe are taken on the left shoulder. The master and disciple put their left hands below them and their rights above. The master says, "This Dharma robe always worn on the upper body is the upper robe; it is a special sign of your distinctness from laypeople and religious fanatics. Wear it as a reminder you are a virtuous ascetic. It is worn as a robe to protect you from heat and cold of sun and wind and from bugs and mosquitoes. Thinking, 'I will keep always an upper cloth like this,' place it on your right shoulder."

The same procedure is then followed with the lower robe. "This is worn below, the lower robe, to keep your nakedness and embarrassing parts covered, to protect you from mosquitoes and so on, and to distinguish you from householders and religious fanatics. Wear it as a reminder that you are a virtuous ascetic. Think, 'I will always keep a lower robe like this,' and wear it. The Buddha wore robes like this, so wear them with mind tamed, with mind calm."

The offering bowl should be filled with a little grain, master and disciple should both hold it with left hand below and right above. The master says:

"This 'offering bowl' is a distinctive sign of being a vessel more receptive than the inferior transcendents of other orders, different from the householders' eating bowls and the fanatics' begging bowls. As it fills with food, your understanding and life should fill with knowledge. As you enjoy the food within it, you should enjoy the Dharma. As the Teacher allowed it as a vessel of receiving alms to avoid the extremes of indulgence and mortification, think, 'I will always keep an offering bowl like this.' The mat is held in the same way. This mat should be used when one rests or sits to protect one from rough surfaces such as grass mats and so on."

Then there is the giving of the water filter. "This water filter manifests the compassion of the Buddha's teaching, since the vow of individual liberation refrains from all harmfulness to other beings, one must abandon harming all beings. Since you need to use water morning, noon, and night, you must keep this filter with you. By this example, all your things must be prevented from harming living creatures."

The assistant helps the initiate wear the lower robe and the upper robe. Then the master makes the initiate take the tips of the robes together and hold his palms together, and the master then places a flower on his head.

The Sangha members chant prayers and scatter flowers, saying, "May his banner of liberation be firm! May he complete his purity of conduct! May he consummate the great heap of ethical behavior! May he enjoy the pure ethics of the transcendent in all his lives!"

Second, the change of attitude: The initiate thinks, "This image is the actuality of the Lion of the Shakyas!"

He bows three times to it and three times to the master. He then kneels before them, putting his palms together at his heart.

"It is very good that you wish to transcend. The reasons are stated in the Sutras about the great difference between householders and transcendents.

All the Buddhas of the three times attained Buddhahood in the life-form of a transcendent; no one did so in the form of a householder. Especially the merit of taking one step toward a monastery with the pure ambition that wishes transcendent renunciation is infinitely greater than the merit of all beings of the three realms giving away their children and wives and so on until the end of the eon. Householders cannot properly achieve the beneficial goal of this life and the future, since their household duties distract them too much; hence they will suffer in this life and in the future. The transcendent is the opposite; their aims and activities are less, and they can achieve readily through learning, reflecting, and meditating; in this and future lives they are able to progress from happiness to happiness and ultimately they are able to attain the exaltation of Nirvana peace. Thus you should think deeply in your heart of the drawbacks of the household and the benefits of transcendence and follow after that very Lion of the Shakyas, intensifying your feeling, 'How good to become a transcendent!' Through this communication, one changes one's attitude. Having transcended, one must no longer adhere to householder's duties or even name or clan, so one receives a name ending with one's Sangha division or the name of one's master."

Now having completed the three changes, in order to effect the acceptance of the actual ethical conduct of a transcendent, one offers three bows each to the Teacher's image and the master, one kneels and lowers one's upper robe from one shoulder. One must repeat the following formulaic expression three times to undertake the ethical conduct. Then, requesting the master's attention, using one's new name, with refuge in the Three Jewels, thinking, "Following the example of the peerless Lion of the Shakyas as long as I shall live, I abandon the signs and outfit of the householder and take up properly the signs and equipment of the transcendent, never to transgress against them!" then one repeats after the master:

"Master, please attend to me! I, so-and-so, from this time forth for as long as I shall live, take refuge in the Buddha, the supreme of two-footed beings! Take refuge in the Dharma, the supreme of desireless things! Take refuge in the Sangha, the supreme of communities! Following the transcendence of the Chief, the Lord, the Transcendent, the Saint, truly perfect Buddha, Shakyamuni, Shakyasimha, Shakyaraja, I transcend. I abandon the householder signs! I truly take up the transcendent's signs!"

One repeats three times. The master says, "That is the method of achieving transcendent renunciation! You are excellent!"

One replies, "This achievement has been excellent!"

CHAPTER 5

Practicing the Loving Spirit of Enlightenment

The Quintessence Segment

Thinking how these pathetic beings were all my mothers
How over and over they kindly cared for me,
Bless me to conceive the genuine compassion
That a loving mother feels for her precious babe!

Not accepting even their slightest suffering,
Never being satisfied with whatever happiness,
Making no distinction between self and other,
Bless me to find joy in others' happiness!

This chronic disease of cherishing myself,
Seeing it the cause creating unwanted suffering,
Resenting it and holding it responsible,
Bless me to conquer this great devil of self-addiction!

Knowing the cherishing of my mothers as the bliss-creating mind,
Door for developing infinite abilities,
Though these beings should rise up as bitter enemies,
Bless me to hold them dearer than my life!

In short, the fool works only in self-interest,
The Buddha works only to realize others' aims,
With the mind that understands these costs and benefits,
Bless me that I can exchange self and other!

Self-cherishing the door of all frustration,
Mother-cherishing the ground of all excellence,
Bless me to put into essential practice
The yoga of exchanging self and other!

Therefore, O compassionate holy Mentor,
Bless all beings to obtain happiness,
Letting my mothers' sins, blocks, sufferings
Entirely take effect upon me now,
Giving them all my joy and virtue!

Though the whole world be full of the fruits of sin,
And unwanted sufferings fall down like rain,
Seeing this as exhausting past negative evolution,
Bless me to use bad conditions in the path!

In short, whatever happens, good and bad,
By practice of the five forces, essence of all Dharma,
Becomes a path to increase the two enlightenment spirits,
Bless me to contemplate indomitable cheer!

Bless me to make my liberty and opportunity meaningful,
By practice of the precepts and vows of mind development,
Applying contemplation at once to whatever happens
By the artistry employing the four techniques!

Bless me to cultivate the spirit of enlightenment,
To save beings from the great ocean of existence,
Through the universal responsibility of love and compassion,
And the magic of mounting give and take upon the breath!

Bless me to intensify my efforts
On the sole path of the all-time victors,
Binding my process with pure messianic vows,
And practicing the three ethics of the supreme Vehicle!

Asanga's Teaching of Great Compassion

(*from* Geshe Wangyal's *Door of Liberation*)

To conceive the spirit of enlightenment, you first must develop equanimity
toward all beings, and then contemplate the sevenfold cause-and-effect
spiritual instruction given by Maitreya to Asanga. First imagine before you
a being who has neither helped you nor harmed you. Think, "From his
own point of view, he wants happiness and does not want suffering, just
like everybody else. I will free myself from attraction and aversion. I will
not feel close to some and help them while feeling distant from others and
harming them. I will develop equanimity toward all beings. Lamas and
gods, enable me to do this!"

Once you feel equanimity toward that neutral person, imagine a person
who attracts you. Try to feel equanimity toward that person. Think, "My
partiality is due to my attraction. Since I have always desired attractive beings, I have been reborn constantly in the miserable life-cycle." Thus restrain your desire and meditate.

Once you feel equanimity toward that attractive person, imagine an unattractive person. Try to feel equanimity toward him. Think, "Because there has been discord between us, I have developed an aversion to him and so lack equanimity. Without it, I cannot conceive the spirit of enlightenment!" Thus restrain your aversion and meditate.

When you feel equanimity toward that unattractive person, imagine both persons together. Think, "These two are the same in that each, from her own viewpoint, wants happiness and doesn't want misery. From my viewpoint, this one who seems so close now has been reborn as my enemy countless times. This one toward whom I feel hostile has been reborn as my mother countless times and has cared for me with love. Which one should I like? Which one should I hate? I will feel equanimity and free myself from attachment and aversion. Lamas and gods, please enable me to do this!"

When you feel such equanimity, extend it to all beings. "All beings are the same. Each wants happiness and doesn't want misery. All beings are my relatives. Therefore I will learn equanimity and be free from attachment and aversion to near and far, helping some and harming others. Lamas and gods, help me to accomplish this!"

Once you have developed the mind of equanimity, implement the first of the seven causal instructions for attaining the spirit of enlightenment. Visualize the lamas and gods before you and contemplate: "Why are all beings my relatives? As there is no beginning to the life-cycle, there has also been no beginning to my rebirths. In passing through these countless lives, there is no form of life which I have not adopted countless times, and there is no country or realm in which I have not been born. Of all beings, there is not one who has not been my mother innumerable times. Each has been my mother in human form countless times, and will become my mother many times again."

When you have fully experienced this truth, contemplate the kindness which living beings have shown you when they were your mother. Visualize the lamas and gods before you, and imagine clearly your mother of this life, when she was young and as she grew old. "Not only is she my mother in this life, but she has cared for me lives beyond number. In this lifetime, she lovingly sheltered me in her womb, and when I was born she lovingly put me on soft pillows and cradled me in her arms. She held me to the warmth of her breasts, and suckled me with her sweet milk. She welcomed me with loving smiles and looked at me with happy eyes. She cleaned my snotty nose and wiped away my excrement. My slightest ailment gave her worse misery than the thought of losing her own life. Scorning all affliction, torments, and abuse, not considering herself at all, she provided me as well as she could with food and shelter. She gave me infinite happiness and benefit, and protected me from measureless misery and harm." Contemplate her very great kindness. Then, in the same way contemplate the kindness of your father and others close to you, for they have also been your mother countless times.

When you have fully experienced this truth, meditate on beings toward whom you feel impartial. "Though it now seems that they have no relationship to me, they have been my mother times beyond number, and in those lives they protected me with love and kindness." When you have experienced this truth, meditate on those beings who are now your adversaries. Imagine them clearly in front of you, and think: "How can I now feel that these are my enemies? As lifetimes are beyond number, they have been my mother countless times. When they were my mother they provided me with measureless happiness and benefits and protected me from misery and harm. Without them I could not have lasted even a short time and without me they could not have endured even a short time. We have felt such strong attachment countless times. That they are now my adversaries is due to bad evolutionary actions. At another time in the future they will again be my mother who protects me with love." When you have fully experienced this truth, meditate on the kindness of all beings.

Then meditate on repaying the kindness of all beings, your mothers. Visualize the lamas and deities before you and contemplate: "From beginningless time these mothers have protected me with kindness. Yet as their minds are disturbed by the demons of addictive passions, they have not obtained independence of mind, and are crazed. They lack the eye to see either the path to the high states of humans and gods or the path to Nirvana, the supreme good. They are without a spiritual teacher, the one who is the leader of the blind. Continually pummeled by the discord of wrong deeds, they slip toward the edge of the terrifying abyss of rebirth in the life-cycle, especially its lower states. To ignore these kind mothers would be shameless. To return their kindness I will free them from the misery of the life-cycle and establish them in the bliss of liberation. Lamas and gods, enable me to do this."

Then meditate love. Imagine a person to whom you are strongly attached, such as your mother. "How can she have undefiled happiness when she does not even have the defiled happiness of the life-cycle? What she now boasts of as happiness slips away, changing to misery. She yearns and yearns, strives and strives, desiring a moment's happiness, but she is only creating the causes of future misery and rebirths in lower states of being. In this life as well, weary and exhausted, she creates only misery. She definitely does not have real happiness. How wonderful it would be if she possessed happiness and all the causes of happiness! May she possess them! I will cause her to possess happiness and all its causes. Lamas and gods, please enable me to do this!"

When you have gained experience of this, continue to meditate, first imagining other persons who are close to you, such as your father, then imagining a person toward whom you feel impartial, then an adversary, and finally all beings.

Then do the meditation of great compassion and universal responsibility: "My kind fathers and mothers, whose number would fill the sky, are helplessly bound by evolutionary actions and fettering passions. The four rivers, the river of desire, existence, ignorance, and fanaticism, sweep them helplessly into the currents of the life-cycle, where they are battered by the waves of birth, old age, sickness, and death. They are completely tied up by the tight and hard to break bonds of various kinds of evolutionary actions. From beginningless time they have entered into the iron cage of holding the concepts 'I' and 'mine' in the center of the heart. This cage is very difficult for anyone to open. Enshrouded by the great darkness of ignorance, which obscures judgment of good and evil, they do not even see the path leading to the happy states of being. Much less do they see the path leading to liberation and enlightenment.

"These wretched beings are ceaselessly tortured by the suffering of misery, the suffering of change, and the all-pervasive suffering of creation. I have seen all beings, my mothers, wretched, engulfed in the ocean of the life-cycle. If I do not save them, who will? If I were to ignore them, I would be shameless, the lowest of all. My desire to learn the Mahayana would be only words, and I could not show my face before the Buddhas and Bodhisattvas. Therefore, no matter what, I will develop the ability to pull all my kind sad mothers from the ocean of the life-cycle and to establish them in Buddhahood."

Think this and generate a very strong and pure universal responsibility.

Finally, meditate the spirit of enlightenment. Ask yourself whether or not you can establish all beings in Buddhahood, and reflect, "I do not know where I am going; how can I establish even one being in Buddhahood? Even those who have attained the positions of disciple or hermit Buddha can accomplish only the minor purposes of beings, and cannot establish beings in Buddhahood. It is only a perfect Buddha who can lead beings to full enlightenment. Therefore, no matter what, I will obtain peerless and completely perfect Buddhahood for the sake of all beings. Lamas and gods, please enable me to do this!"

Eight Verses on Mind Development

by Geshe Langri Tangpa Dorjey Sengey

Through my ambition to achieve
The supreme of goals,
Far better than any wish-granting gem,
May I always dearly cherish every being!

Whenever I associate with anyone,
May I see myself as lower,
And with deep determination
May I cherish the other as superior!

In all acts, inspecting my own mind,
As soon as addictive feelings arise,
So troubling to myself and others,
May I stop them, using forceful methods!

When I meet beings of evil nature,
Driven by fierce sin and suffering,
May I cherish them as the rarest find,
Like chancing upon a treasury of jewels!

When others feel jealous of me
And abuse and attack me wrongly,
May I take the defeat unto myself,
And grant to them the victory!

When those in whom I have invested
The greatest hopes of getting benefit,
Instead irrationally inflict great harm,
May I see them as my best spiritual teachers!

In short, may I give to all, my mothers,
All help and happiness in this and future lives!
And may I secretly take upon myself
All my mothers' harms and sufferings!

And may all of them not be touched
By tainted notions of the eight concerns,
Being detached, freed from all bonds
By the wisdom knowing all things as illusions!

Shantideva's Teaching of Great Compassion
Tolerance, Remedy for Anger

Whatever my virtuous deeds,
Devotion to Buddhas, generosity, and so on,
Amassed over a thousand eons,
All are destroyed in a moment of fury.

There is no sin as harmful as hate,
No penance as effective as tolerance,
Thus by all possible means I should
Cultivate tolerance with intensity.

Keeping the mind wounded by hate,
I will never experience peace,
I will have no joy or happiness,
Lose sleep and writhe with discontent.

Even a lord whose magnanimity is vital
To those he gives wealth and status,
Is nonetheless in danger of being killed,
If he has hatred for them.

Hate wears out friends and relatives;
Though attracted by giving, they will not trust us.
In sum, there is no way to live happily
Together with the fire of rage.

Anger, my real enemy,
Creates such sufferings as these.
But who controls and conquers it
Finds happiness here and hereafter.

Hate finds its food in the mental discomfort
I feel, faced with the unwanted happening
And the blocking of what I want to happen;
It then explodes and overwhelms me.

Seeing that, I should carefully eliminate
That food that gives life to the enemy;
For that enemy has no activity at all
Other than causing me harm.

Whatever happens, I must not allow
My cheerfulness to be disturbed.
Being unhappy won't fulfill my wish
And will lose me all my virtues.

Why be unhappy about something
If it can be fixed?
If it cannot be fixed,
What does being unhappy help?

Unwanted for me and my friends
Are suffering, contempt,
Harsh words, and disrepute;
For enemies it is just the opposite.

Cause for happiness sometimes happens;
Causes of suffering are very many.
But without suffering there is no transcendence,
So, my mind, you must be brave!

Pointlessly, penitents and flagellants
Endure the sensations of cuts and burns;
Why then, my mind, are you afraid
To suffer for the sake of freedom?

There is nothing that does not become
Easier to bear through constant practice;
Thus by practicing with little pains,
You should learn to endure great pains.

Who has not experienced this with accidental pains,
Bites of insects and of snakes,
Pangs of thirst and hunger and so on,
And irritations such as rashes?

I should not become intolerant
Of such as heat, cold, rain, and wind,
Sickness, death, bondage, and blows;
For it only adds to the hurt.

Some become even more brave and heroic
When they see their own blood spilling;

Others feel faint and pass out completely
Just seeing another bleeding.

These things come from the mind,
Whether its habit is brave or timid;
Therefore I should disregard injuries
And not let sufferings get to me.

Even though they experience sufferings
The wise don't let the mind cloud or agitate;
In making war on the addictions,
The battle will bring much harm.

Disregarding all sufferings,
Conquering enemies such as hate,
These are truly victorious heroes—
The rest just slaughter corpses.

Further, suffering has its benefits;
Being tired of it dispels our arrogance,
It stirs our compassion for cyclic creatures,
It makes us shun sin and love virtue.

I am not angry with the major sources
Of sufferings, ill-humors such as bile,
So why am I angry with mental beings,
All driven by conditions as they are?

As all the while unwillingly
This illness inevitably occurs,
So all the while unwillingly
Addictions arise compulsively.

Not thinking "I should be furious,"
People helplessly feel fury;
And not thinking "I must develop,"
Fury itself automatically develops.

Whatever evils can be found
And the various kinds of sin,
All arise by the force of conditions,
And not willfully at all.

Those conditions gathered together
Have no intention "let us produce harm,"
Nor does their product, harm itself, intend
"I am going to be produced."

Even the postulated agents, "soul-stuff,"
And the theoretically imagined "self,"
Would never act thinking voluntarily,
"I must arise as the cause of harm."

Since such are unproduced and nonexistent,
So also their will to produce (harm or any action),
Since their focus on their object must be permanent,
It could never become terminated (in action).

If the self were permanent (as claimed),
It clearly must be inactive just like space,
Even on encounter with other conditions
What could it do without changing itself?

And if when acted upon it stays the same as before,
Then what would the action have affected?
Though we say, "This is the action of this,"
What could possibly be its relation (to anything)?

Thus everything is in the power of other things
Themselves in the power of still others;
Knowing that, I will never be angry
With things being as unreal as apparitions.

"If all were unreal, then what is eliminated by whom?"
Surely eliminating anger would be irrational.
It is not improper to eliminate anger, if you want
To interrupt the continuous stream of suffering.

Thus if I see enemy or friend
Do something wrong,
I will keep my good cheer, thinking,
"This comes from mechanical conditions.

If it were voluntarily happening,
Since no one wants to suffer,
No embodied being whatsoever
Would ever experience suffering."

Through carelessness,
People hurt themselves with thorns and so on,
And to win a woman and so on,
They become obsessed and wasted.

Some kill themselves jumping off cliffs,
Taking poison and vile food,
And hurt themselves
With unmeritorious acts.

If in the power of addictive emotions
They kill even their cherished selves,
How would they fail to cause harm
To the bodies of other beings?

Thus compelled by addictions,
When they try such things as killing me,
Perhaps it's hard to feel compassion,
But what's the point of getting angry?

If it is natural for the immature
To cause harm to others,
It is wrong to get angry with them,
Like resenting fire for burning.

Even if beings are gentle natured
And the evil of harm is occasional,
It is still wrong to be angry;
Like resenting space for filling with smoke.

Though sticks and so on really hurt me,
I get angry with the thrower;
But he is also a tool, thrown by hate,
So I am only rightly angry with hate.

Long ago I inflicted
Harm of this kind on beings,
So causing injury to them,
Now this harm comes back to me.

His weapon and my body
Both are causes of my suffering;
He made the weapon, I the body,
With whom should I be angry?

Blind with craving, if I cling
To this human form so prone to suffering,
Agonizing to the touch like an open sore,
Whom should I hate when it is hurt?

The immature don't want suffering
Yet thirst for suffering's causes
And so are hurt by their own evil;
What's to resent in others?

Just like the keepers in the hells
And the forest of razor-sharp leaves,
This pain is produced by my own evolution.
With whom should I be angry?

Compelled by my evolutionary actions
Others come forth to harm me;
When that sends them to hell,
Have I not caused their downfall?

Relying on them with tolerance,
Do I not purge myself of many sins?
Yet when they relate to me with harm,
Do they not suffer long the pains of hell?

Since thus I injure them,
And thus they benefit me,
Why so perversely, savage mind,
Do you feel anger toward them?

If I have the excellence of tolerance,
I'll never stay in hell;
Though I protect myself this way,
How will it be for them?

Yet if I retaliate by harming them,
That will not serve to protect them;
My own conduct will be destroyed,
And all my discipline will be for naught.

My mind is not itself embodied,
So no one can conquer it in any way;
But its deep attachment to the body
Lets it be harmed by sufferings of the body.

But since contempt,
Harsh words, and disrepute
Can never injure the body,
Why, mind, do you get so angry?

Because others will dislike me!
But that will not consume me
Either in this life or the next;
So why should I dislike it?

"Because it will block my worldly gain!"
Even if I don't like that,
I will leave my profits behind me here,
While I will go on riding on my sins.

Better that I die right now,
Worse that I live long by evil deeds;
Though I might hang on for quite a while,
Reality comes out in the suffering of death.

You dream of happiness for a hundred years,
And then you waken.
You dream of happiness for an instant,
And then you waken.

In both these wakings
The happiness will not return;
Whether life is long or short,
Like that at death it ends the same.

Even if I gain great good fortune
And enjoy happiness for a long time,
Just as if I was robbed by a thief,
At death I go on destitute with empty hands.

If I live and have good fortune,
I can wipe out sin and save up merit.
But if I use anger to attain that fortune,
Do I not consume all merit and accomplish sin?

If I am destroying the very merit
For the sake of which I am alive,
What is the use of living,
When all I do is intensify my sins?. . .

"I should be angry when people slander me,
Since they thereby ruin others' confidence!"
Then why don't you also get angry
When they slander others?

When the deficiency points to others,
I can tolerate lack of confidence;
But why can't I tolerate slander,
Since it just points out my mental addictions?

Should people slander or even destroy
Icons, sacred monuments, or Scriptures,
My hatred would be inappropriate,
Since Buddhas and such cannot be injured.

I should stop my anger toward people
Who harm mentors, relatives, and friends,
Seeing as in the above cases
How it arises from mechanical conditions. . . .

When I have understood this,
I should scrupulously make merit,
Using every way to turn everyone
Toward mutually loving attitudes. . . .

If others take pleasure in praising
An excellent person (who is my rival),
Why don't you also, O my mind,
Take pleasure and praise him? . . .

When my excellence is discussed,
I want others to be happy too;
But when others' excellence is the topic,
I don't even want myself to be happy.

Since I conceived the spirit of enlightenment
By wanting all beings to find happiness,
Why do I become angry
When they find happiness on their own? . . .

If I don't like others to get any good,
Where is my spirit of enlightenment?
How could I have that spirit
If I get angry about others' fortune? . . .

Praise and so on are but distractions,
They destroy my disillusion with cyclic life,
They stir my rivalry with the excellent
And destroy my chance of real success.

Thus those who aim to destroy
My reputation and so on,
Are they not also deeply engaged
In preventing my fall to the lower depths?

Dedicated to achieving liberation,
I don't need bonds of gain and status.
When one frees me from my bonds,
How can I resent him?

Those who want me to suffer
Are like Buddhas blessing me,
They elevate me beyond all dangers;
Why should I resent them?

"But if he obstructs my gaining merit?"
It's not right to be angry with him even then,
For there is no penance as good as tolerance,
And doesn't he help me abide in it?

If I, by my own shortcomings,
Fail to remain tolerant of him,
I have finally only obstructed myself
From using this occasion for merit.

If one thing won't happen without another,
And if it does happen when it's there,
That other thing is the cause of the one;
How can it become its obstructor?

When I make a gift, the recipient
Will not obstruct my generosity.
The bestowers of monastic graduation
Do not obstruct monastic graduation.

There are plenty of recipients in this world,
But the one who causes harm is rare;
If I don't cause them harm,
Beings usually won't harm me.

Therefore I should rejoice in my enemy;
He helps my practice of enlightenment,
Being just like a treasure found at home
Without having to go out and get it.

I can practice tolerance with him;
So he deserves my first offering
The fruits of tolerance to him,
Since he is the cause of tolerance.

"But that enemy does not deserve such veneration,
Since he does not intend my tolerance-practice!"
Then why venerate the holy Dharma,
Since it too is but a cause for practice.

"But this enemy is not to be venerated
Since he does have the intention to harm!"
How could I ever practice tolerance
If all strove only to help me, just like doctors.

Thus since tolerance is developed
Relying on those with hate in their hearts,
They are as fit for veneration as the holy Dharma,
Since both are causes of tolerance.

Therefore the Muni said
The buddhaverse is the world of beings;
The many who have satisfied those beings
Have thereby attained transcendence.

Beings and Buddhas are alike
As both cause gain of Buddha qualities;
As I adore the Buddhas,
There is no way not to adore beings. . . .

Further, since Buddhas are beings' true friends,
Who accomplish their measureless benefits,
What other way is there to repay such kindness
Than to love and satisfy those beings?

Having given their bodies and entered hells for beings,
Gratitude to Buddhas means helping those same beings;
Thus even if beings cause the greatest harm,
I must treat all with most resourceful goodness. . . .

When beings are happy, Buddhas are pleased;
When they are harmed, Buddhas are harmed.
I will love them and delight the Buddhas;
For if I hurt them, I will hurt the Buddhas.

Just as the senses can find no pleasure
When the body is ablaze with flames,
So when beings are being harmed
There is no way to delight the Compassionate.

Thus since I have harmed these beings,
And caused displeasure to the Compassionate,
I now repent and confess these sins,
And beg your indulgence for such displeasure.

In order to please the transcendent lords,
From now on I will control myself and serve the world,
Let the many beings kick me, trample my head, or kill me—
May the World Saviors rejoice as I do not retaliate. . . .

Why don't I see that all comes from pleasing living beings,
Not only my future attainment of Buddhahood,
But also great glory, fame, and happiness
In this very lifetime.

Even in cyclic living, tolerance bestows
Beauty, health, and fame,
Supporting a very long life,
And the happiness of a universal monarch.

Compassion

Thus having considered the excellence of solitude
By the many themes appreciating its value,
I must calm my conceptual agitations
And cultivate the spirit of enlightenment.

First of all let me strive to contemplate
The equality of self and other;
Since we are equal in pleasures and pains,
I should guard all others as I do myself.

Though parts of the body such as hands are many,
They are one in needing to be protected;
So all different beings in pleasure and pain
Are just like me in wanting to be happy.

If my pain
Does not harm the bodies of others,
Still that pain of mine becomes
Unbearable only when identified as "mine."

So the pains of others
Do not affect me directly.
Still, if I identify their pains as mine,
They too become hard to bear.

So I must dispel the pains of others,
Because they are pains just like my own.
I must help others,
Because they are beings, with bodies like mine.

When I and others both
Are alike in wanting happiness,
What's so special about me
That I strive for my happiness alone?

When I and others both
Are alike in not wanting pain,
What's so special about me
That I guard myself, not others?

I don't guard them
Since their pains don't hurt me.
Why then do I guard myself from future pains,
Since they also don't hurt me now?

To think "I will experience that"
Is a mistaken notion;
For the one who dies here
Is almost totally different from the one reborn.

When someone has a pain,
That one should guard himself against it.
But the foot's pain is not the hand's;
Why then does the hand guard against it?

Though this self-concern is not rational,
It happens because of the self-habit.
But what is irrational for self and other
Should be abandoned as much as possible.

"Continuum" and "mass" are false constructions,
Just like rosaries and armies;
There is no possessor of pain,
So who can take control of it?

There being no owner of pain,
All are without distinctions (of self and other).
It must be dispelled because it is pain.
What has certainty got to do with it?

Why should the (unowned) pain of all be abolished?
This is no sound argument.
To abolish my own I must abolish all,
Otherwise, I, like beings, must stay in pain.

Since compassion increases my pain,
Why should I insist on developing it?
Think about the pains of beings,
How could compassion increase them?

If a single pain
Could abolish many pains,
A loving person would feel compelled
To undergo that pain for self and other.

Thus she who attunes her mind like this
Delights in eradicating others' pains
And can plunge into the worst of hells
Like a wild goose into a lotus lake.

The vast ocean of joy
When all beings are free,
Am I not satisfied with that?
What to do with a solitary freedom?

Thus doing the welfare of beings,
I should not be conceited or amazed with myself;
Enjoying single-mindedly the welfare of others,
I need not expect any rewarding fruit.

Thus, just as I protect myself
From unpleasant things however slight,
I should have a protective concern
And a compassionate attitude for others.

Through the power of familiarization,
I have come to regard as "myself"
A few drops of others' sperm and ovum,
In themselves quite insubstantial.

Likewise, why cannot I come to regard
Others' (well-developed) bodies as "myself"?
After all, it is not hard to posit
My own body as some other thing.

Having understood the flaws in self-concern,
And the ocean of advantages in other-concern,
I must abandon self-preoccupation
And cultivate concern for others.

Just as the hand and so on are accepted
As inalienable limbs of the body,
Why should not embodied beings
Be accepted as inalienable limbs of life?

Just as custom creates a sense of self
About this body that utterly lacks a self,
Why cannot habit create the sense of self
About any other living being?

Therefore I have no pride or wonder
About performing altruistic deeds,
Just as I expect no great reward
For having given myself some food.

Thus, just as I protect myself
From unpleasant things however slight,
I should cultivate a protective concern
And a compassionate attitude for others.

Therefore the Savior Lokeshvara,
From great compassion for all beings,
Blessed his name alone to clear away
All terrors of the cyclic life.

I should not shrink from what is hard;
For such habituation is so powerful,
Fear at the mention of a person's name
Can create displeasure even when they're absent.

One who desires as soon as possible
To give refuge to self and others
Should practice the holy secret teaching
Of the transposition of self and other. . . .

"If I give it, what can I enjoy?"
Such selfish thinking is the demon's way.
"If I enjoy it, what can I give?"
Such altruism is the way of gods.

If I hurt others for my own sake
I will suffer in hell and so on.
If I hurt myself for the sake of others,
I will achieve all success.

One who wants himself to be higher
Finds bad realms, foul and stupid.
But shifting the highness to the others,
He gains pleasant realms and honor.

Using others for my purposes,
I end up as a servant and such.
Exercising myself for others' sake,
I end up lord and master.

All happiness in the world
Arises from the wish for others' happiness.
All suffering in this world
Arises from the wish for one's own happiness.

What need to say a great deal more?
The immature work for their own sake,
Buddhas work for the sake of others;
Just look at the difference between them!

If I don't truly exchange
My happiness for others' sufferings,
I won't attain Buddhahood
And will not find even cyclic happiness.

Forget about the future life—
My servants will do no work for me,
My masters will give me no rewards,
I will not achieve even the goals of this life.

In pursuit of happiness in this life and the future,
I throw away this art of supreme delight
And contribute to the sufferings of others,
My delusion so causing me unbearable pains.

Since all the violence there is,
The terror and suffering in the world,
All come from this habit of the self,
What can I do with this great devil?

If I don't give myself up completely,
I won't be able to abandon suffering,
Just as you can't stop burning yourself
As long as you don't let go of the fire.

Thus to heal my own injuries
And relieve the sufferings of others,
I must give myself up to others
And attend to others as myself.

"I am under the power of others!"
Make sure of this, you my mind!
Now you should think of nothing other
Than achieving the goals of beings.

It is not right for these eyes belonging to others
To work to achieve my own goals;
It is wrong for them to do anything
That counters the goals of others.

Thus beings should be the main concern;
Whatever I notice on my body,
I should steal and use it
For the benefit of others.

Taking inferior, equal, and superior beings as myself,
And taking myself to be another,
With my mind free of conceptual thoughts,
I should cultivate pride, competitiveness, and envy. . . .

The Bodhisattva Commitment from
Tsong Khapa's Stages of the Path

In a clean . . . place . . . one sprinkles sandalwood water and scatters sweet-smelling flower petals. One then puts on an altar images of the Three Jewels, statues, Scriptures, and so on. One adorns it with fine cloth, flowers, music, food, and jewels. There must be an image of Shakyamuni and a copy of the *8,000-Line Transcendent Wisdom Sutra*. Then . . . the host of holy ones is invited . . . and praises sung. Then the disciples . . . join their palms together. The lama helps them generate intense faith from their hearts in the excellencies of the refuge host, and they think that the Buddhas and Bodhisattvas are sitting just before each of them; slowly they should recite the sevenfold preliminary prayer. Then they should imagine that the mentor is the Teacher, Shakyamuni, make three prostrations, offer the symbolic universe, kneel on the right knee, join palms together, and then make the formal request for the spirit of enlightenment.

"Just as all the ancient perfect Buddhas, transcendent saints, and great Bodhisattvas on the spiritual stages first conceived the spirit of unexcelled, perfect enlightenment, may I, named [so-and-so], please be allowed by the Master to conceive the spirit of unexcelled, perfect enlightenment."

One should repeat this three times. One should then take the special refuge in the Lord Buddha, the Dharma of the truth of path (mainly the Universal Vehicle Nirvana), and the Sangha of the nonregressing holy Bodhisattvas, from this time forth until reaching the seat of enlightenment, especially in order to provide refuge for all beings, thinking strongly never to regress:

"Master, please attend to me! I, named [so-and-so], from this time forth until I reach the seat of enlightenment, take refuge in the Lord Buddhas, best of humans! Master, please attend to me! I, named [so-and-so], from this time forth until I reach the seat of enlightenment, take refuge in the best Dharma, peaceful freedom from desire! Master, please attend to me! I, named [so-and-so], from this time until I reach the seat of enlightenment, take refuge in the best Community of nonregressing holy Bodhisattvas!"

One repeats this three times. One then should hear the precepts of the refuge from the mentor, then recite again the seven-branch prayer, then purify the mind by reflecting on love and compassion immeasurably for all beings.

Then the actual rite. Before the master, one kneels on the right knee, joins the palms together, and conceives the spirit. This is not just the spiritual conception "I will attain Buddhahood for the sake of others" but the conception "Mindful of my spiritual conception, I will never give up until I reach the perfect enlightenment." Such a commitment. If one cannot educate oneself in the precepts of such a willing spirit, one should not make it. But whether or not one can educate oneself in those precepts, one can participate in the rite with only the conception "I will become a Buddha for the sake of all beings." In conceiving the *willing* spirit, either type of person is allowed, but one who cannot educate himself at all in the precepts cannot participate in the rite to conceive the *acting* spirit. Now the actual rite to uphold the spirit:

"May all the Buddhas and Bodhisattvas of the ten directions please attend to me! May the Master please attend to me! I, named [so-and-so], by that root of virtue of the nature of giving and ethical action and meditation that I do, get others to do, and rejoice in others' doing, in this life and in all of my other lives, just as all the Buddhas, Saints, Transcendent Lords, and great Bodhisattvas in the exalted spiritual stages conceived the spirit of unexcelled perfect enlightenment, so may I, named [so-and-so], from this time forth until I reach the seat of enlightenment, conceive the spirit of unexcelled perfect enlightenment! May I free those beings not yet freed! May I deliver those not delivered! May I console those not consoled! May I release those not ultimately released!"(Three times.)

Bodhisattva Vow Ceremony

Kneel with folded palms. Recite three times: "O teacher, please grant to me the authentic taking of the vow of the Bodhisattva ethic! If there is no objection, out of compassion for me, please hear my plea and rightly grant it to me!"

The Teacher gives general instructions, giving the particulars of the vow and the dangers of not keeping it.

Repeat three times: "Please, teacher, quickly grant me true undertaking of the vow of the Bodhisattva ethic!"

Actual taking of the vow: The teacher recites the traditional words three times; after each time, the vow takers say, "I undertake them!" "Gentle son or daughter, named [so-and-so], do you undertake all the precepts and the ethical actions of all the Bodhisattvas of the past, all the precepts and the ethical actions of all the Bodhisattvas of the future, and all the precepts and all the ethical actions of all the Bodhisattvas of the present everywhere, all of those precepts and ethical actions, the ethics of vowed restraint, the ethics of amassing virtue, and the ethics of helping beings?" "I undertake them."

One recites three times: "Guru, Buddhas, and Bodhisattvas, please attend to me! As ancient Buddhas conceived the will to enlightenment and systematically lived by the Bodhisattva precepts, I also, to help beings, must conceive the enlightenment spirit and systematically live by the Bodhisattva precepts!

"Now my life becomes fruitful! I have succeeded as a human being! Today I am born in the Buddha family! I have become a child of Buddha!! From now on may all my actions suit that family tradition! May I act never to disgrace this family so impeccable and holy!

Shantideva's Bodhisattva Vow

May I be the doctor and the medicine
And may I be the nurse
For all sick beings in the world
Until everyone is healed.

May a rain of food and drink descend
To clear away the pain of thirst and hunger
And during the eon of famine
May I myself turn into food and drink.

May I become an inexhaustible treasure
For those who are poor and destitute;
May I turn into all things they could need
And may these be placed close beside them.

Without any sense of loss
I shall give up my body and enjoyments
As well as all my virtues of the three times
For the sake of benefiting all.

By giving up all, sorrow is transcended
And my mind will realize the sorrowless state.
It is best that I now give all to all beings
In the same way as I shall at death.

Having given this body up
For the pleasure of all living beings,
By killing, abusing, and beating it
May they always do as they please.

Although they may play with my body
And make it a thing of ridicule,
Because I have given it up to them
What is the use of holding it dear?

Therefore I shall let them do anything to it
That does not cause them any harm,
And when anyone encounters me
May it never be meaningless for him.

If in those who encounter me
A faithful or an angry thought arises,
May that eternally become the source
For fulfilling all their wishes.

May all who say bad things to me
Or cause me any other harm,
And those who mock and insult me,
Have the fortune to fully awaken.

May I be a protector for those without one,
A guide for all travelers on the way;
May I be a bridge, a boat, and a ship
For all who wish to cross (the water).

May I be an island for those who seek one
And a lamp for those desiring light;
May I be a bed for all who wish to rest
And a slave for all who want a slave.

May I be a wishing jewel, a magic vase,
Powerful mantras, and great medicine;
May I become a wish-fulfilling tree
And a cow of plenty for the world.

Just like space
And all the great elements such as earth,
May I always support the life
Of all the boundless creatures.

And until they pass away from pain
May I also be the source of life
For all the realms of varied beings
That reach unto the ends of space.

Just as the previous Lords of Bliss
Conceived the enlightenment spirit,
And just as they successively lived
By the Bodhisattva practices,

Likewise for the sake of all that lives
Do I conceive the spirit of enlightenment,
And likewise shall I too
Successively follow the practices.

In order to further increase it from now on,
The intelligent who have vividly taken
The spirit of enlightenment in this way
Should extol it in the following manner:

"Today my life has borne fruit;
Having well obtained this human existence,
I've been born in the family of Buddha
And now am one of Buddha's children.

Thus whatever actions I do from now on
Must be in accord with the family tradition.
Never shall I do anything to disgrace
This holy, faultless family!

Just like a blind man
Discovering a jewel in a heap of trash,
Likewise by some coincidence
I have found the enlightenment spirit within me.

It is the supreme elixir
That overcomes the lord of death;
It is the inexhaustible treasure
That eliminates all poverty in the world.

It is the supreme medicine
That cures the world's disease.
It is the evergreen tree that shelters all beings
Wandering tired on the roads of life.

It is the universal bridge
That frees beings from wretched lives,
It is the rising moon of the mind
That dispels the torment of addictions.

It is the great sun that burns away
The misty ignorance of the world;
It is the quintessential butter
From the churning of the milk of Dharma.

For all guests traveling the path of life
Who wish to experience the true happiness,
This spirit will satisfy them with joy
And exalt them in the highest bliss.

Today in the presence of all the saviors
I invite the world to be my guests
At the feast of temporal and ultimate bliss.
May gods, titans, and all be joyful!

The All-Good Prayer

To the Bliss Lords of the three times,
Those Human Lions of all ten directions—
With full clarity of body, speech, and mind,
I bow down in reverent salutation!

Through the power of the prayer of all-good deeds,
I manifest in the mental presence of all the Victors;
In their lands as numerous as the atoms of the earth
I bow my bodies to salute them all!

Buddhas as numerous as the world's atoms in each atom
Sit amidst retinues of their Buddha-children;
Thus I believe all realities in every direction
Are filled with glorious Victors!

With endless oceans of sincere praise,
With all sounds, oceans of poetry,
I express the great virtues of all the Victors;
I praise all the Lords of Bliss.

I now offer to each supreme Victor
Sacred garlands of exquisite flowers,
Precious parasols and sweet-toned cymbals,
The best incense and finest lamplight.

I now offer to each supreme Victor
The finest of clothes and perfumed oils,
Powders and food piled high as Mount Meru,
All in arrays of supernal beauty!

And any supreme unexcelled offerings
All I yearn to offer to the Victors;
By faith in the power of the prayer of all-good deeds,
May I offer my reverence to all the Buddhas.

Under the influence of desire, anger, and ignorance,
With my body, speech, and also with my mind,
Whatever the sinful acts I have committed
I now lay them bare before the Victors.

In all the merits of the Buddhas and Bodhisattvas,
In all the virtue of disciples and hermit Buddhas,
In all the merit of every living being
I fully rejoice with a heart of gladness.

Those brilliant lamps of every world system
Won Buddha-detachment through the stages of enlightenment.
I exhort those Saviors in all ten directions
To turn the unexcelled wheel of Dharma.

With hands folded in sincere supplication,
I beg those who consider showing final Nirvana
To remain for as many eons as atoms of the world
For the joy and benefit of beings.

Whatever little merit I might have amassed
From saluting, praising, offering, confessing,
Rejoicing, exhorting, and imploring
I dedicate all to enlightenment for the sake of all beings!

I shall learn the ways of all the Victors,
Completely perfecting all good deeds;
May my ethical actions be taintless and pure;
May they be always faultless and undefiled.

In the tongues of the gods, Nagas and yakshas,
In the languages of demons and men,
With a voice as vast as the sounds of sentient beings
In every tongue I will proclaim the Buddhadharma.

Peacefully striving for the transcendences,
I shall never forget my precious spirit of enlightenment.
May whatever obscurations arise from my sins
Be without exception completely cleansed.

Liberating all sentient beings in all ten directions
From evolution and the effect of the misery from sin—
Thus will I act like a lotus that the ripples cannot moisten;
Like the sun and moon in a cloudless sky.

I will alleviate the suffering in all the hell realms—
Vast as the worlds and the ten directions;
Placing all beings in a state of bliss,
Thus will I benefit sentient beings.

Fully perfecting the all-good work,
Acting in accord with sentient beings,
I will teach them to accomplish good deeds—
Even in the endless eons to come!

Whoever practices in such a way
May I always meet and befriend him or her;
And with our bodies, speech, and minds,
May our activity and our prayers be joined.

To those I meet who long to befriend me
May I always teach them to do good deeds,
May I always find them wherever I go,
And may I never push them from my mind.

May I always clearly see the Victors,
Guarded by a retinue of their children;
Tirelessly throughout the eons to come,
May I offer them endless offerings.

Holding to the holy Dharma of the Victors,
May I always manifest enlightened action;
Acting completely through good deeds,
May I do so in all time to come.

In all the turns of the wheel of existence
May I endlessly seek merit and wisdom;
May I endlessly accomplish the merits
Of wisdom, method, meditation, and liberation.

On as many worlds as the particles of each atom
Buddhas unencompassable by thought
Sit in the midst of a Bodhisattva retinue;
Thus may I see them as they do enlightened deeds.

And without exception may all ten directions
And the three times be but the size of a hair.
So will I enter the expanse of Buddhas,
The ocean of worlds, and the expanse of eons.

With speech, the ocean of words,
The pure, poetic aspect of all the Victors,
With poetry like the thoughts of sentient beings,
So will I always engage in the Buddha speech.

The victorious Transcendent Lords of the three times
Turn the wheel of Dharma in many ways;
By the power of mind I will follow their methods
And speak in their inexhaustible poetry.

May I enter into the eons to come,
And may I do it in but one instant.
I will enter into all time's eons
Whose measure is the space of an instant.

In the space of a single instant, may I see
The Bliss Lords of the three times, those Lion-humans;
May I always engage in their sphere of activity
Through the power of the illusory liberations.

All the planetary arrays of the three times
Shall become manifest on a single atom.
In that way in all directions without exception
I shall enter into the arrays of the Victors.

May all those lamps of the worlds who have not yet come
Turn the wheel of the stages to Buddhahood.
They teach the limit of peace as Nirvana.
May I draw ever closer to those survivors.

Always through the swift power of miracles,
Completely through the might of the vehicles,
Always through the strength of virtuous action,
May I be always filled with the power of love.

Completely through the power of virtue and merit
And the powerful wisdom of desirelessness,
Through the strength of wisdom, method, and meditation,
May I achieve the might of enlightenment.

The power of evolution shall be purified,
And the power of misery defeated;
Evil shall be rendered powerless,
And I shall perfect the strength of good activity.

Fully purifying the vast expanse of worlds,
I shall fully free the ocean of beings.
Seeing the vast expanse of realities,
I shall fully know the ocean of perfect wisdom.

Fully purifying the vast expanse of activity,
I shall completely perfect the ocean of prayers.
Making offerings to the vast expanse of Buddhas,
I shall act tirelessly in the ocean of future time.

All of the special paths of enlightened prayer
Of all the blissful Victors of the three times,
And through good activity, enlightened Buddhahood,
All that without exception I shall perfect.

That saint, the son of all the Victors,
Who is known as All-Good Samantabhadra,
In order to unite my deeds with his,
All of this merit I fully dedicate.

Fully purifying my body, speech, and mind,
And completely purifying good activity and all worlds,
Like the dedication of wise Samantabhadra
May I too dedicate in communion with him.

For the full virtue of these good deeds
I shall accomplish the prayers of Manjushri,
And tirelessly in the eons to come
May I perfect all of those vows.

Pure activity is immeasurable;
Virtue is without end.
Remaining in the endlessness of activity,
May I attain all magical powers.

Sentient beings are as numerous
As the immeasurable breadth of space;
Suffering's extent is the same.
May the vastness of my prayer equal them all.

May all the limitless worlds of the ten directions
Be beautified with jewels and offered to the Victors.
For as many eons as the atoms of the earth
The joys of men and gods I will also offer.

Whoever hears this king of dedications,
And yearning for supreme enlightenment,
Develops but once a firm faith,
This will become for him or her the highest virtue.

Whoever offers this prayer of good deeds
Will avoid all hellish rebirths,
Will abandon all unwholesome friends
And soon come to see the supreme light.

Meeting all needs, she will live joyfully
And appreciate this precious human life;
And whatever are the ways of Samantabhadra,
She will eventually, unimpeded, become the same.

He who, under the power of misknowledge,
Committed the five heinous crimes
By saying this prayer of good deeds
will quickly purify that evil.

In the wise manner of the savior Manjushri,
And also through the deeds of Samantabhadra,
In order to follow the discipline of those beings,
I fully dedicate all of these merits.

Through the dedication praised as supreme
By the transcendent victors of the three times,
I fully dedicate all this root of virtue
Toward the living practice of all-good deeds.

CHAPTER 6

Practicing the Liberating Wisdom

The Quintessence Segment

Bless me to perfect the wisdom transcendence,
Through the yoga of ultimate-reality-spacelike equipoise,
Connected with the intense bliss of the special fluency
Derived from wisdom of discrimination of reality!

Bless me to complete the magical samadhi,
Understanding the procedure of truthless appearance
Of outer and inner things, like illusions, dreams,
Or the reflection of the moon in water!

Bless me to understand Nagarjuna's intended meaning,
Where life and liberation have no iota of intrinsic reality,
Cause and effect and relativity are still inexorable,
And these two do not contradict but mutually complement!

The Three Principles of the Path Segment

Who sees the inexorable causality of things,
Of both cyclic life and liberation
And destroys any objectivity conviction
Thus finds the path that pleases Victors.

Appearance inevitably relative
And voidness free from all assertions—
As long as these are understood apart,
The Victor's intent is not yet known.

But when they coincide not alternating,
Mere sight of inevitable relativity
Secures knowledge beyond objectivisms,
And investigation of the view is perfect.

More, as experience dispels absolutism
And voidness clears away nihilism,
You know voidness dawn as cause and effect—
No more will you be deprived by extremist views.

Foundation of All Excellence Segment

And bless me to cease attraction to false objects,
And through precise analysis of ultimate reality,
Swiftly to produce within my spiritual process
The integrated path of quiescence and transcending insight!

In Sanskrit: Bhagavatī Prajñāpāramitā-hṛdaya
In English: The Heart of Transcendent Wisdom,
the Lady Buddha

Thus did I hear on a certain occasion. The Lord was dwelling on the Vulture Heap Peak at Rajagerha, together with a great community of monks and a great community of Bodhisattvas. At that time, the Lord entranced himself in the samadhi of teaching called "Illumination of the Profound."

At the same time, the holy Bodhisattva Avalokiteshvara, the great messiah, was contemplating the practice of the profound transcendence of wisdom; and he realized that those five body and mind processes are void in their intrinsic reality.

Thereupon, influenced by the psychic power of the Buddha, the venerable Shariputra addressed the holy Bodhisattva Avalokiteshvara, the great messiah, thus: "When any noble son wishes to engage in the practice of the profound transcendence of wisdom, how should he learn?"

Then the holy Bodhisattva Avalokiteshvara, the great messiah, addressed the venerable Shariputra thus: "Shariputra! When any noble son or noble daughter wishes to engage in the practice of the profound transcendence of wisdom, he or she should realize it in this way: those five body and mind processes should be truly realized to be void of any intrinsic reality. Matter is voidness. Voidness is matter. Voidness is not other than matter; neither is matter other than voidness. Likewise, sensations, conceptions, emotions, and consciousnesses are also void. Shariputra! Thus all things are voidness: signless, uncreated, unceased, stainless, impeccable, undecreased, and unincreased. Shariputra! Therefore, in voidness there is no matter, no sensation, no conception, no emotion, no consciousness, no eye, no ear, no nose, no tongue, no body, no mentality, no form or color, no sound, no scent, no taste, no texture, no idea. There are no sense media, from eye to mentality; and there are no consciousness media from visual- to mental-consciousness media either. There is no ignorance and no cessation of ignorance, and so on up to no old age and death and no cessation of old age and death either. Likewise there is no suffering, no origination, no cessation, no path, no intuitive wisdom, no attainment, and no nonattainment either.

"Therefore, Shariputra, because the Bodhisattva is without attainment, he lives in reliance on transcendent wisdom; his spirit is unobscured and free of fear. Passing far beyond all confusion, he succeeds ultimately in Nirvana. And all the Buddhas who live in past, present, and future rely on transcendent wisdom to reach manifestly perfect Buddhahood in unexcelled, perfect enlightenment. Such being the case, there is the mantra of transcendent wisdom; the mantra of the great science, the unexcelled mantra, the uniquely universal mantra, the mantra that eradicates all suffering. It is not false and should be known as truth; the transcendent wisdom mantra.

"TADYATHA/—GATE—GATE—PARAGATE—PARASAMGATE—BODHI—SVAHA//

"Shariputra! Thus should the Bodhisattva, the great messiah, learn the profound transcendence of wisdom!"

Thereupon, the Lord arose from that samadhi and applauded the holy Bodhisattva Avalokiteshvara, the great messiah: "Excellent! Excellent! Noble son! Such it is! Such it is! One should practice the profound transcendence of wisdom in just the way you have taught it. And even the Transcendent Lords will joyfully congratulate you!"

When the Lord had spoken thus, the venerable Shariputra, the holy Bodhisattva Avalokiteshvara, the great messiah, everyone in that audience, and the whole world, with its gods, humans, titans, and fairies, all rejoiced; and all applauded what the Buddha said.

The Treasury of Wish-Fulfilling Gems

by Kunkyen Longchen Rabjam

Chapter Eighteen:

ESTABLISHING THE NATURE OF REALITY

Once you have completed such contemplations,
You should develop experiential wisdom in your process.
Among the three paths of transcendence in the three Vehicles,

Here you enter the unexcelled, essential import.
First, devote yourself to understanding the nature of reality.
Although this takes many forms, depending on the Vehicle,
The definitive essence is the indivisible reality
Which is the secret treasury of the Buddhas.

It is the natural transparency intuition
Beginninglessly peaceful, free from perplexity.
Like sun and sky, spontaneous and uncreated.
Since its natural great purity is primally present,
It is vision and voidness inseparable,
Free of proof and rejection, going and coming.
Beyond the realm of superficial determinations and distinctions,
Beyond dual-reality notions, it resolves all perplexities.
Its indivisible reality is neither proven nor unproven,
Experientially vision and voidness are naturally nondual;
This reality is called "indivisible."

When analyzed by the conventional two realities,
All things in cyclic life are mistaken appearances;
Untrue and deceptive, they are superficial realities.
Things of Nirvana are profound peace of translucency,
Accepted as ultimate reality, changeless in nature.

This manifold appearance is thus superficial.
Illusion, like the reflection of the moon in water,
It lacks the intrinsic reality it appears to have.
When examined, it lacks basis, root, and substance,
Free of intrinsic identity, empty as space.
When unexamined, this illusory, enticing diversity
Evolves as a relativistic distortion of instinct.

Thus, just like a *datura* hallucination,
These things are selfless and unreal.
Since that, in reality, is their way of being,
The "ultimate" appears but superficially,
Though appearing, in reality it is unborn;
So naturally its reality is indivisible.
Its natural primal purity
And its transparent ultimacy are nondual,
So the life-cycle and liberation are nondual,
And its reality is indivisible.

Since the life-cycle appears while lacking reality,
In that ultimate realm of intrinsic realitylessness
Nothing can be distinguished as separate and distinct,
And life-cycle and liberation are taught as equality.
Other ideas are false intellectual notions,
Quite confused about the nature of reality.
Causality exists as it appears to deceptive experience,
So cherish understanding of ethical choice.

The changeless nature of ultimate reality
Is transparency, the Bliss Lord essence, spontaneity,
Natural indivisible awareness of clarity-void.
This is the mandala of natural spontaneity
Primal natural perfection, essence of enlightenment,
Purity, unfabricated, free from partiality,
Profound peace, body and wisdom inseparable.

It has examples known to all beings;
Known by the wise as like underground gold,
A lamp in a vase, a body in a lotus.

Just as a pauper has a treasure underground
But doesn't know and so stays poor,
Though you possess natural enlightenment,
It is hidden by the earth of body, speech, and eightfold mind,
So you stay poor, impoverished by the ills of life.

Just as a clairvoyant person can see
And find a way to take out the treasure
To perfect the wealth of self and other,
So the holy ones teach that reality
And show how enlightenment can be found within,
The wish-granting gem that fulfills both aims.

Just as a lamp in a vase might be bright
But cannot illuminate, blocked by the vase,
So the essential Truth Body abides within
Yet does not show, blocked by the vase of obscuration.
But it does show when the vase is broken,
Just as the world lamp illumines all the lands,
When all obscurations are removed.

Though the Bliss-Lord Body is in the lotus,
It does not show when the lotus is closed
So the thousand petals of subjects and objects block
One's vision of the self-luminous Lord of Victors.
When the petals open, it is clear,
There is great liberation from the lotus of duality.
The three Buddha Bodies become naturally evident.
Thus please understand the reality
That ultimate-realm translucency
Exists within yourself!

This reality has names of many different kinds.
It is "the realm" that transcends life and liberation
And the primally present "natural spontaneity,"
As the "essential realm" obscured by defilements,
As the "ultimate truth," the condition of reality,
As the originally pure "stainless translucency,"
As the "central reality" that dispels extremisms,
As the "transcendent wisdom" beyond fabrications,
As the "indivisible reality" clear-void-purity,
As the "Suchness" reality free of death transitions.
Such names are accepted by the clear-seeing wise.

Not understanding this, one adopts a nihilistic voidness,
Though claiming to avoid extremes of being and nothing,
Since one does not know the ground of freedom
And longs to escape to the peak of existence,
One falls outside this profound teaching,
Sits empty-minded, fit to rub with dust!

The Teacher taught the treasury of Dharma,
The path of the pinnacle, clear light, essence of all,
The "reality of the ground spontaneity."
Understanding this ultimate profound view,
Liberates one from resistance and obscuration,
Frees from all absolutism and nihilism.
One's practice is fruitful, one soon becomes enlightened,
One gains the eye to see all Sutras and Tantras.
Therefore be sure to realize the reality of clear light!

Tsong Khapa's Medium-Length Transcendent Insight

Benefits of Meditating on Quiescence and Insight

The Buddha stated in the *Elucidation of Intention Sutra* that all mundane and transcendent excellencies of Individual and Universal Vehicles are the effects of mental quiescence and transcendent insight.

One might object, "Well, aren't quiescence and insight themselves excellencies of character of one who has already attained the fruits of meditation? In that case, how is it correct for all those excellencies to be the effects of those two?"

Since actual quiescence and insight, as will be explained, are indeed excellencies of character of one accomplished in the fruits of meditation, it is granted that all excellencies of Individual and Universal Vehicles are not their effects. However, there is no contradiction, since all samadhis beyond one-pointedness toward virtuous objectives are classified under the heading of "insight." With this in mind, the Lord said that all excellencies of the three vehicles are the effects of quiescence and insight.

He further states in the *Elucidation of the Intention Sutra:* "If a person practices quiescence and insight, he will become liberated from the bondages of bad conditioning and signification." Ratnakarashanti explains in the *Instruction in Transcendent Wisdom* that this means that "bad conditioning" bondages, which are the instincts lying in the mental processes capable of generating ever-increasing distorted subjectivities, and "signification" bondages, which create those instincts in the form of prior and posterior attachment to distorted objects, are abandoned by insight and quiescence, respectively. Now those are the benefits of what are designated as "quiescence" and "insight," and the meaning is the same even if you do not so designate them, as when you designate them the benefits of "meditation" and "wisdom." They still are to be known as the benefits of these two, quiescence and insight.

How the Two Contain All Samadhis

The Buddha also stated in the *Elucidation* that all samadhis of Individual and Universal Vehicles that he ever mentioned are included in quiescence and insight. Therefore, since those eager for samadhi cannot possibly explore all separate categories of samadhis, they should explore thoroughly the method of cultivation of quiescence and insight, which provide a general framework for all samadhis.

The Identification of Mental Quiescence

Buddha states in the *Elucidation*: "One sits alone in isolation, one absorbs oneself within, one impresses in the mind the well-considered teachings, and one goes on impressing this within the mind continuously, the very mind that is doing the impressing. Entering in this way and repeatedly abiding therein, when physical and mental fluency emerge, it is called 'mental quiescence.' This means that when the mind no longer vacillates but works continuously, naturally abiding with its chosen object, and when the joyous ease of mental and physical fluency is produced, then that samadhi becomes (actual) mental quiescence. This is produced just from holding the mind within without wavering from its chosen object and does not require any realization of the thatness of things.

The Identification of Transcendent Insight

The Buddha said in the *Elucidation,* "Then, after attaining the physical and mental fluency, one abandons the mode of keeping the mind focused on one thing, and one individually investigates the well-considered things arising as internal images in the realm of the samadhi; one confronts each one of them. Thus, with regard to those objects of knowledge that arise as images in the objective sphere of samadhi, their discernment, investigation, examination, thorough analysis, tolerance, acceptance, differentiation, viewing, and discrimination; all these are called 'transcendent insight.' And in this way, the Bodhisattva becomes expert in transcendent insight."

According to Ratnakarashanti and Asanga, quiescence and insight are not differentiated according to their chosen objects, since each of them can take either ultimate or relative as their object. There is such a thing as an insight that does not realize voidness. Therefore one is called "quiescent stability" because it is a quieting of the mind's attraction toward external objects and a stabilizing of the mind on the inner object. And the other is called "transcendent insight" because there is an "intensifying" or "excelling" experience.

Now there are some who assert that quiescence is the lack of the sharp clarity of the intellect through keeping the mind thought-free, and insight is the presence of such sharp clarity. But they are mistaken, since such contradicts all of the above explanations, and since that difference is merely the difference between samadhi afflicted by depression and samadhi without depression. All quiescence samadhis must definitely be cleared of depression, and all samadhis free of depression definitely arrive at sharp clarity of mind. Therefore we must recognize whether or not a samadhi or wisdom is oriented toward voidness by whether or not the intellect involved understands either of the two selflessnesses, since there are innumerable samadhis that have bliss, clarity, and thoughtfulness without having any interest in the objective ultimate reality. It is established by experience that to generate insight it is not enough to hold the mind completely free of thought and not discover the view that understands the real situation. Failure to understand voidness in no way precludes the development of nondiscursive samadhi. By the power of holding the mind thought-free for a long time, one develops fitness of neural energies. This is marked by the arisal of joy and bliss in body and mind; so lack of realization of voidness does not preclude the creation of bliss. Once that has been created, by the power of the vividness of the feeling of bliss, clarity dawns in the mind. Therefore one cannot represent all blissful, clear, and thought-free samadhis as realizing thatness. Thus, while it does happen that nondiscursive bliss and clarity occur in samadhis realizing voidness, it also often happens in samadhis not at all oriented toward voidness. So it is necessary to distinguish the difference between the two.

Reason for the Necessity to Meditate on Both

Why is it not sufficient to meditate on quiescence and insight one by one but rather to meditate upon both together?

For example, if one is in a temple at night and wishes to view the wall paintings and so lights a lamp, one can see the painted deities quite clearly if one has both a bright lamp and it is undisturbed by the wind. If the lamp is not bright, or if its brightness is too agitated by the breeze, one cannot see the deities clearly. Similarly, to view the impact of the profound, one can see thatness clearly if one has both the wisdom that ascertains unerringly the import of thatness and also the unwavering concentration that stays focused on its chosen object. Even though you might have the nondiscursive samadhi, which stays put without being distracted elsewhere, if you do not have the wisdom to be aware of the real situation, however much you may cultivate that samadhi, it will be impossible for you to realize the real situation. And, even if you have the view that understands selflessness, if you do not have the stable samadhi where the mind stays put on one point, it will be impossible for you to see clearly the impact of the real situation. Therefore both quiescence and insight are necessary.

Then what is the way in which quiescence must precede insight? Here the generation of insight is in the context of the common individual who has not previously generated meditative realization and must newly do so. In that context, except for the exceptional way, to be explained below, in which a distinctive subjectivity for the realization of voidness meditates on selflessness, in the usual context of the Transcendence Vehicle and the three lower Tantra divisions, analytic meditation is necessary, since without practicing analytic meditation, which cultivates wisdom's analysis of the import of selflessness, meditative realization will not emerge. Now in that case, one seeks the understanding of selflessness, repeatedly analyzing its meaning, before one has achieved quiescence, and if quiescence has not been achieved already, it is impossible to achieve based on that sort of analytic meditation. Further, while quiescence is achieved by the practice of focusing meditation apart from analysis, there is no method to practice insight apart from the practice of quiescence. Therefore insight must be sought subsequently; and therefore, ultimately, you cannot get around the order that quiescence is first sought and then insight is meditated based on the achieved quiescence.

Of course, this order of quiescence and insight is in terms of their initial development. Once attained, there is no fixed order, since sometimes one will first meditate insight and later quiescence.

Conditions Necessary for Transcendent Insight

General Setup

(Kamalashila), in his *Second Stages of Meditation,* states the three conditions for transcendent insight to be reliance on a holy person, eagerness to hear the teachings, and suitable reflection upon them. More explicitly, the reliance on an expert who knows unerringly the essentials of the Buddha's Scriptures, the study of the flawless scientific treatises, and the development of the view that realizes thatness by the wisdoms of learning and reflection—these constitute the indispensable preconditions for transcendent insight. If there is no penetrating certainty about the import of actual reality, it is impossible to generate that realization which is the transcendent insight into the nature of reality.

One must seek such a view by relying on teachings of definitive meaning, and not on those of interpretable meaning. And one comes to understand the impact of the definitive discourses by knowing the difference between interpretable and definitive discourses. Further, if one does not rely on the philosophical treatises that elucidate the Buddha's inner thought, written by one of the great champions who personified living reason itself, one is like a blind person wandering in a dangerous wilderness without any guide. Thus one should rely upon the flawless scientific treatises.

On what sort of person should one rely?

The holy Nagarjuna was renowned through the three realms and was quite clearly predicted by the Lord himself in many Sutras and Tantras as the elucidator of the essence of the teaching, the profound import free of all extremes of being and nothingness. So, one should seek the view that realizes voidness by relying on his treatises. Aryadeva also was taken as equal in authority to the Master by the great centrists such as Masters Buddhapalita, Bhavaviveka, Chandrakirti, and Shantarakshita. Hence, since both Father Nagarjuna and Son Aryadeva were the sources for the other centrists, the old-time scholars called these two the "grandmother treatise centrists" and the others, the "partisan centrists."

Which one of these masters should one follow to seek the ultimate intention of Nagarjuna and Aryadeva, the Holy Father and Son?

The eminent former mentors in the line of my oral tradition followed the practice of the Lord of Masters Atisha in holding the system of Chandrakirti as the supreme one. Master Chandrakirti perceived that, among the commentators on the *Wisdom,* it was Master Buddhapalita who most completely elucidated the intention of the noble ones. He took the latter's system as his basis, and, when he worked out his own elucidation of the noble intention, while he used many of the good statements, he refuted points that seemed slightly incorrect in the work of Master Bhavaviveka. Therefore, since I see the explanations of these two masters, Buddhapalita and Chandrakirti, as very much superior in explaining the treatises of the Noble Father and Son, I will follow them here in determining their intention.

The Method of Determining the View: Identification of Addictive Misknowledge

Misknowledge is the basis of all ills and faults since all the Victor's teachings to counter other addictions such as attachment are only partial remedies and only his teaching against misknowledge is a comprehensive medicine. As Chandrakirti says in the *Lucid Exposition:* "Buddhas are renowned in this world as regulating the activities of people by their nine modes of teaching such as *Sutras,* based on the two realities. Therein, teachings dispelling lust will not bring hatred to an end. Teachings dispelling hatred will not bring lust to an end. Teachings dispelling pride and so on will not conquer the other taints. Thus, those teachings are not all-pervasive and do not bear the great import. But teachings dispelling delusion conquer all addictions, for Victors declare that all addictions truly depend on delusion."

That being so, the meditation on thatness is necessary as the medicine for misknowledge and since one does not know how to cultivate the medicine without identifying misknowledge itself, it is very important to identify misknowledge.

Misknowledge is the opposite of knowledge, and knowledge here should be taken not as whatever type of common knowledge but as the wisdom of the knowledge of the thatness of selflessness. The opposite of that, again, is not properly understood as the mere absence of that wisdom, as merely something else than that, but as its very antithesis. That is precisely the reification of a self, and, as there are two reifications of selves, of persons, and of things, the subjective self-habit and the objective self-habit together constitute misknowledge. As for the manner of that reification, it is the habitual sense that things have intrinsically objective, intrinsically identifiable, or intrinsically real status.

These reasons bring out the mode of the habitual sense of truth status, the negatee which is the habitual notion that the apparent intrinsic reality of things is not merely imposed by force of beginningless mental construction but is established within objects as their own objectivity. The presumed conceptual object of that habit pattern is called "self" or "intrinsic reality." Its absence in the designated "person" is called "personal" or "subjective selflessness," and its absence in things such as eyes, ears, and so forth is called "selflessness of things" or "objective selflessness." It is thus understandable by implication that the habitual sense of the existence of that intrinsic reality in persons and things is the two "self-habits." As Chandrakirti says in his *Four Hundred Commentary:* "The 'self' is the 'intrinsic reality' which is that objectivity in things independent of anything else. Its absence is selflessness. It is understood as twofold by division into persons and things, called 'personal selflessness' and 'objective selflessness.'"

With regard to the innate egoistic view that also is the self-habit, in the *Introduction*, Chandra refutes the position that its object is the aggregates and comments that its object is the dependently designated self. He also states that the conventional self is not the mere conglomerate of the aggregates. Thus, as its object is neither the conglomerate of the aggregates at any one time nor the conglomerate of the temporal continuum of the aggregates, one must take the mere "person" and the mere "I" as the objective basis of the mere thought "I." Thus one should not put either the separate or the conglomerate aggregates as the substance of that "I." This is the unexcelled distinctive specialty of this dialecticist centrist system, which I have explained extensively elsewhere.

The object of the innate egoistic view that is the property habit is the actual "mine," object of the innate cognition that thinks "mine," and is not held to be objects such as one's eye and so on. The manner of this habit is the habitual holding of the objects perceived as "mine" as if they were intrinsically identifiably property.

As for the innate objective self-habit, its objects are the form aggregate and so on, the eyes, ears, and so forth of both self and others and impersonal inanimate objects and so on. Its mode is as explained above.

In the *Introduction Commentary*, Chandra affirms that "delusion is misknowledge, which functions as the reification of the intrinsic objectivity of nonobjectively existent things. It is superficial, with a nature of obscuration, seeing intrinsic realities in things." Further, in saying "thus, by the force of the addictive misknowledge included in the 'existence' member," he equates that misknowledge which is the truth habit about objects with addictive misknowledge. Thus, while there are two systems of classification of objective self-habits either as addictive or as cognitive obscurations, this system chooses the former way.

This is also the statement of the Noble Father and Son, as in the *Voidness Seventy:* "Reification of the reality in things born of conditions, the Teacher called it 'misknowledge'; therefrom the twelve members arise. Seeing truly and knowing well the voidness of things, misknowledge does not occur, is ceased; thereby the twelve members cease." Here "reification of the reality in things" indicates the habitual perception of "truth" or "reality status" in those things.

In the *Jewel Rosary*, Nagarjuna also states in the same vein that "as long as there is the aggregate habit, so long will there be the 'I' habit." That is, that egoistic views will not be reversed as long as the truth habit about the aggregates is not.

The context here is the identification of that "delusion" which is one of the three poisons and hence equivalent to addictive misknowledge. To get rid of that misknowledge, he declares it necessary to understand the import of the profound relativity, which happens when the import of voidness arises as the import of relativity. Therefore one must interpret addictive delusion according to Chandrakirti's explanation in the *Four Hundred Commentary* as the reification of reality in things.

This system was lucidly proclaimed by Chandrakirti, following Buddhapalita's elucidation of the intention of the noble ones.

Now that just-explained misknowledge which is thus habituated to the two selves is not the conscious holding of persons and things hypostatized by the distinctive beliefs of Buddhist and non-Buddhist philosophers, such as unique, permanent, and independent person; objects that are external yet are the aggregates of indivisible atoms without eastern and so on directional facets; subjects that are internal cognitions yet that are consciousness-continua composed of indivisible instantaneous consciousnesses without any temporal prior and posterior components; and such as a true nondual apperception devoid of any such subjects and objects. It rather consists of the two unconscious self-habits, which exist commonly both for those affected by theories and for those unaffected by theories and which have persisted from time immemorial without having depended on any theoretical seduction of the intellect. Therefore it is that same unconscious self-habit which is here held as the root of the egocentric life-cycle.

This reason reveals that all living beings are bound in the life-cycle by the unconscious misknowledge. Further, since intellectual misknowledge exists only for those philosophers, it is not properly considered the root of the egoistic life-cycle.

It is extremely important to come to an exceptional certitude about this point. If one does not know this at the time of determining the view, one will not know how to hold as principal the determination of the nonexistence of the hypothetical object held by unconscious misknowledge, while keeping the negation of the intellectually held objects subordinate. And if one refutes the two selves and neglects the negation of the habit pattern of unconscious misknowledge, then one will have determined a selflessness that is merely a rejection of those "selves" hypothesized by the philosophers, as explained above. Even at the time of meditation, one's meditation will be just the same, since the "determination of the view" involves meditation as well. Thus even in meditation only the manifest habits will be involved in the final analysis, and one will experience only the absence of the two selves that are merely those hypothesized by the intellectual habits. To think that this will eliminate the unconscious addictions is a great exaggeration.

One should also understand according to the statement of Dharmakirti in the *Commentary on Validating Cognition:* "Who sees a self always reifies an 'I' there; supposing one identifies with that; identifying, one becomes obscured with faults. Seeing qualities, one desires them, one grasps their attainment as 'mine.' Thus, as long as one is attached to the self, so long will one revolve in the life-cycle."

First, once one holds to intrinsic identifiability in the objective basis of the thought "I," attachment to the self arises. Therefrom craving for the happiness of the self arises. Then, since the self's happiness cannot arise without dependence on one's property, craving arises for property, the "mine." Then, being obscured by such faults, one begins to see the qualities in those things. Then one grasps onto the property as the means of accomplishing the happiness of the self. Through the addictions thus produced, conceptually motivated action occurs, and from such action, the life-cycle itself is constantly held together. As Nagarjuna says in the *Voidness Seventy*, "Action has its cause in addictions; construction's nature is from addictions; the body has its cause in actions; and all three are empty of intrinsic reality." In such a way one must practice finding certainty in the sequence involved in the evolution of the egoistic life-cycle.

Reason for the Need to Seek the View That Understands Selflessness, Wishing to Abandon Such Misknowledge

It appears extremely necessary to will to abandon utterly the above misknowledge, the twofold self-habit, so one should intensely cultivate such a will. Even so, having such a desire, not to strive to understand how self-habits become the root of the life-cycle, and, having seen a part of that, not to strive to develop in mind a pure view of selflessness, having properly negated the objects held by self-habits with the help of the definitive scriptures and sound reasoning, such a person has to have extremely dull faculties, since he thinks nothing at all of completely losing the life of the path leading to liberation and omniscience.

Thus Chandrakirti teaches that the truth habit positing things is the cause of all addictive views. And all other addictions are abandoned by the realization of the real condition of things as not intrinsically really produced, by reason of their relativity. For the vision of their intrinsic realitylessness will not arise without negation of the object held as the intrinsically real status of things.

That is, he states that by cultivating the understanding of voidness, as voidness of the intrinsically real status of things, the egoistic views are eliminated, and by eliminating them all other addictions are eliminated, since it is impossible to understand selflessness without negating the object of the personal self-habit.

In short, the many supreme experts in elucidating the meaning of the profound discourses investigate with many references and reasonings when they determine the import of thatness. And, seeing that selflessness and voidness cannot be understood without seeing that the self, as held by the false habits, is not existent and is void, they spoke thus as above; because it is crucially important to find certitude about this.

If one does not meditate on the import of this negating of the object of the error fundamental to cyclic bondage, even if one meditates on any other would-be-profound import, it will not disturb the self-habits at all; because it is impossible to eliminate self-habits without applying the intelligence to the thatness of selflessness and voidness; and because even though without negating the object of self-habits one can at least withdraw the mental gravitation toward that object, that is not acceptable as applying the mind to selflessness.

The reason for this is that when the mind is applied to an object, there are three habits: one holding that object in truth, one holding it as truthless, and one holding it without either qualification. So just as the nonholding of truthlessness is not necessarily the truth habit, so the disconnection from the two selves is not necessarily the application to the two selflessnesses; because there are limitless states of mind included in the third option.

The two self-habits, further, function through perceiving things chiefly as persons and objects, and therefore it is necessary to determine right on the very basis of error the nonexistence of that thereon so held; otherwise it is like searching for footprints in the house of a thief already gone into the forest.

Therefore, since errors will be terminated by meditating on the import thus determined, such a voidness is the supreme import of thatness. And if some other false import of thatness is determined, it is no more than wishful thinking, and you should consider it outside the meaning of the scriptures.

Thus the misknowledge in truth habits about fabrications of persons such as males and females and things such as forms and sensations is eliminated by finding and meditating upon the view that understands the voidness that is selflessness. When misknowledge is eliminated, eliminated too are the conceptual thoughts that are improper attitudes reifying the signs of beauty and ugliness and so on by perceiving the objects of truth habits. When they are eliminated, all other addictions, desire and so on, which have egoistic views as their root, are eliminated. When they are eliminated, actions motivated by them are eliminated. When they are eliminated, involuntary birth in cyclic life as propelled by actions is eliminated.

Considering this process, the firm determination "I will attain liberation!" is generated, and thence one seeks the utterly incisive view of thatness.

In regard to the sequence of generation of the two self-habits, it is the objective self-habit that generates the personal self-habit. Nevertheless, in entering the truth of selflessness, it is by first generating the view of personal selflessness that one must later generate the view of objective selflessness. As Nagarjuna states in the *Jewel Rosary:* "A creature is not earth, water, fire, wind, space, or consciousness; if it is none of these things, what else might a creature be? Since the creature as collocation of elements is not real in itself, so each element, itself a collocation, is not really real either."

Thus he first declares the nonreality of the person and then the nonreality of its designative bases, the elements earth and so on.

As for the reason why one must understand it that way, while there is no variation of degree of subtlety in the selflessness to be ascertained in the basic person or in the basic thing, because of the essentiality of the subject of concern, it is easier to ascertain selflessness in the person and harder to ascertain it in the thing. For example, it is difficult to ascertain objective selflessness in the eye, ear, and so on but easy to ascertain it in things such as images, and this can be used as an example of the varying cases in determining selflessness with regard to things and persons above.

If one knows well the condition of the "I" anchoring the concept of self that thinks "I," and one applies the reason about it to internal things such as eye and nose and external things such as vases, one should come to understand them in just the same way. Then, knowing the nature and seeing the reality of one thing, one can be able to know and see the natures of all other things.

"Person" is a term used in contexts such as the six species of persons such as gods, or the types of persons such as individual persons or holy persons, and in referring to the accumulator of evil and good action, the experiencer of their effects, the traveler in cyclic life, the practicer of the path for the sake of liberation, and the attainer of liberation. Chandrakirti in his *Introduction Commentary* quotes a standard Scripture: "The demon-mind 'self,' it forces you to adopt its view; this aggregate of emotions is void, therein no sentient being. Just as one says 'chariot,' depending on its aggregate of components, so depending on the aggregates, one says 'superficial sentient being.'"

The first sentence teaches the personal selflessness that is the ultimate absence of "person"; the first phrase calls the personal self-habit the "demon-mind"; the second phrase shows the holder of that habit to be the victim of evil views; and the third and fourth phrases state that the aggregates are devoid of any personal self. The second verse teaches the conventional existence of the self, the first two phrases giving the example and the last two applying it to the meaning. It teaches that the "person" is a mere designation based on the aggregates, because this Scripture states the aggregate-conglomerate must be understood as either the simultaneous conglomerate of aggregates or their sequential conglomerate. Thus neither the spatial conglomerate nor the temporal continuum of the aggregates can be posited as the "person." When the conglomerate is posited as designative base, that which is conglomerated is also posited as a designative base; so it is illogical for either to be the "person" itself.

Here one uses the first of the four key procedures for determining self-lessness, analyzing one's own mental process in order to identify one's own mode of habitual adherence to a personal self. This has been already explained.

The second key procedure (is as follows): If that person has intrinsically real status, it must be established as actually the same or actually different from the aggregates of body and mind, and thus one decides that there is no way for it to be established in any other way. In general, in regard to such things as pots and pillars, if one determines them on one side as matching, one excludes them on the other side from differing, or such a thing as a pot, if determined here as differing, is excluded on the other side from matching—as this is established by experience, there is no third option other than sameness or difference. Therefore one must become certain that it is impossible for a self to exist and to be neither the same as nor different from the aggregates.

The third key procedure is to see the faults in the hypothesis that the person and the aggregates are intrinsically really the same.

The fourth key procedure is to see well the faults in the hypothesis that the person and the aggregates are really different. Thus, when these four keys are complete, the pure view realizing the thatness of personal selflessness is developed.

To rehearse the third key procedure, if self and aggregates were the same entity with intrinsically real status, three faults would accrue. The first is that there would be no point in asserting a self, since if the two were intrinsically really established as a single entity they would never be at all differentiable, since the two being absolutely established as a single entity could necessarily never appear as different to a cognition that perceived them. The reason for this is that, while there is no contradiction for a superficial thing's appearance being different from its real mode of existence, such a difference does preclude any truth status in that thing, since a true thing must really exist in just the way it appears to any cognition.

Thus the postulation of an intrinsically objective self is (only) for the sake of establishing an agent for the appropriation and discarding of the aggregates, and this is not plausible when the self and the aggregates have become the same. As Nagarjuna states in the *Wisdom*, "When it is asserted that there is no self but for appropriation, then that the appropriation itself is the self; and then that self of yours is nonexistent." The second fault is that the self would become a plurality. If the self and the aggregates were really the same, then just as one person has many aggregates, so one would come to have many selves; or, as the self is no more than one, the aggregates would become one. Chandrakirti says in the *Introduction:* "If the aggregates were the self, as they are many so the self would become many."

The third fault is that the self would become endowed with production and destruction. As Nagarjuna says in the *Wisdom:* "If the aggregates were the self, then it would become endowed with production and destruction." That is, just as the aggregates are endowed with production and destruction, so the self would become endowed with production and destruction, since the two are a single entity.

Now, if one thinks this is merely an acceptance of the momentary production and destruction of the self or the person each instant, while it is admitted that there is no fault in accepting this merely conventionally, the opposition here asserts the intrinsic identifiability of the person and so must assert the intrinsically objective production and destruction of that person, which assertion has three faults, as Chandrakirti states in the *Introduction.*

First, "Things intrinsically identifiably separate are not rationally included in a single continuum"; that is, it is illogical for things that are objectively established as different, in being former and later, to relate with the later depending on the former; because the former and later things are self-sufficiently and independently established and cannot properly relate to one another. Thus, since it is incorrect to include them in one continuum, the "I" cannot rightly remember its former life, "At that time I was like that," just as two different persons such as Devadatta and Yajña cannot remember each other's lives. In our system, though things are destroyed in every instant, conventionally there is no contradiction for former and later instants to be included in a single continuum, so it is possible for former lives to be remembered. Those who do not understand this point generate the first of the four wrong views mentioned in Scripture as relating to a former limit. When the Buddha often says, "I was this former person," they think that the person at the time of Buddhahood and the person of this former life are the same, or that, since created things are instantaneously destroyed, they cannot be the same, so both of them must be permanent, and so forth. In order not to fall into such (views), one must understand properly the way—at the time of remembering former lives—in which the general "I" is remembered without specifically qualifying it as to country, time, and nature.

The second fault is the fault of the effect of action committed becoming lost, when, if the person were intrinsically identifiable, it would be impossible to bring the agent of the action and the experience of the evolutionary effect together on a single basis, the mere "I."

The third fault is that of receiving the evolutionary effect of actions not performed; if such could happen, there would be the extreme absurdity that a single personal continuum would experience all the evolutionary effects of all the actions performed and accumulated by other different personal continua. These two faults, as explained above in the *Introduction*, accrue through the key point that if the person has objectively real status, it is impossible for his former and later instants to be included in a single continuum. As Nagarjuna says in the *Wisdom*, "If the god and the man are different, they cannot logically belong to one continuum."

Here you may wonder, "Granting these faults if persona and aggregates are the same, what is the fault if you assert the intrinsically real difference of person and aggregates?"

Nagarjuna gives the fault in the *Wisdom*: "If the self were different from the aggregates, it would be devoid of the nature of the aggregates." If the self were objectively different from the aggregates, it would have to lack the created nature of the aggregates; it would have no production, no duration, and no destruction, just as a horse lacks the nature of an ox, being a different creature. Our opponent here thinks, "Well, isn't that just how it is, after all?" However, if the personal self were utterly different from all relational things, it would not be logical for the instinctive mental self-habit to perceive it as the object that supports the conventional designation "self," because it is not a created thing, subject to ordinary contacts and relations, just like a skyflower or a state of Nirvana. Further, if it were really different from the nature of such as the aggregates, which is material and so on, it should be perceived as such, just as matter and mind are perceived as different things. But since the self is not perceived in such a manner, the self is not something different from the aggregates. As Nagarjuna says in the *Wisdom*: "It is not correct for the self to be something different from the processes of appropriation; if it were, logically it should be perceived apart from appropriation; but it is not." And Chandrakirti says in the *Introduction*, "Thus the self does not exist apart from the aggregative processes since its perception beyond them is not established."

By means of such reasons, one should cultivate a firm certainty that sees the faults of the self being objectively different from those of the aggregates. If you do not derive a correct certainty about the faults of these two positions of sameness and difference, your decision that the person is intrinsically realityless will merely be a premise, and you will not discover the authentic view.

Determination of the Nonreality of "Mine"

Thus having inquired rationally into the existence or absence of intrinsically real status in the self, when you negate its intrinsic reality by not finding any self either the same or different from the aggregates, that same rationality analytic of thatness will not discover any intrinsic reality in one's property. If you cannot perceive the son of a barren woman, his property such as eyes and so on will also not be perceived. Thus that rationality which determines the lack of intrinsically objective status of one's own "I" or "self" or "person" should realize the entire import of the thatness of personal selflessness, that all persons and their property, from hell beings up to Buddhas, have no intrinsic reality as the same or as different from their designative bases, whether they be contaminated or uncontaminated aggregates. And thereby one should also understand the method of establishing the lack of intrinsic reality of all those beings' property. . . .

Arising as Illusion

The method of understanding other things as like the example of illusion is as follows: For example, when a magician manifests an illusion, though there never was any horse or ox there, the appearance of horse and ox undeniably arises. In the same way, things such as persons, although they were always empty of any objectively established intrinsic reality as objects, are understood as undeniably appearing to have that status. Thus the appearances of gods and humans are represented as persons, and the appearances of forms and sounds and so on are represented as objects, and although not even an atom in persons and objects has intrinsically identifiable intrinsic reality, all the functions of relativities such as accumulation of evolutionary actions and seeing and hearing are viable. Voidness is not nihilistic, since all functions are viable because of it. Since one simply becomes aware of that voidness, things having always and ever been void, neither is it just a mentally made-up voidness. Since all things knowable are accepted in that way, it is not a partial voidness, and when one meditates upon it, it serves as the remedy for all the automatic reifications of the truth habits.

That profound import is not at all objectively inaccessible to any sort of cognition but can be determined by the authentic view and can be taken as object by meditation on the meaning of reality; so it is not a voidness that cannot be cultivated in the context of the path, that cannot be known, and cannot be realized, a sort of utter nothingness. . . .

Thus, to the perception of one experienced in meditating in samadhi, there is an understanding that apparent things such as pots and cloths are void of what they appear to have; but this is not the same as the understanding of their illusoriness and dream-likeness, which is their lack of intrinsically real status. Therefore one must investigate thoroughly the distinctive mode of arisal as illusory stated in the definitive meaning scriptures and the scientific treatises in order to generate realization of illusoriness and dream-likeness.

False Mode of Arising as Illusory

When one has not properly identified the measure of the negatee as explained above, when one's analysis of the object cools down, one first begins to imagine that the object does not exist, then one comes to experience the analyzer also as likewise (nonexistent), then even that ascertained as nonexistence ceases to have existence, and one comes into a state wherein there is no ground of ascertaining anything at all as "this is it" or "this is not it." There then arises perception of a fuzzy, foggy appearance, occurring from the failure to distinguish between intrinsically real existence and nonexistence and mere existence and nonexistence. Such a voidness is the kind of voidness that destroys relativity, and therefore the arisal of such a fuzzy, foggy perception derived from such a realization is definitely not the meaning of illusoriness.

Therefore when one analyzes rationally and one comes to consider that such a "person" is not present even in the slightest upon any intrinsically established object, sustaining that consideration one might have perceptions that arise in a fuzzy, foggy manner; just this is not very difficult. Such experiences occur for all those who admire the centrist philosophies and have a casual learning of the teachings that demonstrate intrinsic realitylessness. But the real difficulty is to negate completely any objectively established intrinsic reality and yet develop a deep certainty about the representation of how that intrinsically unreal person itself is the accumulator of evolutionary actions and the experiencer of evolutionary effects and so on. When the combination of those two facts—realitylessness and the ability to represent those things—is carried to the extreme limit of existence, that is the view of the central way, so extremely difficult to discover. . . .

When one investigates with the rationality analytic of ultimate reality, nothing whatever is discovered that can withstand analysis such as a person who is born, does actions, and transmigrates. Nevertheless, illusory things occur as the evolutionary effects of good and bad actions. One must develop one's understanding according to this statement of the Buddha.

Furthermore, when one does not practice in equipoise by concentrating upon the view that has decisively penetrated into reality, but merely finds stability in one-pointedness on not holding anything at all in one's mind, then, when one arises from the power of that samadhi, appearances such as mountains no longer appear solid and substantial but appear indistinct like fine smoke or like a rainbow. But this is not the arisal of illusoriness explained in the Scriptures, because this is an appearance within a voidness of coarse substantiality and is not an appearance within the voidness of the intrinsically real status of those apparent things; and because the absence of solid substantiality is definitely not the meaning of voidness that is intrinsic realitylessness. Otherwise there would be the fault that it would be impossible for the truth habit to arise when perceiving a rainbow as a qualified object, and it would be impossible to develop the wisdom-realizing truthlessness when considering substantiality as the qualified object.

Correct Arisal in Illusoriness

For example, when the visual consciousness sees an illusory horse or ox, one depends on the certainty in mental consciousness that the apparent horse or ox does not exist, and one generates a certainty that the horse or ox appearance does not exist as it seems. In the same way, one depends on both the undeniable appearance of person and object in conventional cognition and the certainty through rational cognition that that very thing is empty of an objectively established intrinsic reality, and thereby one generates the certainty that that person is an illusory or false appearance. By that key one reaches the essence of the meditation on voidness as like space wherein one's concentration allows not even an iota of mental orientations that are substantivistic sign-habits. When one arises from that concentration, and one regards the arisal of apparent objects, the aftermath illusory voidness arises. In that manner when one investigates repeatedly with the rationality analytic of the presence or absence of intrinsically objective status in things, after one has generated an intense certitude about intrinsic realitylessness, one's observation of the arisal of appearances is the arisal in illusoriness, and there is no separate method of determining the voidness that is illusoriness. Thereupon, when one engages in activities such as prostrations and circumambulations, the certitude from the above analysis is taken into account, and the engagement in those activities becomes the education in the arisal of illusoriness. One should perform those activities from within the actuality of that awareness. When one purifies that, the mere remembrance of the view causes those things to arise in illusoriness.

To express the method of seeking that certainty in an easily understandable way: Having initiated the proper arisal in general of the above-explained rational negatee, one should identify it by considering thoroughly how one's own misknowledge reifies intrinsic realities. Then, considering specifically the pattern wherein if such intrinsic reality exists it will not go beyond sameness or difference with its basis of designation, and the process wherein devastating negations accrue to the acceptance of either alternative, one should derive the certainty that is aware of the negations. Finally, one should confirm the certitude that considers that there is not even the slightest intrinsically real status in the person. And one should cultivate repeatedly such certainty-derivation in the voidness orientation. Then one should become involved in the appearance of the convention "person" undeniably arising as object of cognition, and one should cultivate the attitude oriented toward relativity wherein that conventional person is represented as the accumulator of evolutionary action and the experiencer of evolutionary effects, and one should discover the certitude about the systems wherein relativity is viable without any intrinsic reality.

When those two facts—that is, the viability of relativity and the absence of intrinsic reality—seem contradictory, one should consider the pattern of their noncontradiction by using the examples of mirror images and so forth. Thus the mirror image of an object, such as a face, although it is void of the reality of the eyes and ears and the like that appear in it, is still produced depending on the object and the mirror, and it is destroyed when either of those conditions is removed. Those two facts—its voidness of the objects and its being produced depending on them—are undeniably coincident in the same phenomenon.

Like that, there is not even an atom of intrinsic reality status in the person, and yet this does not contradict its being the accumulator of evolutionary actions, the experiencer of evolutionary effects, and its being produced depending on the actions and addictions of previous lives. One should cultivate this consideration. Thus one should understand illusoriness in this way on every such occasion. . . .

Objective Selflessness

"Objects" are the five aggregates that are the person's designative base, the six elements such as earth, and the six media such as eye and so forth. Their voidness of objectively established intrinsic reality is the selflessness of those things. There are two parts to the way of determining this: one negating objective self by the reasonings mentioned above, and the other negating it by other reasonings previously unmentioned. . . .

The Royal Reason of Relativity

The reason of relativity is clearly stated in the *Dialogue with Sagaramati Sutra* as logically negating the intrinsic reality-status of things: "Things that occur relativistically do not exist with intrinsic objectivity." In the *Dialogue with Anavatapta Sutra*, Buddha also clearly states, "What is produced from conditions is unproduced, it is not produced through any intrinsic objectivity. I declare that everything produced from conditions is void. Who knows voidness, he is consciously aware." This kind of statement is extremely common in the precious Scriptures.

In the latter quotation, the "unproduced" in the first line is explained by the "not produced through any intrinsic objectivity," which thus qualifies the negatee in the negation of production. Chandra, in the *Lucid Exposition,* cites the *Visit to Lanka*, "intending the lack of intrinsically real production, I say all things are unproduced!" Thus the Teacher himself explicates his own inner intent in the discourses, explaining for those who worry that perhaps the unqualified statements of productionlessness mean that all things produced do not exist at all, that it rather means that there is no production through any intrinsic reality.

In the third line, the Buddha states that conditionality of dependence on conditions is equivalent to voidness of intrinsic objectivity, which is tantamount to the equation of voidness of intrinsic reality with relativity. This shows that the Buddha does not intend a voidness of functional efficacy, which would be the negation of mere production.

Nagarjuna also, in the *Wisdom*, states, "Whatever is relatively occurrent is peace in its objectivity." That is, things are peaceful, or void, with respect to intrinsic objectivity, by the reason of their relativity. Thus one should understand that these statements clear away the darkness of erroneous opinions such as that the central way system must advocate nonproduction with respect to even relative production.

Such a reason of relativity is extremely praiseworthy. The Buddha states in the *Questions of Anavatapta Sutra,* "Wise persons will realize the relativity of things and will no longer entertain any extremist views." That is, one no longer entertains extremist views once one realizes relativity. Furthermore, Chandra declares in the *Introduction*, "Since things are occurrent in relativity, such reifications cannot be attached to them. Hence this reasoning of relativity cuts open the whole network of bad ideas." This is the unexcelled distinctive specialty of the eminent beings Nagarjuna and his son. Therefore here, among all reasonings, we should celebrate the reason of relativity.

Here there are two chief points of resistance that obstruct the realistic view. One is the reificatory view or absolutist view that has a fixed orientation toward truth habits that hold to the truth status in things. The other is the repudiative view or nihilistic view that goes too far by not appreciating the measure of the negatee and becomes unable to incorporate in its system the certitude about cause and effect within relativity, losing all ground of recognition about anything such as "this is it" and "this isn't it." These two views are completely eliminated by the negation of intrinsic reality based on the reason that brings certitude that from such and such a causal condition such and such an effect occurs. For the ascertainment of the import of the thesis radically refutes absolutism, and the ascertainment of the reason radically refutes nihilism.

Therefore all things—inner, such as emotions, and outer, such as sprouts—that occur in dependence on misknowledge and so forth and seeds and so forth, respectively, being thus relative are not correctly established as intrinsically identifiable. For if they were to be intrinsically objectively established, it would be necessary for each to have an independent, self-sufficient reality status, which would preclude their dependence on causes and conditions. As Aryadeva says in the *Four Hundred*, "What exists relativistically will never become independent. All this is without independence; hence the self does not exist."

By this one should realize that persons and things such as pots have no intrinsically real status, since they are designated in dependence on their own aggregation of components; this is the second formulation of the reason of relativity. Since things are dependently produced and dependently designated, they are not objectively the same as what they depend upon; for if they were the same, all actions and agents would become the same. Neither are those two objectively different; for if they were, any connection could be refuted and that would preclude any dependence.

Thus having derived certitude about the voidness that is the voidness of all the objectifying attitudes of substantivism, it is extremely praiseworthy to assume responsibility for ethical choice by not abandoning the certitude about the relevance of the evolutionary effects of actions. As Nagarjuna states in the *Disclosure of the Spirit of Enlightenment*, "Knowing this voidness of things, the one who still takes responsibility for evolutionary actions and effects, this one is even more wondrous than wonder, even more miraculous than miracles!"

To achieve this, one must distinguish between intrinsically real existence and mere existence, and between lack of intrinsically identifiable existence and nonexistence.

If you do not distinguish these kinds of existences and nonexistences, you will not get beyond the two extremisms of reification and repudiation, since as soon as something exists it will have objective existence, and once something lacks objective existence it will become utterly nonexistent.

Therefore, in our system, we are free from all absolutisms by the absence of intrinsic objectivity, and we are freed from all nihilisms by our ability to present an intrinsically unreal causality in that very actuality of voidness of objectivity.

Nagarjuna, thinking that the truthlessness of uncreated things such as space, calculated cessation, uncalculated cessation, and thatness could be easily proved once the truthlessness of persons and created things was proved by the above-explained reasonings, stated in the *Wisdom*, "If created things are utterly unestablished, how can uncreated things be established?"

As for the way in which it is easy to prove: Once intrinsic reality in created things is negated as above, their nonreality is established as sufficient for the presentation of all functions such as bondage and liberation, cause and effect, and objects and means of knowledge. That being established, then uncreated things also, such as reality and calculated cessation, even though also lacking truth status, can still be well represented as the goals of the paths, objects of knowledge, and as the Dharma jewel, refuge of disciples. It is never said that "if one does not maintain these things as truths, the systems that must present those things are invalid." Therefore there is no point in maintaining the truth status of these (uncreated) things, since truth status is not required for conventional viability.

Even if one did claim their truth status, one would still be required to maintain their presentability as characterized by such and such characteristics, as their being disconnected causes and disconnected effects, and as their being cognized by such and such validating cognitions. And in that case, if they are claimed to be not connected with their own means of attainment, characteristics, and means of cognition, then one cannot avoid the fault of all unconnected things being characteristic and characterized in relation to each other and so forth. And if it is claimed that they are connected, then, since it is impossible for a true, intrinsically real thing to depend on anything else, the claim of connection cannot be sustained.

Thus one should negate truth status through the analysis of sameness and difference. If this rational analysis cannot refute the truth status of these uncreated things, then one cannot refute even in the slightest the truth status of anything, since created things are completely similar.

Former scholars held many opinions about the grounds of differentiation into the two realities. Here, knowable objects are the ground of differentiation, following Shantideva's statement in the *Education Manual.* "Knowable objects are comprised by the superficial and ultimate realities."

They are divided into the two realities, superficial and ultimate, according to Nagarjuna's statement in the *Wisdom:* "The reality of the social superficial and the reality of the ultimate object."

In the *Lucid Exposition,* Chandrakirti explains "superficial" in three ways, as "a covering over reality," as "mutual dependence," and as "social convention." The latter of these is explained as having the nature of the expressed and its expression, the knowable and its knowledge, and so forth, but by this the superficial reality is not to be understood either as including all expressibles and knowables whatsoever, or as merely the expression and cognition of subjective conventions. Now, the first of the above three is the superficial represented as reality in superficial cognitions of forms and so on. This is also the misknowledge that reifies existence of intrinsic reality in things lacking in any intrinsically real objective status. For, truth status being objectively impossible, truth is (merely) represented in cognition, and there is no representation of truth in a cognition free of truth habits.

Actual Transcendent Insight

When you discover the view that realizes the two selflessnesses from the above teaching of the necessary conditions for transcendent insight, you should meditate on transcendent insight.

How many transcendent insights are there?

Here I have not mainly taught the high stages of transcendent insight but have emphasized the transcendent insight to be meditated by common individuals. To completely analyze that type of transcendent insight, there are the insights of the four realities, the insights of the three doors, and the insights of the six investigations.

The insights of the four realities are stated in the *Elucidation of the Intention* as the four, "discernment" and so forth. Among them, "discernment" takes the contents of reality as its object, and "investigation" takes the nature of reality as its object. The first contains thorough examination and thorough analysis, and the second contains examination and analysis, since they respectively discern coarse and subtle objects. The identification of these four is stated in the *Stages of the Disciples* and in the *Instruction in Transcendent Wisdom.*

The insights of the three doors are stated in the *Elucidation of the Intention* as the insights arisen from signs, arisen from thorough investigation, and arisen from individual discrimination. As for the description of these three, taking the import of selflessness as an example, first, selflessness is identified, then it is taken as object, and then its significance is imprinted in the mind without engaging in repeated determinations. The second stage of insight consists of determinations in order to ascertain what was not previously certain. The third stage of insight is the analysis as above of the identified import.

The insights of the six investigations are the thorough investigations and individual discriminations of meaning, object, nature, orientation, time, and reason. Insight investigating meaning investigates whether "the meaning of this expression is this"; investigating objects considers "this is internal" or "this is external," and so forth; investigating nature, it investigates whether "this is a particular nature or a general nature," or "this is a common nature or an uncommon nature"; investigating orientation, it investigates the faults and disadvantages of negative orientations and the virtues and benefits of positive orientations; investigating time, it investigates "such happened in the past, such happens in the present, and such will happen in the future." Insight investigating reason, investigates through the four types of reasoning; it investigates relational reasoning by viewing how effects occur depending on causes and conditions, considering specifically the objects of superficial and ultimate realities; it investigates functional reasoning by investigating how things perform their specific functions, such as fire by burning, considering "this is the phenomenon, this is the activity, and this is the function it accomplishes"; it investigates logical reasoning by investigating how things are established without contradicting validating cognitions, considering whether "this is supported by perceptual, inferential, or scripturally testimonial validating cognitions or not"; and it investigates natural reasoning by investigating the commonsensical natures, the inconceivable natures, and the ultimate natures of things such as the heat of fire and the wetness of water, respecting those natures and not considering other possibilities. The presentation of these investigative insights as sixfold is to be understood by the yogin, but they can definitely be included in three categories, as concerned with verbal meanings, with phenomenal objects, and with ultimate natures. The first investigative insight is in terms of the first concern, objective investigation and particular nature investigation are concerned with the second, and general nature investigative insight and the other three are concerned with the third. The first-explained four insights operate through three doors and manifest six modes of investigation, and therefore the insights of the three doors and the insights of the six investigations are included in the insights of the four realities.

The four conscious attitudes explained above in the quiescence section, such as the "balancing" attitude, are explained in the *Stages of Disciples* as being common to both quiescence and insight, and thus there are also four conscious attitudes in insight.

As for the way of practice, it is the procedure of first seeking quiescence and then, based on that, subsequently practicing insight, and that is the reason why quiescence and insight are differentiated by their different procedures in practice, even though they may both take the same object, such as selflessness. Especially, since the meditation of the two transcendent insights—that concerned with the levels of peace through specific discernment of the faults and virtues of the higher and lower realms, and that concerned with selflessness cultivated through analysis with the wisdom of the specific discrimination of the meaning of selflessness—is indispensably necessary to generate a firm and intense certainty, it has the greater power to abandon specific abandonees, defilements, and obscurations. As for the phenomenologically concerned transcendent insight, it is not only the meditation concerned with levels of peace that abandons the manifest addictions, but it is also stated by Ratnakarashanti in the *Instruction* to be the analytic meditation that discerns the nature of the eighteen elements, by which illustration one can understand the other insights meditated by distinguishing phenomenal objects.

Although Ratnakarashanti explains in the *Instruction* that one must generate quiescence and insight on the stage of yoga oriented toward the phenomenological before generating quiescence and insight oriented toward the ontological, here, following the view of Shantideva and Kamalashila and others, insight is generated after first generating whatever sort of quiescence, and I mean here the transcendent insight oriented ontologically toward ultimate reality.

The *Esoteric Communion* also explains the orientation toward mind-only, as taught in the *Visit to Lanka:* "depending on mind alone, do not imagine any external objects"; the orientation toward thatness; and the teaching of the three stages of the yoga of nonappearance. It also appears to explain, as above, the procedure of practice of quiescence and insight through focused meditation and analytic meditation in the first two stages. Thus it accepts a similar procedure of developing quiescence and insight in the mental process oriented toward reality. My own interpretation is that in the context of the Unexcelled Yoga the procedure of developing the understanding of the view must be practiced according to the central way treatises. In practice, however, although sometimes there are conscious attitudes analytic of thatness during the aftermath intuitions of the creation stage and perfection stage, and although the perfection stage yogin who has achieved the ability to concentrate on the essentials in the body must definitely meditate through concentration on top of his or her view when cultivating thatness in equipoise, there is no practice of the analytic meditation of transcendent insight as explained in other treatises. Therefore in that context you should not employ one-pointed reality meditation of transcendent insight as explained in other treatises. Instead in that context you should employ one-pointed reality meditation upon your view in alternation with your employment of analytic meditation. . . .

If you do not discover the view of selflessness, no matter what method of meditation you practice, your meditation will not abide on the import of thatness. So you must discover that view. And even if you have an understanding of the view, if you do not remember the view when you meditate on thatness and focus your meditation upon that, you will have no meditation on reality. Further, if after each new session of analysis of the view you focus your mind on not holding anything at all, it is not the cultivation of reality of thatness. Further, practicing by remembering that view and just focusing upon it is no more than the above practice of quiescence, and the meaning of the treatises is not just to practice insight in alternation with that. Therefore you should practice through the specific analysis by means of wisdom of the import of selflessness, as explained above.

If you practice analytic meditation by itself, the quiescence you previously developed will decline, so you should practice analytic meditation mounted on the horse of quiescence, now and then blending in periods of focused meditation. Moreover, if you practice analytic meditation often, your focusing decreases, so you should often return to focused meditation, engaging in quiescence by itself. If the focused meditation is overdone, you become averse to analysis or you ignore the functioning of your analysis, and your mind becomes obsessed with one-pointed quiescence, and so you should often return to analytic meditation. Your meditation has the greatest power if you practice quiescence and insight in balanced proportion, so that is how you should practice.

Thus it is not correct to hold that all thoughts occurring in analytic practice are substantivistic sign habits that are truth habits and therefore terminate them; because, as I have repeatedly established, truth-habit thought is only one tendency of thought. If you decide that rational negations overwhelm whatever is held by discriminating thought, this becomes the nihilistic repudiation that has overextended the rational negatee, and it is not the meaning of the scriptures, as I have established. Yet you may still think that, even if you do not assert that with regard to other subjects of concern, whatever is held in cognition regarding ultimate nature is merely the product of substantivistic sign habits that conceptualize truth status in things. In fact, those sign habits are the fault of a defective habit pattern of mind and do not function with regard to all objects cognized, because it is stated that the egocentric individual desiring liberation must investigate reality from many scriptural and rational perspectives.

Again you may think that the meditation on thatness, as it is for the purpose of generating nondiscrimination, is not produced by analytic discrimination, since cause and effect must correspond in nature. The Lord himself clearly answered this concern, in the *Kashyapa Chapter:* "Kashyapa, for example, when you rub two sticks together, they produce fire and are themselves completely consumed in the process. In the same way, Kashyapa, authentic analytic discrimination produces the faculty of holy wisdom, and, being produced, it serves to consume that authentic discrimination itself." Here he clearly states that the holy wisdom is generated by discrimination. Similarly Kamalashila states in his *Middle Meditation Stages*, "When the yogi analyzes with wisdom and does not cognize as ultimately certain any intrinsic objectivity of anything, he enters the samadhi free of discriminative thought, and he realizes the utter nonexistence of the intrinsic objectivity of things but merely meditates exclusively on the abandonment of all conscious attitudes; he never eliminates that particular discrimination of that absence of mental function, and he will never realize the utter nonexistence of intrinsic objectivity, since he is devoid of the illumination of wisdom. Thus, from the authentic specific discrimination arises the fire of the true wisdom of reality, like fire arisen from rubbing sticks, which then burns the sticks of discrimination. This is what the Lord stated." Otherwise it would never happen that the uncontaminated would arise from the contaminated, the transcendental from the mundane, a Buddha from a living being, a holy person from an alienated individual, and so forth. For in all these cases the effect is dissimilar from the cause.

Nagarjuna states in the *Disclosure of the Spirit of Enlightenment* that "where discriminations occur, how could there be voidness? The Transcendent Lords do not perceive any mind in the form of discriminated and discrimination; where there is discrimination and discriminated, there is no enlightenment." But here he is teaching that enlightenment will not be attained when truth status is perceived in discriminated and discrimination and does not negate discriminative wisdom or the mere function of discriminated and discrimination. Otherwise it would contradict his extensive determination of thatness through many discriminative analyses in that text; and if mere discrimination were meant, their not being seen by Buddha means their nonexistence. Again Nagarjuna states in the same text, "Voidness, called 'nonproduction,' 'voidness,' and 'selflessness,' if it is contemplated as anything less, it does not serve as meditation on that." This does not refute meditation that takes voidness and selflessness intrinsically unproduced as its object, but it refutes meditation on an inferior voidness, the lesser nature that is conceived by holding those voidnesses as having themselves truth status. As he states in the *Transcendental Praise*, "As you taught the nectar of voidness to cure all mental constructions, you reject those who adhere to it as true in itself." Likewise he said in the *Jewel Rosary* that "thus neither self nor selflessness is apprehended in reality. Therefore the Great Sage eliminated the views of self and selflessness." Both self and selflessness have no objective status in reality, and so the view that holds both as truly existing is eliminated. But this does not refute the view of selflessness, because, as in the previous quote from the *Rebuttal of Objections*, if it is not the case that there is realitylessness of intrinsically real status, then intrinsically real status would become existent.

These ways of meditation occur also in the old instructions on the stages of the path. Geshe Potowa says, in his *Collected Sayings*, that "some say that you should rationally determine intrinsic realitylessness at the time of study and reflection but meditate only on nondiscrimination at the time of meditation. But such leads to an irrelevant voidness, which will not serve as a remedy, since it is meditated as something else. Therefore, even at the time of meditation, one should discriminatingly investigate the absence of sameness and difference, or relativity, whatever you are used to, and also fix oneself slightly in nondiscrimination. If you meditate like that, it remedies the addictions."

If you meditate through investigation by discriminating wisdom in that way, until you have achieved the previously explained ecstatic fluency, you have a simulated transcendent insight. Once that ecstatic fluency is generated, you have the genuine transcendent insight. The actuality and method of generating fluency is as already explained. Further, this must occur without weakening of quiescence, and there is a fluency developed from that, so merely having fluency is not enough. Then what is? If you can develop ecstatic fluency through the power of the practice of analytic meditation itself, that then becomes transcendent insight. This is the same whether it involves the transcendent insight oriented toward the contents of reality or the transcendent insight oriented toward the nature of reality.

Such a way of the integration of quiescence and insight must be understood according to the teachings of the original treatises, and one should not rely on other explanations that presume it to be otherwise. And you should understand from my extensive *Stages of the Path* the extensive details (of the teachings) of the "stages of the path of enlightenment" (tradition) on the conclusive analyses through reasoning, the supportive scriptural references, and the processes of meditation.

Praise of Buddha Shakyamuni for His Teaching of Relativity: The Short Essence of Eloquence

by Tsong Khapa

Reverence to the Guru, Manjughosha!
I bow to that perfect Buddha, Supreme Philosopher,
Who taught us relativity, free of destruction, creation,
Nihilism, absolutism, coming, going, unity, and plurality;
The calm beyond all fabrications, the bliss supreme!

I bow down to Him whose insight and speech
Make Him unexcelled as Sage and Teacher;
The Victor, who realized ultimate truth,
Then taught us it as relativity!

Misknowledge itself is the very root
Of all the troubles in this fleeting world;
Who understood that and then reversed it
Taught universal relativity.

Thus how could it be possible
That the geniuses would not understand
This very path of relativity
As the vital essence of Your teaching?

Such being the case, who could discover
Anything even still more wonderful,
To sing Your praises for, O Savior,
Than Your teaching of relativity?

"Whatever depends upon conditions
Is empty of intrinsic reality!"
What excellent instruction could there be
More marvelous than this discovery?

Though the naive can seize upon it
As just confirming their extremist bonds,
The wise use that same (relativity)
To cut open fabrication's net.

This teaching is not seen elsewhere,
So You alone are titled Teacher,

Mere flattery for fundamentalists,
As when you call a fox a lion!

Wondrous Teacher! Wondrous Refuge!
Wondrous Philosopher Supreme!
Wondrous Savior of the world!
I pay full homage to that Teacher
Who proclaimed universal relativity!

O benefactor! To heal all beings
You proclaimed (profound relativity),
The unrivaled reason to ascertain
Voidness, the essence of the teaching.

How can one who understands
The process of relativity
As contradictory, or unestablished,
Ever understand Your art?

Your position is that when one perceives
Voidness as the fact of relativity,
Such voidness of reality does not preclude
The viability of activity;

Whereas when one perceives the opposite,
Activity is impossible in voidness,
Voidness is lost during activity;
One falls into anxiety's abyss.

Thus experience of relativity
Is most recommended in Your teaching,
Neither that of utter nothingness
Nor that of intrinsically real existence.

The nonrelative is like a sky-flower,
So there is nothing nonrelational.
Things' existence with objective status
Precludes dependence on cause and condition.

Thus You said that just because no thing
Exists beyond relational occurrence,
So nothing can really exist beyond
Voidness of intrinsic reality.

You said if things had any self-reality,
Since such could never be reversed,
Nirvana would become impossible,
Since fabrications could not be reversed.

Dauntless in the assemblies of the wise,
You clearly uttered Your lion's roar,
"Let there be freedom from identity!"
Who would presume to challenge it?

All systems are completely viable,
Since the lack of intrinsic reality
And relativity do not conflict;
Never mind they complement each other.

"By the reason of relativity,
There are no grounds to hold extremist views!"
For this excellent statement, You, Savior,
Are unexcelled among philosophers!

"All this objectively is voidness!"
And "From this cause comes this effect!"
These facts are mutually nonexclusive;
Certainties, they reinforce each other.

Than this, what could be more wondrous?
Than this, what miracle could more awe?
For this one principle, if You are praised,
It is real praise; and otherwise not so.

Those held in the thrall of delusions
Rise angrily to challenge You;
No wonder they should find unbearable
Your declaration of identitylessness!

But those who formally accept relativity,
The precious treasury of Your speech,
When they cannot bear the roar of voidness,
That really does amaze me!

The unexcelled relativity,
Doorway to identitylessness,
They hold it as a nominal identity;
How they deceive themselves!

These should be led by whatever art
Into that good path which pleases You,
The matchless haven well frequented
By all the supreme Holy Ones.

Intrinsic reality, uncreated and nonrelative,
And relativities, created and relational;
How can these two facts coincide
In a single instance without contradiction?

Therefore the relatively occurrent,
Though ever free of self-reality,
Appears as if intrinsically real;
So You said all this is like illusion.

From this very fact one well understands
The (centrists') statement that, the way You taught,
Those who would challenge Your teaching,
Rationally can find no fallacy.

Why? Because this Your elucidation
Makes utterly remote the tendencies
To reify and repudiate things
Empirical and hypothetical.

This very path of relativity,
Proof that Your speech is matchless,
Also generates complete certitude
Of the validity of Your other statements.

You speak well from experience of reality,
And those who train themselves under You
Go far beyond every kind of trouble,
Having abandoned the root of all evil.

But those who turn their backs on Your teaching,
Though they have struggled for a long time,
Decry many faults once outside again,
Because of a firm conviction about the self.

O wonder! The wise one understands the difference
Between following and not following your teaching.
Then how could he fail to feel most deeply
Great respect for You (and Your teaching)?

What need is there to mention Your many teachings?
To find even a rough, general certainty
About the precise meaning of even a small part
Confers, even that, the supreme happiness!

Alas, my mind conquered by confusion,
Though I came from afar to seek refuge
In the profusion of Your excellence,
I could not embody its smallest part.

Yet when I stand before the lord of death,
And the stream of life is not quite ended,
I will consider myself fortunate
To have even this slightest faith in You.

Among teachers, the Teacher of relativity,
Among wisdoms, the wisdom of relativity;
These are like imperial victors in the world,
Making You world champion of wisdom, over all.

Whatever You taught is penetrated
By means of relativity itself,
And since that really becomes Nirvana,
No deed of Yours does not deliver peace.

Yea! Whoever hears Your teaching
Finds liberating peace in everything;
So who could possibly not respect
The upholders of such a teaching?

As it overcomes all oppositions,
Is free from internal contradictions,
And fulfills both goals of human beings,
My delight ever grows for this system.

For the sake of this, You gave away
Again and again during innumerable aeons
Sometimes body, other times life,
Loved ones, and great wealth of possessions.

When I see such excellence of Yours,
I see that Your great heart brings forth the teaching,
Just like the fishhook drags out the fish;
What a sorry fate not to hear it from You!

But even with the force of that sorrow,
I will not let my mind waver (from the teaching),
As the mind of the mother
Always goes after her beloved child.

And even when I think upon Your speech,
"That Teacher, full-orbed with nets of light-rays,
Blazing with glory of auspicious signs and marks,
Spoke in this way with his Brahma voice!"

Then the image of great Shakyamuni
Just dawning in mind, heals me well,
As moon-rays heal the pains of fever.

Though that good system is thus marvelous,
Inexpert persons get totally confused
In every respect, as if they were
Tangled up in jungle grasses.

Having understood this problem,
I schooled myself in writings of skilled sages,
Studying with manifold exertions,
Seeking Your intent again and again.

And I studied numerous treatises
Of the Buddhist and the non-Buddhist schools,
Yet unremittingly my intellect
Was still tormented in the trap of doubt.

So I went to the night-lily garden of Nagarjuna's works,
Prophesied to elucidate correctly
The art of Your final Vehicle,
Free of the extremes of being and nothing.

There I saw, by the kindness of the Mentor,
All illuminated by garlands of white light
The true eloquence of the glorious Chandra moon,
Whose expanding orb of taintless wisdom
Courses freely in the sky of Scripture,
Dispels the darkness of extremist hearts,
Eclipses constellations of false truths;
And then my mind at last obtained relief!

Of all His deeds, His speech is the supreme.
And for this very reason, true sages

Should commemorate a perfect Buddha
For this teaching of relativity. . . .

I renounced the world on the example of that Teacher,
My study of the Victor's speech is not inferior,
I am a Buddhist monk, energetic in yoga practice;
And such is my respect for that great Seer!

By my Mentor's kindness, I was thus fortunate to meet
The liberating teaching of the unexcelled Teacher,
And I dedicate this virtue as a cause of all beings'
Being looked after by the holy spiritual teachers.

May the teaching of that Benefactor, 'til world's end,
Be undisturbed by the winds of wrong prejudices,
And, finding faith in the Teacher by understanding
The natural way of the teaching, may it ever increase!

May I uphold the wholesome system of Shakyamuni
That illumines the principle of relativity,
Through all my lives, though I give up body and even life!
And may I never give it up, even for an instant!

May I spend all day and night reflecting
On the methods to propagate this teaching,
Achieved by that best Leader through boundless hardships,
By making strenuous efforts the essence (of His lives!)

As I strive in this way with pure high resolve,
May Brahma, Indra, and the world protectors,
And Mahakala and the other Dharma defenders,
Always befriend me without fail!

Discovery of Mother Voidness

by Jankya Rolway Dorje

O thatness of profound Relativity—O Wonder!
May the Guru who nakedly reveals this as it is,
His kindness irrepayable, be enthroned in my heart!
I will speak spontaneously whatever comes to mind!

I was like a mad child, long lost his old mother,
Never could find her, though she was with him always!
But now it seems I'm about to find that kind old Ama,
Since Big Brother Relativity hints where she hides,
I think, "Yes, yes!"—then, "No, no!"—then, "Could it be, really!"
These various subjects and objects are my Mother's smiling face!
These births, deaths, and changes are my Mother's lying words!
My undeceiving Mother has deceived me!
My only hope of refuge is in Brother Relativity!

The sole chance for freedom is just old Mother's love;
If this subject-object situation were all there was to it,
The three-time Buddhas could find no way to save us!

But liberation *is* possible, since these various changes
Are but the changes of my unchanging Mother!

The mutual interdependence
Of ineffable Mother where nothing has status,
And Relativity where everything appears,
Is exactly what must be understood!

Seeking my old Father, and just not finding,
Is the actual finding of my old Mother,
Then from my Mother's lap I find my old Father—
I, child of such kind parents, cry out for their refuge!

When Mother's neither one nor many faces
Seemed to be there ineffably reflected
In the clear mirror of Big Brother Relativity—
How crazy I was, not to start this quest!

The generous testaments of Nagarjuna and Chandrakirti
Were but papers blowing in the wind, until Tsong Khapa,
Manjugarbha, sent his retriever hawk to get them.
Then was I saved the trials of far questing
And allowed to see my old Mother, natural here with me.

Nowadays some of the bright ones of our school,
Fond of terms such as "self-sufficiency" and "truth status,"
Seem to put aside what obviously appears before them
And seek some fabulous unicorn to be critiqued!
They never acknowledge this obvious appearance.

They explain and explain, not reaching the crux,
And that old Mother completely escapes them!

Though things surely do exist somehow,
Their reality seems not to be this horny incompatibility,
Since the intimacy of Father-Mother union
Seems inseparably tender and cozy!

The systematists, traditionists, and idealists,
And the dogmaticist centrist masters,
Describe the Mother's snow-white elephant body
With such a wide variety of designations—
"The fierce striped tiger of substantial objects!"
"The brainless, mad monkey of pure subjectivity!"
"The powerful bear of self-sufficient nonduality!"
But they all miss the presence of old Mother!

The many sages of Sakya, Nyingma, Kagyu, Drugpa, and so on
Proclaim their traditions' various conventions for Her;
"Subjectless clarity-voidness-self-awareness!"
"Primal, spontaneous true face of Samantabhadra!"
"Nonartificial, innate Great Seal!"
"Freedom from assertions beyond something and nothing!"
All these are fine, they all do hit on the real situation,
But let them press down a little on their own noses
And ask themselves honestly, "Is it really so?"

Cheer up, you realists, no need to be nervous,
Since external things are not done away with!
Cheer up, you idealist philosophers,
Validation works, even without apperception!
Cheer up, you dogmaticist centrist masters,
Relativity has beauty even without identifiability!

No need to worry, you holders of personal lineages,
It's fine even to hold clarity-voidness union!
Your mystic sages need not insist on all-goodness,
Since even in primal purity good and bad apply!
You wise old sages need not be too stubborn,
Since the innate will arise even in willful meditation!
And you hardheaded critics, don't get too excited,
It's fine to assert freedom from something and nothing!

I acknowledge of course that those unfamiliar with texts
Cannot know the technicalities of using conventions,
So it is not that I do not respect their attainments;
If any feelings are hurt, please forgive me!

Though by no means am I an heir to omniscience,
Through skill with the reins of analysis and devotion,
I rode well the fine stallion of the ancestral texts
And won my way to freedom from the abyss.

No need to seek her, she's the seeker himself!
Don't cling to her truth; she is utter falsehood!
Don't negate her falseness, it is truth itself!
It's sufficient to rest in the unabsolute unceased!

Though I don't see my Mother, by her mere name
It seems I meet my long-lost kind parents,
As if face to face!
Great thanks, O Nagarjuna and sons!
Great thanks, O Tsong Khapa Lama!
Great thanks, O kind Mentor Lama!
As the way to repay all your kindness,
I thus honor our Mother the Void!

My unproduced, inexpressible old Mother
Cradles gently the tiny infant of intellect;
With the banquet of her perfectly good expressions,
May she lead all beings to true happiness!
E MA LA—Rolway Dorje!
A O LA—I dance with joy!
A HO LA—I worship the Three Jewels!

CHAPTER 7

Practicing the Creation Stage

The Quintessence Segment

Then bless me to embark in the boat to cross the ocean of the
    Tantras,
Through the kindness of the captain Vajra-master,
Holding vows and pledges, root of all powers,
More dearly than life itself!

Bless me to perceive all things as the deity body,
Cleansing the taints of ordinary perception and conception
Through the yoga of the first stage of Unexcelled Tantra,
Changing birth, death, and between into the three Buddha bodies!

Glorious Esoteric Communion Self-Creation Yoga

by Lama Tsong Khapa

NAMO GURU MANJUGHOSHAYA!
May the glorious, precious root Mentor
sit in the lotus of my heart
and sustain me with his great kindness.
May he grant attainments of body, speech, and mind!

I invoke the glorious Losang Drakpa,
who lovingly teaches just as he sees
the complete essence of the path of all Sutra and Tantra,
who holds the complete holy Dharma of the Victor.

I invoke the feet of the Holy Mentor,
supreme guide leading beings to liberation,
seeing this life impermanent as a bubble
and samsara coreless like a plantain tree.

I invoke the feet of the Omniscient One,
perfect fruit of enlightenment's evergreen tree,
grown on the ground of equanimity,
from compassion-seeds watered by the rain of love.

I invoke the effortless servant of others,
in ordinary form for the sake of the less intelligent,

yet complete with the mandala of thirty-two deities,
the five families with the four consorts and so on.

I invoke the Omnipresent Lord Vajradhara,
who achieves beings' aims with limitless incarnations,
with the vow of the inseparable vajra union,
base of the whole mandala, residents and environment.

I invoke the feet of Lodro Rinchen
... Savior Nagarjuna,
... Matangipa,

I invoke the feet of Tilopa, Sri Jnana,
who, attaining powers, went to the pure land of bliss,
and blessed by the holy Dakini-angel,
performed more deeds than a thousand Buddhas.

I invoke the feet of Narotapa,
in whose heart was born the illusory samadhi,
who performed many very difficult feats
in the eastern city, as the Dakini prophesied.

I invoke the feet of the translator Marpa,
... Wangi Dorje,
... Sonam Rinchen,
... Tsultrim Kyab,
... Zhonu O of Serding,
... Choku Ozer of Deding,
... Phagpa O of Lake Jo,
... Khyungpo Lhaspa, supreme master,
... Losang Drakpa,
Zang Kyongwa, who sees all things,
Sherap Senge, crown jewel of the wise, and
Palden Zangpo, master of the triple canon.
Jamyang Gedun Pelwa, best master, bright as Manjushri,
Trashi Pagpa, vajra holder, and
Samdrup Gyatso, unconfused in all things.
Tzondru Pagpa, who reached the stage of accomplishment,
Dorje Zangpo, who attained the supreme discipline, and
Sangye Gyatso, the holder of the discipline.
Kaydrup Gyatso, transcendent in realization,

Konchok Yarpel, holder of the treasury of oral traditions,
and Ngawang Tzondru, knower of the five sciences.
Gedun Puntsog, holding the freedoms of mind,
Gyachen Tso, treasury of supreme and common powers,
Wangchuk Jay, wise and adept in the essential.
The wise and loving Vajradhara, Ngawang Chogden,
Kelsang Gyatso, Ocean Savior, ambassador of Buddhas.
Lozang Penden Yeshe, whose compassion exceeded all Victors,
and Losang Jampel, springtime of bounty of the ocean of Victors.

I acknowledge and repent to all the Saviors,
whatever proscribed and natural evil actions I performed,
had performed, and rejoiced at,
while gripped by addictions in former times.
I invoke the live and ancestral masters,
may they bless my mental stream;
embarking on the ship of the profound two stages,
may I enter the ocean of omniscient wisdom!
May I swiftly attain the exaltation of Vajradhara,
never parting in all lives from the true masters,
enjoying the glory of the Dharma and perfecting
the virtues of the stages and paths!

Instantaneous Self-Creation

In a split second I myself become the blue-black Fury Vajra, with three
faces, black, white, and red; six arms holding vajra, wheel, and lotus in the
right, and bell, jewel, and sword in the left; embraced by Touch Vajra similar to myself. We are both adorned with the eight jeweled ornaments, our
shoulders draped with heavenly shawls, our waists covered with divine
silken robes.

Inner Sacrifice

OM AH VIGHNANTAKRT HUM.
OM SHUNYATA JNANA VAJRA SVABHAVA ATMAKO HAM.

All becomes emptiness. From the actuality of emptiness comes HUM YAM
HUM, from the gray-blue YAM arises a semicircular blue-green disk of wind,
adorned on the two sides by two five-point vajras, arising from the HUMS.
Upon that, there is HUM RAM HUM, from the red RAM arises a triangular
red fire plane, adorned on the two sides by two vajras arising from two

HUMS. Upon that arising from OM AH HUM, a tripod of human heads and above that arising from AH a skull, red inside and white outside. Within it from an AH arises an eight-petaled red lotus marked with AH. In its center are the five meats and the five nectars. In the sky above them on a solar seat, arising from HUM is a five-point white vajra, whose center is marked by HUM. From it light radiates, wind stirs, fire blazes, and the substances in the skull melt and boil. The vajra with its solar seat falls within, and the substances become equal in flavor. All taints are purified, and it becomes translucent as milk-white crystal. The lotus with its AH melts, and a light bright as sunlight blazes forth, and all naturally becomes the nectar of wisdom. The light-rays of OM like a laser hook attract the wisdom of all Transcendent Lords of the ten directions; merging it expands into an ocean. OM AH HUM (7x)

Sense Offerings

OM AH VIGHNANTAKRT HUM.
OM SHUNYATA JNANA VAJRA SVABHAVA ATMAKO HAM

HUM All becomes emptiness. From the actuality of emptiness from AH, there are vast expansive skull bowls; inside each is its letter, such as AM, PAM, PUM, adorned with a squiggle. Therefrom arise offering water, water for the feet, water for the mouth, food, flowers, incense, light, scent, food, music. Their nature is bliss emptiness, their aspects are the offering substances, and their function is to give special uncontaminated bliss to the six sense bases.

OM ARGHAM AH HUM. OM PADYAM AH HUM. OM ANCAMANAM AH HUM. OM PROKSHANAM AH HUM. OM PUSHPE AH HUM. OM DHUPE AH HUM. OM ALOKE AH HUM. OM GANDHE AH HUM. OM NAIVIDYE AH HUM. OM SHABDA AH HUM.

Mandala Offering to Mentors

OM VAJRA BHUMI AM HUM. The golden ground of great power
OM VAJRA REKHE AH HUM. The outer iron mountain wall around
OM HAM SUMADHYA MAIRAVE NAMA. Mount Sumeru in the center
OM YAM PURVAVIDEHAYA NAMA. Purvavideha in the east
OM RAM JAMBUDVIPAYA NAMA. Jampudvipa in the south
OM LAM APARAGAVCARYA NAMA. Aparagaucarya in the west
OM VAM UTTARAKURAVE NAMA. Uttara Kuru in the north
OM YAM UPADVIPAYA NAMA. (2x) Lu and Pupag islands

OM RAM UPADVIPAYA NAMA (2X)—Ngayab and Ngayabshen islands
OM LAM UPADVIPAYA NAMA (2X)—Yoden and Lamchoktro islands
OM VAM UPADVIPAYA NAMA (2X)—Draminyen and Draminyenjida islands
OM YAM GAJA RATNAYA NAMA—precious elephant
OM RAM PURUSHA RATNAYA NAMA—precious minister
OM LAM ASHVA RATNAYA NAMA—precious horse
OM VAM STRI RATNAYA NAMA—precious queen
OM YAM KHADGA RATNAYA NAMA—precious general
OM RAM CHAKRA RATNAYA NAMA—precious wheel
OM LAM MANI RATNAYA NAMA—precious jewel
OM VAM MAHANIDHI RATNAYA NAMA—great treasure
OM SURYAYA NAMA—sun
OM CANDRAYA NAMA—moon

Taking up in mind the all-good precious mandala with the mass of totally good offerings with the forces of virtue of past, present, and future enjoyments of body, speech, and mind of myself and others, I offer it to the Mentor, deities, and the Three Jewels. Accepting it out of your great compassion, please look after us.

IDAM GURU RATNA MANDALA KAM NIRYATAYAMI

Refuge

I always take refuge in the Bliss Lords, who practice the play of mind like a taintless moon, using the limitless arts of their holy compassion—may they always abide in my mind!

I always take refuge in the holy Dharma, the reality uniformly experienced in all things, ground of the successes of all holy spiritual heroes, sure liberator from all superstitions!

I take refuge in the Community of the lords of discipline, truly freed from all bonds, endowed with the glory of best compassion, established on stages such as the joyous!

May I conceive the holy spirit of enlightenment, the mind adorned by intense aspiration, wherein the instincts for all obscurations are eradicated by the purification of thought and evolutionary effects. (3x)

Vajrasattva Meditation

From PAM on my crown a lotus and from AH a moon disk, upon them from HUM a five-pointed white vajra, marked in the center with HUM. From that vajra light radiates, then from its gathering together there arises a white Vajrasattva with one face, two arms holding vajra and bell. His consort, white Vajradhatvishravi, has one face and two arms holding skull and diamond chopper, embracing him. Both are adorned with various jeweled ornaments. He sits in the vajra position; upon a moon in his heart there is a white HUM radiating light, inviting wisdom heroes similar to himself.

OM VAJRASATTVA SAPARIVARA
ARGHAM PADYAM PUSHPE DHUPE ALOKE
GANDHE NAIVIDYE SHABDA PRATICCHA HUM SVAHA
JAH HUM BAM HOH

May they become indivisible! Again, light radiates from the heart HUM, inviting consecration deities

OM PANCHAKULA SAPARIVARA ARGHAM PADYAM PUSHPE DHUPE
ALOKE GANDHE NAIVIDYE SHABDA PRATICCHA HUM SVAHA

May all Transcendent Lords openly please confer consecration. When I pray thus, they hold up a vessel filled with wisdom nectar and confer consecration upon him.

OM SARVA TATHAGATA ABHISHEKHATA SAMAYA SHRIYE HUM

The body becomes filled with wisdom nectar, and he becomes adorned on the crown by Akshobhya. "Lord Vajrasattva, please cleanse and purify all losses of vows and all sins and obscurations of myself and others." By praying thus, light radiates from the heart HUM purifying the sins and defilements of all beings, also offerings are given to the Buddhas and Bodhisattvas, and all their virtues are concentrated into light, dissolving into the heart HUM making his luster and energy outstanding.

OM VAJRASATTVASAMAYAM. ANUPALAYA VAJRASATTVENOPA-
TISHTHA. DRDHO ME BHAVA. SUTOSHYO ME BHAVA. SUPOSHYO ME
BHAVA. ANURAKTO ME BHAVA. SARVASIDDHIM ME PRAYACCHA. SARVA
KARMASUCHA ME. CHITTAM SHRIYAM KURU HUM. HA HA HA HA HOH

BHAGAVAN. SARVA TATHAGATA VAJRA MA ME MUNCHA. VAJRI BHAVA. MAHA SAMAYA SATTVA AH HUM PHAT. (21X)

"O Mentor, my protector, please give refuge, deluded by my ignorance I have broken and lost my vows. Chief holder of the vajra, whose nature is great compassion, I take refuge in the leader of beings."

Vajrasattva says: "Gentle son, all your sins and broken vows are purified." He dissolves into me and my body, speech, and mind become indivisible from his.

Refuge Evocation

I myself become the luminous Akshobhyavajra. The blue HUM on the variegated lotus and sun disk in my heart emits light-rays like laser hooks that draw the deities of the Akshobhya mandala, indivisible from the vajra master, down from their natural abodes. The light-rays return to my own heart.

OM SARVATATHAGATA ARGHAM ... PADYAM ... PUSHPE ... DHUPE ... ALOKE ... GANDHE ... NAIVIDYE ... SHABDA ... RUPA ... SHABDA ... GANDHA ... RASA ... SPARSHE PUJAMEGHASAMUDRA SPARANASAMAYA SHRIYE AH HUM

I salute those magnificent deities like Bodhichittavajra, including forms, sensations, notions, emotions, cognitions, the six media, the six faculties, and earth, water, fire, air, and space!

I salute those magnificent deities like Bodhichittavajra, including ignorance, pride, lust, and those of vajra clan, emerged from constant contact with the knowledge consort, manifesting wild joy of various delights!

I salute those magnificent deities like Bodhichittavajra, Takkiraja, Niladanda, Mahabala, Achala, Sumbharaja, Ushnisharaja, Yamantaka, Prajnantaka, Hayagriva, and Vighnantaka!

In the presence of the greatly compassionate ones, I confess and repent with proper rites all mistakes caused by misperceptions in this timeless ocean of existence.

I rejoice heartily in all the virtues accomplished by perfect Buddhas, Bodhisattvas, or by other saints, and I dedicate them to final enlightenment.

I always take refuge in the Bliss Lords, who practice the play of mind like a taintless moon, using the limitless techniques of their holy compassion—may they always abide in my mind!

I always take refuge in the holy Dharma, the reality uniformly experienced in all things, ground of the successes of all holy spiritual heroes, sure liberator from all superstitions!

I take refuge in the Community of the lords of discipline, truly freed from all bonds, endowed with the glory of superior compassion, who have reached the stages such as joy!

May I create the holy spirit of enlightenment, adorned by the lofty aspiration, which purifies the resolve and maturity to eradicate the instincts for all obscurations!

May that mind which is the actuality of perfect enlightenment now truly abide on the sole path of all Bliss Lords, the way of tenfold pure excellence, such as generosity and so on!

May all the Buddhas and the Bodhisattvas please think of me! I, Akshobhyavajra, from this time forth until I come to the seat of enlightenment, may I conceive the holy, unexcelled spirit of enlightenment, just as the three-times protectors certainly accomplished their enlightenment. I will uphold firmly all three ethics, that of the vow of restraint, that of achieving virtue, and that of helping beings. I uphold from now on the vow arisen from the Buddha yoga of the unexcelled Three Jewels: Buddha, Dharma, and Sangha. I will truly uphold also the holy masters. I will always give the four kinds of gifts each day at the six times in keeping the delightful vow of the great supreme jewel clan. In regard to the great pure lotus clan arising from the great enlightenment, I will hold each Dharma of the Three Vehicles: outer, inner, and secret. I will uphold truly each and every vow I have in the great supreme karma clan, and I will do what I can of ritual offerings. I will conceive the holy unexcelled spirit of enlightenment for the sake of all sentient beings. I will uphold all the vows completely. I will save those not yet saved. I will deliver those not yet delivered. I will console those not consoled. I will establish sentient beings in Nirvana.

May the members of the assembly field return to their own abodes!

Ordinary Protection Wheel

TAKKI HUM JAH—around the terrible ones there is a fence of iron vajras
TAKKI HUM JAH—outside that a water fence
TAKKI HUM JAH—outside that a fire fence
TAKKI HUM JAH—outside that a wind fence

From HUM upon the iron fence a vajra tent like a stupa, under the tent upon the fence a vajra canopy. Beneath this to the ground from HUM the vajra ground. In all the outer directions there is a net of arrows radiating, fiercely blazing with wisdom fire. On the crown moon of the deities a white OM, on the throat lotus a red AH, and on the heart sun a blue HUM—OM AH HUM (3x).

Creation of the Mandala Universe

There being no things, there is no meditator, nothing to meditate upon, and no meditation; since things are without reality, meditation is not to be perceived.

Since all animate and inanimate things are ultimately without reality, they have the nature of emptiness, signlessness, and wishlessness, wherein meditated, meditation, and meditator are not perceived.

From the actuality of emptiness in a split second, in the center of the complete vajra ground, replete with fence, tent, canopy, and fire mountain, there is a white triangular reality source standing upright with an expansive top and tapered base. Within its fine lower point in the center of a lotus there is HUM YAM HUM. From the blue-gray YAM comes a blue bow-shaped wind mandala, and from the two HUMS come two vajras to adorn the two sides. Upon that HUM RAM HUM from the red RAM comes a red triangular fire mandala, and from two HUMS come two vajras to adorn the two sides. Upon that HUM RAM HUM from the white RAM comes a round white water mandala, and from the two HUMS come two vajras to adorn the two sides. Upon that HUM LAM HUM from the yellow LAM comes a square yellow earth mandala, and from the two HUMS come two vajras to adorn the two sides. These being in reality the four goddesses, Lochana and so on, from the merging into one of the four mandalas there arises a double vajra on which is manifest a white BHRUM radiating light-rays of clouds of Buddhas, from which arises the square four-doored divine palace.

Its walls have five layers, from the outside in, white, yellow, red, green, and blue. Near the top of the wall is a red jewel frieze, adorned with jeweled squares and triangles. Its plate is formed by four golden colonnades. Over that protrude rafters shaped like crocodile heads, from whose mouths hang pearl nets and half nets. Outside that, jewel pendants hang from the edge of the roof. Above that is a balustrade in the shape of half lotus petals. It is beautified by eight banners and eight victory standards, which stand in golden vases. Four royal umbrellas adorn the four outer corners. At the foot of the outer wall there is a red ledge, on which dance offering goddesses in various postures and colors, worshiping and making offerings. Vajra-decorated red gems stand on half moons in the outer portals of the gates and arches and at the inner and outer corners of the walls.

In front of each of the four doors there are gold triumphal arches, each supported by four pillars rising from vase-shaped footings, holding up the arch's facade of eleven layers, decorated with gold disks, pendants, jewels, silver horseshoes, munnam jewels, waranda stripes, pendants, jewels, hooves, and a parapet. At the peak of each arch there is a Dharma wheel flanked by a buck and a doe. On the right and left sides of the arches are wish-fulfilling gem trees growing from fine vases, bearing the seven precious necessities of a kingdom. All around are yogin Adepts. Goddesses leaning from the clouds hold garlands of flowers and beautify the mansion. On the floor of the divine palace, halfway within the mandala, is a raised circular beam with five-color lights on the outside and with three-pointed vajras on the inner side. Upon this in the east is a wheel, the south a jewel, the west a lotus, and the north a sword. There are two pillars on each side, which support the diamond roof beams that beautifully uphold the roof, its peak adorned with a jewel and a vajra.

On the right and left of each cardinal section of this upper stage are two jewel vessels each filled with nectar, with eight vessels in all. This supreme good palace of qualities exceeding gods and humans is clearly transparent from the outside in and clearly transparent from the inside out.

All the surfaces above and below are white in the east, yellow in the south, red in the west, green in the north, and blue in the center. Within there are thirty-one lotus seats; the central one and the ten terrible ones have sun cushions, the easterners, such as Vairochana, have moon cushions, Mamaki has a vajra seat, and the other southerners have jewel seats; westerners have red lotus seats, and northerners have crossed vajra seats. Upon these seats, in a split second by merely intense aspiration, all thirty-two deities simultaneously become perfectly manifest.

On the central seat is myself as blue Vajradhara: three faces, blue, white, and red; six arms holding vajra, wheel, and lotus in the right, and bell, jewel, and sword in the left, hair tied up in a crown ornament; adorned by the thirty-two marks and eighty signs. My consort is blue Sparshavajra with Akshobhya crown: three faces, blue, white, and red; six arms holding vajra, wheel, and lotus in the right, and bell, jewel, and sword in the left. Her hair in the half-bound coiffure, extremely graceful with a smiling face, beautiful with gestures such as sidelong glances. Her beauty is fully mature, and she playfully delights with the five objects of desire. With our first two arms, we hold each other in mutual embrace. We are adorned with the eight jeweled ornaments: jeweled crown, jeweled earrings together with a blue utpala flower beautified with ribbons, jeweled necklace, pearl sash, precious bracelets, anklets, and jeweled belt sash. Our shoulders are draped with heavenly shawls, and our waists covered with divine silk. We sit in an aura of light in the enlightened hero posture.

In the east there is white Vairochana with Akshobhya crown: three faces, white, black, and red; six arms holding wheel, vajra, and white lotus in the rights, and bell, jewel, and sword in the lefts. In the south yellow Ratnasambhava with Akshobhya crown: three faces, yellow, black, and white; six arms holding jewel, vajra, and wheel in the rights, and bell, yellow lotus, and sword in the lefts. In the west red Amitabha with Akshobhya crown: three faces, red, black, and white; upper left hand holding bell with the stem of a red lotus, upper right hand holding a flowering lotus at the heart, other right hands a vajra and wheel, left hands a jewel and sword. In the north green Amoghasiddhi with Akshobhya crown: three faces, green, black, and white; six arms holding sword, crossed vajra, and wheel in the rights, and bell, green lotus, and jewel in the lefts. Southeast, white Lochana with Vairochana crown: three faces, white, black, and red; six arms holding wheel, vajra, and pundarika in the rights, and bell, jewel, and sword in the lefts. Southwest, blue Mamaki with Akshobhya crown: three faces, blue, white, and red; six arms holding vajra, wheel, and purple lotus in the rights, and bell, jewel, and sword in the lefts. Northwest, red Pandaravasini with Amitabha crown: three faces, red, black, and white; upper left holds bell and root stems of a red lotus, upper right opens it at her heart. Northeast, green Tara with Amoghasiddhi crown: three faces, green, black, and white; six arms holding crossed vajra, wheel, and vajra-marked lotus in the rights, and bell, jewel, and sword in the lefts.

In the second row out, southeast, white Rupavajra with Vairochana crown: three faces, white, black, and red; two upper hands holding a red mirror, other right hands a vajra and pundarika, left hands a jewel and sword. Southwest, yellow Shabdavajra with Ratnasambhava crown: three faces, yellow, black, and white; two upper hands playing blue lute, other right hands wheel and purple lotus, left hands a jewel and sword. Northwest, red Gandhavajra with Amitabha crown: three faces, red, black, and white; two upper hands holding a conch vessel of scent, other right hands a vajra and wheel, left hands a jewel and sword. Northeast, green Rasavajra with Amoghasiddhi crown: three faces, green, black, and white; two upper hands holding vessels of flavors, other right hands a wheel and vajra-marked lily, left hands a jewel and sword. All eight of the goddesses have hair in half-bound coiffures, extremely graceful with smiling faces, beautiful with gestures such as sidelong glances. Their beauty is fully mature, and they playfully delight with the five objects of desire. They sit in vajra position in their seats in the center of a shining halo of light.

On the (facing center) right and left seats at the eastern door are respectively white Maitreya and Kshitigarha with Vairochana crowns: three faces, white, black, and red; six arms holding wheel, vajra, and pundarika in the rights, and bell, jewel, and sword in the lefts. Maitreya also holds in the upper right a wheel-marked naga tree flower. On the right and left seats at the southern door are respectively yellow Vajrapani and Aksagarbha with Ratnasambhava crowns: three faces, yellow, black, and white; hand implements like Ratnasambhava. On the right and left seats at the western door are respectively red Lokeshvara and Manjushri with Amitabha crowns: three faces, red, black, and white; hand implements like Amitabha. On the right and left seats at the northern door are respectively green Sarvanivarana Viskhambhini and Samantabhadra with Amoghasiddhi crowns: three faces, green, black, and white; hand implements like Amoghasiddhi. All deities from Vairochana to Samantabhadra have hair in royal topknot wearing jeweled crowns, jeweled earrings together with a blue utpala flower beautified with ribbons, jeweled necklaces, pearl sashes, precious bracelets, anklets, and jeweled belt sashes. Upper bodies are draped with cloth of heavenly shawls and the lower bodies covered with divine silks. Adorned by the thirty-two marks and eighty signs. At peace in an orb of radiant light, each one is seated in the vajra position.

In the eastern door black Yamantaka with Vairochana crown: three faces, black, white, and red; six arms holding staff, wheel, and vajra in the rights, and noose over chest with threatening gesture, bell and ax in the lefts. In the southern door white Prajnantakrt with Ratnasambhava crown: three faces, white, black, and red; six arms holding vajra-marked white staff, and sword in the rights, and noose over chest with threatening gesture, bell and ax in the lefts. In the western door red Hayagriva with Amitabha crown: three faces, red, black, and white; six arms holding lotus, sword, and pounder in the rights, and bell on the hip, ax and noose in the lefts. In the northern door black Vighnantakrt with Amoghasiddhi crown: three faces, blue, white, and red; six arms holding double vajra, wheel, and spear in the rights, and noose over chest with threatening gesture, bell, and ax in the lefts. In the southeast black Achala with Vairochana crown, three faces, black, white, and red; six arms holding sword, vajra, and wheel in the rights, and threatening gesture over heart, ax and noose in the lefts. In the southwest door blue Takkiraja with Ratnasambhava crown: three faces, black, white, and red; first two hands held in the Humkara gesture, other two rights vajra and sword, lefts noose and iron hook. In the northwest blue Niladanda with Amitabha crown: three faces, blue, white, and red; six arms holding blue staff marked with vajra, sword and wheel in the rights, and noose over chest with threatening gesture, lotus and ax in lefts. In the northeast blue Mahabala with Amoghasiddhi crown: three faces, black, white, and red; six arms holding vajra-marked black staff, vajra and wheel in the rights, and noose over chest with threatening gesture, trident and ax in the lefts. Above blue Ushnishacakravarti with Akshobhya crown: three faces, blue, white, and red, first two hands in the *ushnisha* gesture, other two rights vajra and lotus, lefts threatening gesture and sword. Below blue Sumbharaja with Akshobhya crown, three faces, black, white, and red; six arms holding vajra, wheel, and jewel in the rights, and noose over chest with threatening gesture, lotus and sword in the lefts.

All ten of the terrible ones have yellowish-red hair flaming up; their brows and eyelashes flare intensely orange. Each face has three eyes and four sharp fangs, which grind horribly. Their fierce, loud laughs HA HA reverberate, and their faces are wrinkled with intensity of expressions. They have big bellies. Their hair is bound by blue Ananta snakes, red Takshaka snakes serve as earrings, striped Kulika snakes adorn the shoulders, white Padma snakes serve as necklaces, yellow Shankhapala snakes serve as bracelets, green Jaya snakes serve as sashes, nectar-colored Vasuki snakes serve as belts, and white Mahapadma snakes serve as anklets. Intense wisdom-fire blazes from their bodies; they stand in the center ready to punish all evil beings.

From my own heart HUM light-rays radiate. All living beings are attracted, streaming into the mandala like vajra heroes, unhindered from the four directions; abiding there, they are consecrated by the light-rays of the enlightenment spirits of the five father-mothers in union and attain the bliss and mental joy of all Transcendent Lords—becoming Vajrasattvas proceeding each to his own Buddhaland.

Conversion of Death into the Truth Body

The laser hook light-rays of the blue HUM of my heart invite the deities from Vairochana to Sumbharaja setting them in my points such as the crown, and they become actually indivisible from my form aggregate and so on. On the crown Vairochana, throat Amitabha, navel Ratnasambhava, groin Amoghasiddhi, navel Lochana, heart Mamaki, throat Pandaravasini, crown Tara, eyes Kshitigarbhas, ears Vajrapanis, nose Khagarbha, tongue Lokeshvara, heart Manjushri, secret organ Sarvanivarana Viskhambhini, joints Samantabhadra, crown Maitreya, doors of the eyes Rupavajras, doors of the ears Shabdavajras, door of the nose Gandhavajra, door of the mouth Rasavajra, door of the vajra Sparshavajra, right hand Yamantaka, left hand Aparajita, mouth Hayagriva, vajra Vighnantakrt, right shoulder's nerve Achala, left shoulder's nerve Takkiraja, right knee Niladanda, left knee Mahabala, crown Ushnishacakravarti, and on the two foot-soles, two Sumbharajas.

The deities of the body dissolve into clear light in sequence: Vairochana, Lochana, Kshitigarbha, Rupavajra, Maitreya, Yamantakrt, and Achala. Then Ratnasambhava, Mamaki, Vajrapani, Shabdavajra, Aparajita, and Takkiraja dissolve in stages into clear light. Then Amitabha, Pandaravasini, Akashagarbha, Gandhavajra, Hayagriva, and Niladanda dissolve in stages into clear light. Then Amoghasiddhi, Tara, Lokeshvara, Rasavajra, Sarvanivarana Viskhambhini, Sparshavajra, Samantabhadra, Vighnantakrt, and Mahabala dissolve in stages into clear light. Then Ushnishachakravarti, Sumbharaja, and Manjushri dissolve in stages into clear light. And then the Lord also dissolves in stages into clear light.

OM SHUNYATA JNANA VAJRA SVABHAVA ATMAKO HAM.

Conversion of the Between into the Beatific Body

Upon the central seat from HUM a solar disk arises and in its center from OM a moon disk and upon that an eight-petaled red lotus, and in the center of that stacked up are OM AH HUM. These merge and become a single moon orb. It emits light-rays, and all animate and inanimate objects gather and dissolve into the moon.

OM DHARMADHATU SVABHAVA ATMAKO HAM.

I am that appearing moon, the mere energy mind, root of all beings and things.

Upon the moon, like water bubbles bursting from water, are white OM, red AH, and blue HUM. They emit light-rays and invite infinite masses of the five Buddha-clans and their retinues from the ten directions. They dissolve and completely transform into a white five-pointed vajra marked at the center with OM AH HUM.

VAJRA ATMAKO HAM

Conversion of Birth into the Emanation Body

The vajra together with the letters completely transforms into myself, the white Primal Protector: three faces, white, black, and red; six arms holding vajra, wheel, and lotus in the rights, and bell, jewel, and sword in the lefts.

Adorned with precious jewels and various robes of silk, from their natural abodes the male and female Transcendent Lords embrace in union, creating streams of enlightenment spirit, which suffuse all the realms of space with hosts of Akshobhyas in order to tame all beings. They bless all beings to experience uncontaminated physical and mental bliss. Then the Akshobhyas merge together in the Mandala Palace and enter into me. I become the blue Emanation Body Vajrasattva, with three faces, blue, white, and red, six arms holding vajra, wheel, and lotus in the rights, and bell, jewel, and sword in the lefts, and adorned with precious jewels and various robes of silk.

The Body Mandala

The front, back, right, and left sides of my body become the Mandala Palace's four corners. The mouth, nose, anus, and urethra become the four doors. The five-colored pure energies that carry thoughts become the fivefold wall. The tongue cognition becomes the precious molding. The intestines become the jeweled nets, and the sinews become the half nets. Parts of the white spirit become the half-moons, the eye cognition becomes the mirrors, and the nose cognition becomes the garland of flowers. The tongue sense becomes the bells, and the body sense becomes the yak-tail fans adorning the nets and half nets. The ear and body cognitions become the banners and victory standards flying on the parapet. The eight limbs, the calves, thighs, forearms, and biceps become the eight pillars. The belly becomes the mandala's interior vases. The ear senses become the half-moon vajras in the corners. The pure five aggregates become the five colors of the Mandala Palace. The four essential places: secret spot, navel, heart, and nose-tip, become the four triumphal arches, and the eye senses become the Dharma wheels above them, with the mind cognition the deer, and the nose sense the triumphal arches' banners. The mind sense becomes the central lotus. Thus all parts of my body become parts of the Mandala Palace.

From my crown to hairline, the reality of the form aggregate, white OM transforms into white Vairochana. . . . From hairline to throat, the reality of the ideation aggregate, red AH transforms into red Amitabha. . . . From throat to heart between the two breasts, the reality of the consciousness aggregate, blue HUM transforms into blue Akshobhya. . . . From the heart to the navel, the reality of the sensation aggregate, yellow SVA transforms into yellow Ratnasambhava. . . . From navel to groin, the reality of the emotion aggregate, green HA transforms into green Amoghasiddhi.

At the navel, the reality of the body's earth element, yellow LAM transforms into white Lochana. . . . At the heart, the reality of the body's water element, blue MAM transforms into blue Mamaki. . . . At the throat, the reality of the body's fire element, red PAM transforms into red Pandaravasini. . . . At the crown, the reality of the body's air element, green TAM transforms into green Tara. . . . At the eyes, the reality of the eye senses, THLIMS transform into white Kshitigarbhas. . . . At the doors of the eyes, the reality of form, JAHS transform into white Rupavajras. . . . The first two arms of both male and female hold each other in mutual embrace. At the ears, the reality of the ear senses, OMS transform into yellow Vajrapanis. . . . At the doors of the ears, the reality of sound, HUMS transform into yellow Shabdavajras. . . . The first two arms of both male and female hold each other in mutual embrace. At the nose, the reality of the nose sense, OM transforms into yellow Akashagarbha. . . . At the door of the nose, the reality of scent, BAM transforms into red Gandhavajra. . . . At the tongue, the reality of the tongue sense, OM transforms into Lokeshvara. . . . At the door of the mouth, the reality of tastes, HOH transforms into green Rasavajra. . . . At the heart, the reality of the mind sense, HUM transforms into red Manjushri. . . . At the vajra, the reality of the body media, OM transforms into green Sarvanivarana Viskhambhini. . . . At the door of the vajra, the reality of textures, KHAM transforms into blue Sparshavajra. . . . The first two arms of both male and female are holding each other in mutual embrace. At the joints, the reality of the joints, SAMS transform into green Samantabhadras. . . . At the crown of the head, the reality of the nerves and sinews, MAIM transforms into white Maitreya. . . . All the gods from Vairochana to Maitreya have ornaments of precious jewels and variegated robes of silk.

At the right hand, its reality HUM transforms into black Yamantakrt. . . . At the left hand, its reality HUM transforms into white Prajnantakrt. . . . At the mouth, its reality HUM transforms into red Hayagriva. . . . At vajra, its reality HUM transforms into black Vighnantakrt. . . . At the right shoulder's nerve, its reality HUM transforms into black Achala. . . . At the left shoulder's nerve, its reality HUM transforms into blue Takkiraja. . . . At the right knee, its reality HUM transforms into blue Niladanda. . . . At the left knee, its reality HUM transforms into blue Mahabala. . . . At the crown its reality HUM transforms into blue Ushnishachakravarti. . . . At the two heels, its reality HUMS transform into blue Sumbharaja with Akshobhya crown: three faces, black, white, and red; six arms holding vajra, wheel, and jewel in the rights, and noose over chest with threatening gesture, lotus and sword in the lefts. All ten terribles have yellowish-red hair flaming up and have all the other manners of ferocity.

Blessing Body, Speech, and Mind

My crown OM becomes a perfect moon disk on which white OM radiates rainbow light-rays, filling all space with a host of Lochanas, whose radiance instantly invites the body-vajra Vairochana host filling all space. I come before the central Lord Vairochana in union with Lochana.

> Holder of the Body of the glorious Buddhas,
> Contemplating the indivisible triple vajras,
> In order to grace me now with blessings,
> Please bestow on me the Vajra Body!
> May all the Buddhas of the ten directions,
> Contemplating the indivisible triple vajra,
> In order to grace me now with blessings,
> Please bestow on me the Vajra Body!

Thus entreated, the emanated Lochanas and the invited Vairochanas are mutually attracted, passionately embrace in union, and experience the bliss of supreme ecstasy. They melt into white light-rays that enter me through the door of Vairochana like Wisdom Heroes. Attaining the wisdom stage, my body is filled and satisfied, and mastery of the body is attained.

> The very body of all Buddhas
> Being fulfilled by my five aggregates,
> By the reality of the Buddha Body,
> May I also become just such!
> OM SARVA TATHAGATA KAYA VAJRA SVABHAVA ATMAKO HAM

My tongue-center AH becomes a red eight-petaled lotus with red AH in the center radiating rainbow light-rays, filling all space with a host of Pandaravasinis. Radiating, they invite the vajra speech Amitabha host, filling all space. I come before the central Lord Amitabha in union with Pandaravasini.

> Glorious path of the Dharma speech,
> Contemplating the indivisible triple vajra,
> In order to grace me now with blessings,
> Please bestow on me the vajra speech!
> May all the Buddhas of the ten directions,
> Contemplating the indivisible triple vajra,
> In order to grace me now with blessings,
> Please bestow upon me the vajra speech!

Thus petitioned, the emanated Pandaravasini and the invited Amitabha hosts are both mutually attracted and passionately enter into union and experience the bliss of supreme ecstasy. They melt into red light-rays that enter into me through the tongue in the manner of a wisdom hero. Attaining the wisdom stage, my body is filled and satisfied, and mastery of the speech is attained.

The very speech of the vajra Dharma,
Perfection of the definitive word,
May my word also be just such,
May I be like you, the Dharma Holder!
OM SARVA TATHAGATA VAGVAJRA SVABHAVA ATMAKO HAM

My heart center HUM becomes a sun disk with a blue HUM in the center radiating rainbow light-rays, filling all space with a host of Mamakis. Radiating, they invite the vajra mind Akshobhya host filling all space. I come before the central Lord Akshobhya and Mamaki in union.

Holder of the glorious vajra mind,
Contemplating the indivisible triple vajra,
In order to grace me now with blessings,
Please bestow on me the vajra body!
May all the Buddhas of the ten directions,
Contemplating the indivisible triple vajra,
In order to grace me now with blessings,
Please bestow upon me the vajra body!

Thus petitioned, the emanated Mamaki and the invited Akshobhya hosts are mutually attracted, passionately embrace in union, and experience the bliss of supreme ecstasy. They melt into black light-rays that enter me through my heart center in the manner of a vajra hero. Attaining the wisdom stage, my body is filled and satisfied, and mastery of mind is attained.

The very Mind of Total Goodness,
With the genius of the Mystic Lord,
May I also become just such,
An equal of the Vajra Holder!
OM SARVATATHAGATAKAYAVAKCHITTA VAJRASVABHAVATMAKOHAM

I become the great Vajradhara, the indivisible triple vajra of body, speech, and mind of all Transcendent Lords!

OM SARVATATHAGATAKAYAVAKCHITTA VAJRASVABHAVATMAKOHAM

In the clear and open heart of myself, the devotee hero blue Vajradhara, is a variegated lotus and moon seat upon which is my red wisdom hero with one face and two arms, holding vajra and bell, embraced by a similar wisdom consort. Through their union in the kiss, their bodies expand. On a moon disk in their heart is a blue five-pointed vajra, and its center is the samadhi hero, a blue HUM; it constantly dawns like a great lamp and becomes a huge mass of sapphire brilliance to destroy the darkness of ignorance. On my devotee hero's crown diadem there is a great white Vajradhara with one face and two arms holding vajra and bell, in passionate union with Vajradhatvishvari, the queen of the vajra realm, with the oozing stream of their enlightenment nectars dripping down into me and satisfying all the deities of my body. From my heart center, the consort of my vajra clan emerges.

OM SHUNYATA JNANA VAJRA SVABHAVA ATMAKO HAM

The consort becomes emptiness. Within the actuality of emptiness emerges KHAM, which becomes a vajra marked by KHAM. It transforms into blue Sparshavajra with Akshobhya crown: three faces, blue, white, and red; six arms holding vajra, wheel, and lotus in the right, and bell, jewel, and sword in the left. Her hair in the half-bound coiffure, she is graceful, smiling, beautiful with gestures such as sidelong glances. Her beauty is mature, and she delights in the five sense objects. From her crown to the hairline, the reality of the form aggregate, white OM transforms into white Vairochana. . . . From the hairline to the throat, the reality of the cognition aggregate, red AH transforms into red Amitabha. . . . From the throat to the heart between the two breasts, the reality of the consciousness aggregate, blue HUM transforms into blue Akshobhya. . . . From the heart to the navel, the reality of the feeling aggregate, yellow SVA transforms into yellow Ratnasambhava. . . . From the navel to the groin, the reality of emotion aggregate, green HA transforms into green Amoghasiddhi. . . . At the navel from LAM, Lochana, at the heart from MAM, Mamaki, at the throat from PAM, Pandaravasini, at the crown from TAM, Tara. At the eyes from JAH, Rupavajra embracing Kshitigarbha, at the ears from HUM, Shabdavajra embracing Vajrapani, at the nose from BAM Gandhavajra embracing Akashagarbha, at the tongue from HOH Rasavajra embracing Lokeshvara, at the vagina from KHAM Sparsavajra embracing Sarvanivarana Viskhambhini.

At the right hand from HUM Vetali, at the left hand from HUM Aparajita, at the mouth from HUM Bhrkuti, at the vagina from HUM

Ekajati, at the right shoulder's nerve from HUM the Buddha consort Vajri, at the left shoulder's nerve from HUM Vishva Ratna, at the right knee from HUM Vishva Padma, at the left knee from HUM Vishva Karma. At the crown from HUM Akasha Vajri, and at the soles from HUMS earth goddesses.

From the unperceivable realm of my secret place HUM transforms into a blue five-pointed vajra, with the central spoke a jewel marked with OM and the hole blocked with a golden PHAT. From the unperceivable realm of my consort's secret place AH transforms into an eight-petaled red lotus with the hole blocked with a golden PHAT. My vajra and her lotus suffuse with five-color light-rays. I become Ratnasambhava.

OM SARVA TATHAGATA ANURAGANA VAJRA SVABHAVATMAKO HAM

I become Vajradhara. HUM—Engaged in union, I feel bliss of supreme joy. I become Amoghasiddhi. PHAT

OM SARVA TATHAGATA PUJA VAJRA SVABHAVA ATMAKO HAM

Drop Mandala, Mandala Triumph

All the gods of the body mandala are satisfied, the melted drop falls into the consort's lotus, and that very drop becomes the fountainhead of all deities, the Transcendent Lords and the five clans and so on. One part of the drop becomes a BHRUM, which transforms into the square four-doored Mandala Palace, replete with all its characteristics, including seats. The other part of the drop becomes the thirty-two parts, each upon a seat. They transform into—

OM AH HUM HUM. OM AH KHAM HUM. OM AH OM HUM. OM AH SVA HUM. OM AH AH HUM. OM AH HA HUM. OM AH LAM HUM. OM AH MAM HUM. OM AH BAM HUM. OM AH TAM HUM. OM AM JAH HUM. OM AH HUM HUM. OM AH BAM HUM. OM AH HOH HUM. OM AH MAIM HUM. OM AH THLIM HUM. OM AM OM HUM. OM AH OM HUM. OM AH OM HUM. OM AH HUM HUM. OM AH OM HUM. OM AH SAM HUM. OM AH HUM HUM. OM AH HUM HUM. OM AH HUM HUM. OM AH HUM HUM. OM AH HUM HUM. OM AH HUM HUM. OM AH HUM HUM. OM AH HUM HUM. OM AH HUM HUM. OM AH HUM HUM.

The thirty-two respectively transform into vajra and vajra, wheel, jewel, lotus, vajra cross, wheel, vajra, blue lotus, vajra cross, red mirror, blue lute, perfume conch, food vessel, wheel-marked naga tree flower, wheel, jewel, jewel, lotus, lotus, sword, sword, staff, vajra, lotus, vajra cross, sword, vajra, blue vajra-marked staff, black vajra-marked staff, vajra and vajra. These in stages transform into the thirty-two deities.

Upon the central seat myself, peaceful blue-black Akshobhya.... Myself as blue Sparshavajra with Akshobhya crown.... At the east, myself white Vairochana.... At the south, myself yellow Ratnasambhava.... At the west, myself red Amitabha.... At the north, myself green Amoghasiddhi.... At the southeast, myself white Lochana.... In the southwest, myself blue Mamaki.... At the northwest, myself red Pandaravasini.... In the northeast, myself green Tara.... In the second row at the southeast, myself white Rupavajra.... At the southwest myself yellow Shabdavajra.... At the northwest myself red Gandhavajra.... At the northeast myself green Rasavajra.... Myself on the right and left seats at the eastern door as respectively white Maitreya and Kshitigarbha.... Myself on the right and left seats at the southern door as respectively yellow Vajrapani and Akashagarbha.... Myself on the right and left seats at the western door as respectively red Lokeshvara and Manjushri.... Myself on the right and left seats at the northern door as respectively green Sarvanivarana Viskhambhini and Samantabhadra.... Myself in the eastern door as black Yamantaka.... Myself in the southern door as white Prajnantakrt.... Myself in the western door as red Hayagriva.... Myself in the northern door as black Vighnantakrt.... Myself in the southeast door as black Achala.... Myself in the southwest as blue Takkiraja.... Myself in the northwest as blue Niladanda.... Myself in the northeast as blue Mahabala.... Myself above as blue Ushnishachakravarti.... Myself below as blue Sumbharaja with Akshobhya crown: three faces, black, white, and red; six arms holding vajra, wheel, and jewel in the right, and noose over chest with threatening gesture, lotus and sword in the left.

All ten of the terrible lords have yellowish-red hair flaring up, their brows and eyelashes flaming intensely orange; each face has three eyes and four sharp fangs that are snarled. Their fierce, loud laugh HA HA reverberates, and their faces have wrinkled expressions, and they have big bellies. They are adorned with various jewel ornaments, their skirts are tiger skins. Their hair is bound by blue Ananta snakes, red Takshaka snakes serve as earrings, striped Kulika snakes adorn the shoulders, white Padma snakes serve as necklaces, yellow Shankhapala snakes serve as bracelets, green Jaya snakes serve as sashes, nectar-colored Vasuki snakes serve as belts, and white Mahapadma snakes serve as anklets. Intense wisdom-fire blazes from their bodies; they stand in the center ready to punish all evil beings. .

Supreme Triumph over Evolution

Akshobhya is attracted to my heart—VAJRADHRK emerges from my heart radiating in the ten directions, accomplishing the Buddha deeds such as turning the wheel of Dharma, especially purifying the hatred of hating beings, establishing them in the exaltation of Akshobhya. All the emanations gather into one and merge indivisibly with the Akshobhya wisdom hero. Consecration is conferred by the enlightenment spirits of the lord and lady of his clan. He returns before me and enters, merging into my heart, and I transform into a peaceful, happy Vajradhara. Then my moon disk seat dissolves into a sun disk seat, and I transform into a blue-black Anger Vajra: three faces, black, white, and red; six arms holding a nine-pointed vajra, wheel, and lotus in the rights, and bell, jewel, and sword in the lefts. In an aura of shimmering red light, I sit in the center of the mandala in the vajra posture.

Sparshavajra is attracted to my heart, SPARSHAVAJRA emerges. . . . Vairochana is attracted to my heart, JINAJIK emerges. . . . Ratnasambhava is attracted to my heart, RATNADHRK emerges. . . . Amitabha is attracted to my heart, AROLIK emerges. . . . Amoghasiddhi is attracted to my heart, PRAJNADHRK emerges. . . . Lochana is attracted to my heart, MOHARATI emerges. . . . Mamaki is attracted to my heart, DVESHARATI emerges. . . . Pandaravasini is attracted to my heart, RAGARATI emerges. . . . Tara is attracted to my heart, VAJRARATI emerges. . . . Rupavajra is attracted to my heart, RUPAVAJRA emerges. . . . Shabdavajra is attracted to my heart, SHABDAVAJRA emerges. . . . Gandhavajra is attracted to my heart, GANDHAVAJRA emerges. . . . Rasavajra is attracted to my heart, RASAVAJRA emerges. . . . Maitreya is attracted to my heart, MAITRI emerges. . . . Kshitigarbha is attracted to my heart, KSHITIGARBHA emerges. . . . Vajrapani is attracted to my heart, VAJRAPANI emerges. . . . Khagarbha is attracted to my heart, KHAGARBHA emerges. . . . Lokeshvara is attracted to my heart, LOKESHVARA emerges. . . . Manjushri is attracted to my heart, MANJUSHRI emerges. . . . Sarvanivarana Viskhambhini is attracted to my heart, SARVANIVARANA VISKAMBHIN emerges. . . . Samantabhadra is attracted to my heart, SAMANTABHADRA emerges. . . . Yamantakrt is attracted to my heart, YAMANTAKRT emerges. . . . Prajnantakrt is attracted to my heart, PRAJNANTAKRT emerges. . . . Hayagriva is attracted to my heart, PADMANTAKRT emerges. . . . Amrtakundali is attracted to my heart, VIGHNANTAKRT emerges. . . . Achala is attracted to my heart, ACHALA emerges. . . . Takkiraja is attracted to my heart, TAKKIRAJA emerges. . . .

Niladanda is attracted to my heart, NILADANDA emerges. . . . Mahabala is attracted to my heart, MAHABALA emerges. . . . Ushnishachakravarti is attracted to my heart, USHNISHACHAKRAVARTI emerges. . . . Sumbharaja is attracted to my heart, SUMBHARAJA emerges from the heart, radiating in the ten directions, accomplishing the Buddha deeds such as turning the wheel of Dharma, especially conquering poisons moving and unmoving, underworld dragons, and earth deities. All emanations condense into one, merging indivisibly with the Sumbharaja wisdom hero. Consecration is conferred by the enlightenment spirits of the lord and lady of his clan. He returns before me and merges with the Sumbharaja in the basement of the palace.

The Mandala Palace is attracted to my heart, OM AH HUM emerges from the heart, radiating in the ten directions, especially purifying the evils and flaws of inanimate objects. All emanations condense into one, merging indivisibly with the palace wisdom hero. It returns before me and merges with the Mandala Palace.

Repetition of Mantras

As one recites the mantras, the individual deity's heart-seed syllable is circled by the letters of the mantra and radiates out the host of deities of the mandala, who accomplish the benefit of beings. These hosts reenter the heart-seed syllables with the mantra letters along with the inhaled wind energy. I recite in this way (alternating) radiating and concentrating.

OM AH HUM. OM AH VAJRADHRK HUM HUM. OM AH SPARSHAVAJRA KHAM HUM. OM AH JINAJIK OM HUM. OM AH RATNADHRK SVA HUM. OM AH AROLIK AH HUM. OM AH PRAJNADHRK HA HUM. OM AH MO-HARATI LAM HUM. OM AH DVESHARATI MAM HUM. OM AH RAGARATI PAM HUM. OM AH VAJRARATI TAM HUM. OM AH RUPAVAJRA JAH HUM. OM AM SHABDAVAJRA HUM HUM. OM AH GANDHAVAJRA BAM HUM. OM AH RASAVAJRA HOH HUM. OM AH MATREYA MAIM HUM. OM AH KSHITIGARBHA THLIM HUM. OM AH VAJRAPANI OM HUM. OM AH KHAGARBHA OM HUM. OM AH LOKESHVARA OM HUM. OM AH MAN-JUSHRI HUM HUM. OM AH SARVANIVARANA VISKAMBHIN OM HUM. OM AH SAMANTABHADRA SAM HUM. OM AH YAMANTAKRT HUM HUM. OM AH PRAJNANTAKRT HUM HUM. OM AH PADMANTAKRT HUM HUM. OM AH VIGHNANTAKRT HUM HUM. OM AH ACHALA HUM HUM. OM AH TAKKIRAJA HUM HUM. OM AH NILADANDA HUM HUM. OM AH MAHA-BALA HUM HUM. OM AH USHNISHACHAKRAVARTI HUM HUM. OM AH SUMBHARAJA HUM HUM. . . . (Recite the hundred-syllable mantra.)

Concluding the Repetitions

Melting in sexual union, the Mother dissolves into the Father. The devotee hero Father dissolves into the wisdom hero. The wisdom hero dissolves into the samadhi hero. The samadhi hero's vowel dissolves into the HA. The HA dissolves into its top. The top dissolves into the moon crescent. The moon crescent dissolves into the drop. The drop dissolves into the squiggle. And finally the squiggle dissolves into clear light translucency.

Then the four goddesses, the realities of the four immeasurables, feel sorrow no longer to see the Lord. They desire to look upon him and so strive to arouse him with sweet songs.

O Thou of Diamond Mind, O Lord who dwells in the realms of beings,
Pray grant refuge to me, who loves the great goal, joy, and pleasure!
O Best Friend, O great Father of living beings,
O Savior, if thou wish me to remain in life,
Pray arise right now to make me happy!

O Thou of Diamond Body, whose wheel of speech benefits all
  beings,
Teacher of the absolute enlightenment essential to win Buddhahood,
O Savior, if thou wish me to remain in life,
Pray arise right now to make me happy,
Through your great love, O Passion's Devotee!

O Thou of Diamond Speech, O Lover and Helper of all,
Always dynamic to accomplish people's necessary aims,
O Savior, if thou wish me to remain in life,
Pray arise right now to make me happy,
With thy ecstatic deeds of perfect goodness!

O Thou of Diamond Passion, essential help of the supreme vow,
O Thou of Equal Vision, best heir of perfect Buddhas,
O Savior, if thou wish me to remain in life,
Pray arise right now to make me happy,
O Treasury of Many Jewels of Excellence!

Thus aroused, through the power of compassion and ancient vows, I arise from the clear light translucency in a body of the nature of the triply enfolded spiritual heroes. All the deities of the mandala clearly behold me. They all declare:

"Reverence to the mystic song, O Akshobhyavajra, O great wisdom, O great expert of the diamond realm, O best three vajras, O triple mandala!

"Reverence to the Diamond Teacher, O Vairochana, greatly pure, O Diamond Peace, O great delight, O best of best, natural clear light!

"Reverence to the Diamond Body, O Jewel King, extremely deep, immaculate like diamond space, naturally pure, without defilement!

"Reverence to the Diamond Speech, O Vajra Amitabha, great king, O holder of the vajra of great space beyond conceptions, O discoverer of the transcendence of passion!

"Reverence to the Diamond Messiah, O Amoghavajra, perfect Buddha, arisen from the natural purity, fulfilling perfectly every being's aspiration.

OM SARVATATHAGATA ARGHAM . . . PADYAM . . . PUSHPE . . . DHUPE . . . ALOKE . . . GANDHE . . . NAIVIDYE . . . SHABDA . . . RUPA . . . SHABDA . . . GANDHA . . . RASA . . . SPARSHE PUJAMEGHASAMU-DRA SPARANASAMAYA SHRIYE AH HUM

Offerings to the Ancestral Mentors

From the KSHUM of my left thumb, the earth foundation. From the ring finger SUM there is Sumeru standing at the middle of the great ocean on the earth and stirring up the essence of nectar. HUM on the tongues of the guests becomes a one-pointed red vajra with a light-ray tube. I make this offering!

To the mouth of the actuality of the concentrated body, speech, mind, excellence, and deeds of all transcendent lords of the ten directions and three times, the origin of the eighty-four thousand masses of teachings, the master of the holy community, the kind root mentor—OM AH HUM.

To the mouth of Victor Vajradhara OM AH HUM
To the mouth of the glorious protector Arya Nagarjuna OM AH HUM
Bodhisattva Matangipa OM AH HUM
Great Adept Tilopa OM AH HUM
Great Pandit Narotapa OM AH HUM
Translator Marpa OM AH HUM
Dharma King Tsong Khapa OM AH HUM
Again to the mouth of Victor Vajradhara OM AH HUM
Bodhisattva Vajrapani OM AH HUM
King Indrabhuti OM AH HUM
Naga Vajra Yogini OM AH HUM
Lord Visukalpa OM AH HUM
Glorious Saraha OM AH HUM
Glorious Arya Nagarjuna OM AH HUM

Glorious Chandrakirti OM AH HUM
Lopa Dorje OM AH HUM
Greatly accomplished Kanhapa OM AH HUM
Master Trinki Shuk Chen OM AH HUM
Lord Go OM AH HUM
Mangrap Sengye Gyaltsen OM AH HUM
Ngok Yeshe Sengye OM AH HUM
Ngok Aryadeva OM AH HUM
Lansta Nima Cham OM AH HUM
Takpa Renchen Trak OM AH HUM
Thur Hlawa Tsultrim Kyab OM AH HUM
Thang Pewa Pagpa Kyab OM AH HUM
Serding pa Zhon nu OM AH HUM
All-knowing Choku Ohzer OM AH HUM
All-knowing Phagpa Oh OM AH HUM
All-knowing Choje Buton Renchen drup OM AH HUM
All-knowing holy master Sonam Gyalsten OM AH HUM
All-knowing Tragyor Namkha Zangpo OM AH HUM
All-knowing peerless great Rendawa OM AH HUM
Dharma King great Tsong Khapa OM AH HUM
Kedrup Gelek Pal Zangpo OM AH HUM
All-knowing Losang Kalsang Gyatso OM AH HUM
Venerable Losang Palden Yeshe OM AH HUM
All-knowing Losang Jampal Gyatso OM AH HUM
Also to the mouths of all those masters who gave initiations, ex-
    pounded the tantras, and gave oral traditional teachings OM AH
    HUM
(To the thirty-two deities of the mandala)
VAJRADHRK OM AH HUM.
SPARSHAVAJRA OM AH HUM.
JINAJIK OM AH HUM.
RATNADHRK OM AH HUM.
AROLIK OM AH HUM.
PRAJNADHRK OM AH HUM.
MOHARATI OM AH HUM.
DVESHARATI OM AH HUM.
RAGARATI OM AH HUM.
VAJRARATI OM AH HUM.
RUPAVAJRA OM AH HUM.
SHABDAVAJRA OM AH HUM.

GANDHAVAJRA OM AH HUM.

RASAVAJRA OM AH HUM.

MAITRI OM AH HUM.

KSHITIGARBHA OM AH HUM.

VAJRAPANI OM AH HUM.

KHAGARBHA OM AH HUM.

LOKESHVARA OM AH HUM.

MANJUSHRI OM AH HUM.

SARVANIVARANA VISKAMBHIN OM AH HUM.

SAMANTABHADRA OM AH HUM.

YAMANTAKRT OM AH HUM.

PRAJNANTAKRT OM AH HUM.

PADMANTAKRT OM AH HUM.

VIGHNANTAKRT OM AH HUM.

ACHALA OM AH HUM.

TAKKIRAJA OM AH HUM.

NILADANDA OM AH HUM.

MAHABALA OM AH HUM.

USHNISHACHAKRAVARTI OM AH HUM.

SUMBHARAJA OM AH HUM.

To the mouth of the deities and mandala gods of the four Tantras OM AH HUM. To the mouth of the oath-bound protectors who saw the previous Buddhas, heard the holy Dharma, relied on the supreme community, who have pledged to protect the doctrine and the four sections of the community, and upon whom the ancient masters relied and practiced—OM AH HUM.

To all the heroes, yoginis, direction protectors, realm protectors, nagas, and so forth, who reside in the twenty-four regions, the thirty-two places, and the eight great cemeteries OM AH HUM.

To the local spirits of natural sites and to all beings as deities OM AH HUM.

OM AMRTA SVADANA VAJRA SVABHAVA ATMAKO HAM

All guests are delighted and satisfied by this nectar of wisdom.

From the unperceivable realm of my secret place HUM transforms into a blue five-pointed vajra, with the central spoke a jewel marked with OM and the hole blocked with a golden PHAT. From the unperceivable realm of my consort's secret place AH transforms into an eight-petaled red lotus with the hole blocked with a golden PHAT. My vajra and her lotus suffuse with five-color light-rays. I become Ratnasambhava.

OM SARVA TATHAGATA ANURAGANA SVABHAVA ATMAKO HAM

I become Akshobhya. HUM I achieve the supreme joy by engaging in dynamic union. I become Amoghasiddhi. PHAT

OM SARVA TATHAGATA PUJA VAJRA SVABHAVA ATMAKO HAM

All the deities of the mandala experience natural bliss and entrance themselves in the samadhi of the indivisibility of great bliss and Thatness; thus they become delighted by the mystic and absolute sacrifice offerings.

The laser hook light-rays of the blue HUM of my heart invite the deities from Vairochana to Sumbharaja, setting them in my vital points such as the crown. On the crown Vairochana, throat Amitabha, navel Ratnasambhava, secret place Amoghasiddhi, navel Lochana, heart Mamaki, throat Pandaravasini, crown Tara, eyes Kshitigarbha, ears Vajrapani, nose Khagarbha, tongue Lokeshvara, heart Manjushri, secret organ Sarvanivarana Viskhambhini, joints Samantabhadra, crown Maitreya, eye-doors Rupavajra, ear-doors Shabdavajra, nose-door Gandhavajra, tongue-door Rasavajra, vajra-door Sparshavajra, right hand Yamantakrt, left hand Prajnantakrt, mouth Hayagriva, vajra Vighnantakrt, right shoulder's nerve Achala, left shoulder's nerve Takkiraja, right knee Niladanda, left knee Mahabala, crown Ushnishachakravarti, and two soles Sumbharajas. Then each part of the divine palace dissolves into each part of my body.

From the sexual contact of myself as Father-Mother in union the light-rays of enlightenment spirit radiate intensely, consecrating all beings, purifying all obscurations and transforming them all into HUMS. These fill the realm of space and then transform into Vajradharas. They are attracted by my light-rays and dissolve into me.

OM YOGASHUDDAH SARVADHARMAH YOGASHUDDHO HAM.
YE DHARMA HETUPRABHAVA. HETUN TESHAM TATHAGATA HYAVA-
DAT. TESHAM CA YO NIRODHO. EVAM VADI MAHA SHRAMANAH.

Esoteric Communion Prayers

By this virtue, may I quickly attain the state of Vajradhara,
The whole essence of all Buddhas! And may all beings attain it too!
May I practice all deeds for the sake of enlightenment,
The deeds taught by both the perfect Buddhas and by
    Bodhichittavajra!

Thus from within the vivid experience of deity body
Luminant voidness like a magic illusion, like a dream,
Among the divine host of the mandala of Akshobhyavajra,
Fabulous collection of victors of ten directions,
Since I have found delight through the wondrous bliss;
Striving here to make outer, inner, and secret offerings,
To praise, to contemplate, and to recite and so on,
Whatever virtue I might thus accumulate,
May I take up the supreme spirit of enlightenment,
Bearing responsibility for liberating beings.
Seeing that all those my mothers
Have fallen into the ocean of samsara just like me,
Seeing that there is no winning enlightenment
Just by conceiving the spirit yet not cultivating
The three kinds of ethics, may I train myself intensely
In practicing the Bodhisattva vow.
Become a vessel through practice of ordinary path,
May I enter with perfect ease
Into that holy haven of well-destined beings,
The Vajra Vehicle, supreme way of all.

By vase initiation anointment in streams of Ganga water,
May all percepts and concepts of the ordinary be cleansed!
By tasting the wisdom elixir of the secret initiation,
May energies in the speech place arise as mantra!
By the goad of orgasmic bliss of the third initiation,
May the mind be drawn into the realm of clear light!
By the fourth initiation's identifying the meaning of communion,
May reifications about the ultimate be cut off!

Then, having found a nonartificial certitude
That the keeping of pure vows and commitments
Is the base of achieving both kinds of powers,
May I always guard them even at the cost of life!

May all appearance dawn as the circle of deities,
Finding extreme and total stability
In the gross and subtle paths of the creation stage,
With four branches of service and practice in four-session yoga
That completely concentrates the energetic stores

Effortlessly, with every movement, utterance, and thought
Free of all suspicion of notions and perceptions of the ordinary!

Depending on the supreme field of the mind mandala
Accumulating the stores with proper rituals
And the yoga of sacrificial gifts free of misappropriation,
May my spiritual process become fully purified!

May all miracle deeds be accomplished by the samadhi
Of the glorious Anger-vajra, accompanied with his retinue
Of the ten furious terrifics, who punish
Evil-minded demons who run around in every direction!

May the yoga of the creation stage be achieved,
Which purifies all percepts and concepts of the ordinary
In the processes of birth, death, and the between,
By gradually generating in the spiritual process
The supreme vajra of proper practice
Of death as the Body of Truth, the between as the Beatific Body,
And of birth as the Body of Emanation—the supreme technique
To realize the exaltation of the Three Bodies!

Through the samadhi in the mode of the great passion,
The swift path to that consummation of one's own aims,
Skilled in technique of devotion to the consort of one's own Buddha
    clan,
May the victors be worshiped by means of orgasmic bliss!

May the best mandala triumph soon be achieved,
Which totally purifies all lands, beings, and environment,
Filling all of space with clouds of emanations,
From the animate and inanimate mandala
Produced when the fury-fires blaze up,
Ignited by the union of the vajra with the realm of space,
Melts the liquid enlightenment spirit into the avadhuti path,
Whence it goes into the lotus of the wisdom consort!

May the outer and inner repetition become perfected,
As well as the yoga of subtle equanimity,
Creating the five-colored jewel, essence of five sugatas,
At the tip of the paths of the vital and evacuative energies,
Expanding in nets of rainbow light-rays,

And in the mustard-seed-size drop of enlightenment spirit,
Completely visualize the symbol and deity mandalas
And focus on them at will vividly and without blur!

Then, depending on the substance, the mantra,
The wheel machine, and on their contemplation,
May I accomplish the eight great realizations,
And the fabulous deeds of pacifying and so on,
And thereby accomplish the best evolutionary triumph!

May I attain the profound path of the five stages,
Together with the three conducts of yoginis,
Which includes completely the six branches,
Withdrawal, contemplation, vitality control,
Stabilization, verification, and samadhi!

May the downward and upward four joys be produced,
Brought forth by the stages of reversal and emergence,
Of the streams of nectar when the sun melts down the moon,
Relying on the mind in the subtle drop in the jewel tip!

Arising from that, amid all appearances that dawn,
May I perfect body isolation withdrawal and contemplation,
By the samadhi of the Diamond Body, arising
As one hundred, five, three, and one classes!

By concentrating the king of drops, the best mantra drop,
On the tip of the lotus of the heart,
May the twelve energies that generate
All notions of subjects and objects
Dissolve into the indestructible drop!

The vibration of the drop of light at the nose tip,
By its dawning as the uncontrived three vajras,
By the samadhi of speech isolation speech vajra,
May I break free from my heart's eggshell of ignorance!

By meditating vitality control of the substance drop
At the root of art, wisdom, and mystic channels,
Clearing away the darkness of conception energies,
May the clear light sun dawn in the center of my heart!

By meditating vitality control of the three drops
At the three nose tips, by the lights of moon and sun

And the dark gloom in the cloudless sky,
May the mind isolation of the three voids arise!

Becoming expert in the key points
Of the complete secret instruction
Of the nine mergers, three to each of three
Magic Body of Beatitude, Clear Light Body of Truth,
And the variegation of the Body of Emanation,
May I perfect the holding of the absolute clear light
By means of the relative Magic Body,
The reverse-order verification practice,
The samadhi of communion, and the three conducts,
Conventional, unconventional, and extremely unconventional!

If I cannot achieve the supreme samadhi here
Or in the between, and am caught by time of death,
May I be able to merge the four voids of the process
Of basic death with the four voids of the path!
Merging the samadhi of illusion with my time
In the between, at the time of taking rebirth,
May I consciously be born in a supreme birthplace
Just as the Beatific Body takes Emanation Body incarnation!

In short, whatever dawns in birth, death, and the between,
Understanding it as an exhortation to virtuous practice
From previous prayers, practicing the three path-conversions,
May my mind's delight expand immensely at the time of death!

Thus may all beings be delivered
By this consummate technology,
This ultimate of this miraculous path,
Practicing it properly without obstructions,
Spreading and expanding it in all directions!

Mentor's Benedictions

The host of deities of the *Esoteric Communion,*
Filling the vastness of space like sesame seeds,
Some cause rains of various flowers to fall,
Some sing sweet songs of blessed fortune.
Others act to conquer the army of malignants,

And all cause you always to abide in glory.
Know this and generate happiness in mind,
As I pronounce this garland of benedictions.

Full beatitude, ablaze with glory of wondrous signs and marks,
Always playing in the feeling of the kiss of bliss and void,
Abandoned the peace extreme with unconditional compassion,
Homage to the Lord with his seven limbs!

Mystic Lord, collecting the communion of all mysteries,
Finder of the supreme through the Communion, King of Tantras,
To Indrabhuti, Nagadakini, Visukalpa, glorious Saraha,
Nagarjuna the vajra-holder and Aryadeva,
Nagabodhi, Shakyamitra, Matangi,
Chandrapada, and so on—
By that good luck of the store of goodness found,
In this distinguished lineage of mentors,
May all your troubles be eliminated
And your fortune increase like the waxing moon,
And may you sport in the glory of perfection!

The five classes of Buddha Father-Mothers, the four heroines,
The eight Bodhisattvas and the ten terrific lords—
The Buddha Jewel of the glorious Communion:
By the good luck of the store of goodness found
In the circle of the thirty-two deities,
May all your troubles be eliminated,
And your fortune increase like the waxing moon,
And may you sport in the glory of perfection!

The Tantric Scripture uttered from the lotus mouth
Of the Universal Lord Glorious Vajrasattva,
Its fine root of thirty-three thousand lines,
The glorious *Communion Root Tantra* and *Explanatory Tantras*,
The four consecrations and the three kinds of vows,
The four vajras of ordinary creation-stage service,
The six branches of supreme perfection-stage service,
The profound five stages and three conducts,
The Dharma jewel of the glorious Communion:
By the good fortune of the store of goodness found
In the textual and practical Dharma wheels,
May all your troubles be eliminated,

Your fortune increase like the waxing moon,
May you sport in the glory of perfection!

The Community Jewel of the glorious Communion
Who dwells in fabulous pure lands in ten directions—
By the good fortune of the store of goodness found
In all who hold more than one dimension of the holy
Textual and practical teachings of the King of Tantras,
May all your troubles be eliminated,
Your fortune increase like the waxing moon,
May you sport in the glory of perfection!

CHAPTER 8

Practicing the Perfection and Great Perfection Stages

The Quintessence Segment

Bless me to realize here in this life
The path of clear light/magic body communion,
Coming from you, Savior, when you put your toe
In my eight-petaled heart-center Dhuti-nerve!

If the path is not complete and death arrives,
Bless me to go to a pure buddhaverse
By the instruction for implementing the five forces
Of mentor-soul-ejection, the forceful art of Buddhahood!

In short, life after life forever,
You, Savior, please care for me never apart,
Bless me to become your foremost child,
Upholding all the secrets of body, speech, and mind!

You, Savior, at your perfect Buddhahood,
May I be foremost in your retinue—
Grant me good luck for easy spontaneous achievement
Of all my goals, temporary and ultimate!

Thus having prayed, may you, Supreme Mentor
Joyously come to my crown to bless me,
Sit surely, your toenails glistening,
In the pistil of my heart-center lotus!

From Nagarjuna's Five Stages of the Perfection Stage

1. VAJRA REPETITION

This art is taught by the perfect Buddhas, like a ladder,
For those stable in the creation stage and ambitious for the perfection stage.
The life energy of beings, doing all work, is called wind.
It is like the mount of consciousness, fivefold and tenfold in nature.
Through realization of creation by mantra, one is trained in vajra repetition.

The yogin abiding in vajra repetition will obtain the mind objective,
Abiding in the illusory samadhi, he is purified by the summit of truth,

Arising from the summit of truth, she will attain nondual intuition.
Abiding in the communion samadhi, there is nothing whatever further to learn.

This is the Perfection Yoga, and the great Vajradhara,
Supreme in all ways, is born from that.
Since the three states, past, present, and future,
Are purified through clear light, he sees them all at once.

These truths abide well sealed, in the glorious *Communion Tantra;*
They should be understood from the mentor's speech,
In accordance with the *Explanatory Tantras.* . . .

Who devotedly always strives in service and worship,
Who retains her learning, such a one
Need not be examined by the superior Mentor—
He should be given the Mentor's grace.

Who falls from the summit of a high mountain
May think, "I mustn't fall!"—but she will fall.
Who obtains the helpful prophecy by the Mentor's kindness
May think, "I should not be delivered," yet he will be delivered! . . .

2. MIND OBJECTIVE

I pay homage and bow down! With homage I bow down!
With homage, homage, homage I bow down!
Offering praises, I pay homage!
Who praises, who is praised?
I myself pay homage to my own intuition,
When will I understand that we are like
Water poured in water, butter poured in fire? . . .

Now it is to be clearly explained by the perfected yogin/i,
Explaining here the purity of the three voidnesses as clear light.
That is called universal voidness, the purity of the three intuitions.
The abode of those intuitions is reality and the unexcelled omni-
science.
Unchanging, not appearing, nondual, and supremely peaceful,
It is not in the range of existence or nonexistence, or of any words.
Then, from the purity of clear light, the three intuitions emerge;
One becomes the omniscient one, supreme in all one's aspects,
Endowed with the thirty-two auspicious signs and the eighty marks.

The *Magnificent Play Sutra* states:
Shakyamuni, accepting this enlightenment,
The clear and transcendent state,
Clearly thought that Buddhahood
Is to be attained from the great voidness.
On the bank of the river Nairanjana,
He sat in the immovable samadhi,
Then the Victors filled all space
With vajras like a scattering of sesame.
They snapped their fingers before the Bodhisattva
And spoke together in a single voice.
"This meditation is not perfection.
By this the ultimate will not be won.
Apprehend the clear light,
Like the realm of space, supreme!
Attaining the realm of clear light,
You will be born in the absolutely joyous body.
Then, in the ecstatic vajra body,
You will attain universal mastery."
When he heard that statement,
He abandoned the immovable samadhi,
And at the time of midnight,
The Bodhisattva saw clear light.
The body was not straight
Nor was it not straight,
There was no exhalation or inhalation,
He did not speak, nor was he silent.
His good eyes were not closed
Nor were they open.
The miraculous universal voidness,
Great intuition, translucent and clear,
Then he clearly beheld it
By the kindness of the actual Mentor.
Then he saw in a single instant
The three states of existence
Of the past, the present, and the future.
Purified by the clear light,
Through the vajralike samadhi,
At the time of the predawn light
He was adorned by the excellence of magic illusion

Like the moon in water, like a mirage, and so on.
Then sitting at the tree of enlightenment
He conquered all the devils.
The Shakya Savior thus attained
The genuine intuition, unexcelled,
And then to help and protect all beings
He manifested that actuality right there.
That perfect enlightenment thus manifested
Is called the intuition of reality. . . .

It is not attachment, and not detachment,
Nor is it apprehended in between.
It is not empty, and not nonempty,
Nor is it apprehended in the middle.
The communion of all Buddhas
Proclaims it as this very reality.
The reality beyond the three intuitions,
Is taught through intentional speech.
Likewise the nature of perfect enlightenment
Is taught by the verse "There is no thing, and so forth."
From the "Enlightenment" chapter
Of the glorious *Secret Communion Tantra*.
And the purity of desire and so on
Is also taught in the *Glorious Paramount Bliss*.
That same reality is also taught by the Transcendent One
As universal voidness.
What is taught as that reality
By various Sutras and Tantras,
It is none other than this realm
Of universal voidness.
From the eighty-four thousand teachings
Taught by the Great Ascetic,
This nature of perfect enlightenment
Is proclaimed the essence of the essence. . . .

3. SELF-EMPOWERMENT

Homage to the Great Vajra,
Chief of all the vajras;
Out of love I will explain
The actual self-empowerment.

First, one gets the empowerment following the creation stage, one understands the intention of the four kinds of Tantras, one has wisdom and knowledge of physical, verbal, and mental isolation. One intensely aspires to both realities, and one truly propitiates the Vajra Master. Having pleased the Mentor and having made the great offerings in group rites, one offers even one's own young mate. Then one gets the private instruction in the self-empowerment from the Mentor's own mouth, and one gets the secret initiation, together with the rosary, water, perfect Buddha, vajra, bell, mirror, name, mastership, and permission initiations. Then one should praise the Mentor with this praise:

> "Your body has no inner void,
> Nor flesh, nor bone, nor blood;
> It is a purposeful manifestation
> Just like a rainbow in the sky. . . .
> Homage to the unconditional you!"

Thus having praised the Vajra Master with these praises, one should pray that he is pleased by these verses:

> "Whose very substance is omniscient intuition,
> Who purifies the wheel of the life-cycle,
> Now please kindly bestow upon me
> The chief jewel of all elucidations!
> Abandoning the lotuses of your feet,
> I take no refuge in any other Lord.
> May the hero of beings, the Great Ascetic,
> Grant me supreme genius!"

> Thus fearlessly praying
> She hears these words,
> Feels compassion with his disciple,
> And begins the self-empowerment.
> To know the stage of self-empowerment,
> One must teach the superficial reality;
> That will be attained in no other way
> Than through the kindness of the Mentor.

> The stage of the self-empowerment—
> Who does not discover it,
> Though she studies Sutras, Tantras, and rites,
> Her pains will ever prove fruitless.
> Who attains the stage of self-empowerment

Is himself the Lord, the essence of all Buddhas,
Without any doubt she will attain
Buddhahood in his very lifetime.
The samadhi of self-empowerment
And alike the realm of clear light,
In their aspects as cause and effect,
Teach the two realities.
By the stage of the self-empowerment
One will attain the clear light.
Therefore the Vajra Master
Teaches self-empowerment first.

All beings are without free will
And do not arise independently.
Self-empowerment's cause is the clear light;
The clear light of universal voidness.
That mind which binds foolish beings
With the chains of cyclic life;
That same mind causes the yogin/i
To proceed to the realm of Lords of Bliss.
Here there is no birth at all
Nor is there any death at all.
One should understand that egoistic life itself
Abides in the nature of the mind.
The nature of mind is not perceived
Without the yoga of the breath.
When that nature of the mind creates,
Evolution and birth then take their course.
That mind really controlling the breaths,
Then the threefold consciousness
Arises as the body of the yogin/i,
It is called the "body of magic illusion."
For this reason it is explained
That all beings are "like illusion,"
Abiding in the illusory samadhi
Everything is seen like that.
Form and also feeling,
Perception and creation,
Consciousness the fifth,
And likewise the four elements,
The eye and so forth and the objects,

And the five consciousnesses,
Divided into internal and external—
All are from nothing other than illusion.
One should understand the magic body
Like an image reflected in a mirror.
Its color like a rainbow,
Its range like the moon in water.
Freed from being and nothingness,
It is like the well-designed Vajrasattva,
His appearance clearly reflected
In a flawless mirror surface.
Superior in all its aspects,
A body one never tires of seeing,
It is taught to that good disciple,
And is called "the self-empowerment. . . ."

And so one enters into the worship of self.
Oneself is all the Buddhas
And all the Bodhisattvas.
Thus with all of one's efforts
One should always worship oneself. . . .

The Great Seal of great bliss
Will be achieved by following oneself. . . .

The private word of the self-empowerment,
Who does not get it from his Mentor
Perceives permanence or annihilation,
And thus becomes prone to regression.

Abandoning all forms of worship,
Engage truly in the worship of the Mentor.
By pleasing him, one will attain
The supreme intuition of omniscience. . . .

The Mentor takes away sin.
The Mentor dispels terrors.
The Mentor delivers one to the far shore
Of the terrors of the ocean of misery. . . .

Who is defiled with pride
Refutes the stage of truth,
Who has contempt for the Dharma
Such a one should not be taught.

Devoted to the Mentor, speaking truth,
Expert in teachings and concentrated,
Keeper of deeds according to her vows,
This stage should be taught to him.

4. UNIVERSAL ENLIGHTENMENT

I pay homage to the Vajra Hero,
Teacher of universal voidness.
I will explain the fourth stage
Of direct enlightenment.
The self-existent Lord,
The sole, great-souled deity;
Greater than him is the Vajra Master,
Because she grants the personal instructions. . . .

Having truly propitiated him
For a year or even for a month,
When that Mentor is well pleased,
Then worship her as much as possible. . . .

The disciple folds his palms
To please the Mentor with worship and praise.
"I pay homage to you, the unconditional,
Liberated from the three realms,
Equanimous as the space,
Not corrupted by all desires. . . .

Grant the vision of direct enlightenment,
Whose nature is universal voidness!"
The disciple should press her palms together,
Praise the Mentor, and then entreat him:
"Great Savior, grant me the vision
Of direct enlightenment,
Free from evolution and birth,
Beyond the three luminances.". . .

Thus the yogin/i should please the Mentor
By expressing her excellencies truly;
Their compassion arises for the disciple,
And she puts forth this very stage.

Night-moon is luminance; the spread of sun-rays is radiance. The interval is
the luminance-imminence; one proceeds through these not just once

through one's own natural instincts. What is neither night nor day nor the interval is free from those instincts. That is the instant of enlightenment, the supreme teaching of the Mentor, the objective of the yogin/i. . . . This instant just before the sunrise is the immaculate ultimate of reality. . . . In an instant she will attain the untroubled inner bliss of Buddha enlightenment. . . .

> The yogin/i attains thus such reality,
> Gaining the inexhaustible body of the sole friend of beings,
> Whose nature is animate and inanimate
> The Human-lion made of intuition,
> The cause of all beings.
> That crooked body becomes straight,
> Firm, and abiding without any abode,
> Whose eyes are wide open even when they are closed,
> Who is entranced even when not meditating.
> Even though she uses words, she is inexpressible.
> Though he has enjoyments, he has no grasping,
> Though she is the savior of the world, she is the slave of others. . . .

> The essence of all things, with the genius of the immaculate
> Teaching gained by the Mentor's kindness,
> Is clear and pure, extremely subtle, natural supreme peace,
> The realm of Buddha Nirvana.
> Free of notions of duality, nature of constant bliss,
> The yogin/i should meditate that reality.
> Liberated from good and evil, herself, here and now,
> Become the Lord Vajrasattva!

5. COMMUNION

> I pay homage to the Protector,
> Whose nature is cause and effect,
> Yet abandons all dualities;
> I will explain the final stage of communion.

> Abandoning the two notions
> Of egoistic life and liberation,
> Wherein they become the same thing;
> That is called "communion."
> Knowing the addictive and purificative
> Both as the absolute itself;

Who knows them as just the same
Knows the communion.

The notion of things with their forms
And the notion of nothingness;
The yogin/is who treat them as the same,
That one knows this communion.

Not having the mind that divides
The two, subject and object,
Having the mind without such differentiation,
That one knows the so-called communion.

Who abandons the cognitions
Of permanence and annihilation,
He is the sage who knows the reality
Of this stage of abiding communion.
Knowing wisdom and compassion as one,
Who acts in such a way
Is said to have "communion."

This stage is the sphere of Buddhas.
Fully concentrating the unification
Of art and wisdom, she has knowledge;
Who abides in this great yoga
Comes to have this communion. . . .

Freedom from the two notions
Of personal selflessness
And objective selflessness
Is the nature of communion.

Knowing the stage of knowing reality,
Who truly brings together
Self-empowerment and clear light,
This is the stage of communion. . . .

The superficial and the absolute,
Each with his own aspects,
Where they truly merge,
Is called "communion."

When the perception of reality itself
Arises (in the magic body),

That is the winning of communion,
The abode of the inexhaustible yogin/i.

Abandoning both the occasions
Of sleeping and being awake,
Freedom from both sleep and wakefulness,
The Teacher proclaimed as communion.

For whom all of these are not,
Abandoning somethings and nothings,
That yogin/i abides in communion,
Liberated from mindfulness and unconsciousness,

Having a constantly occurring character,
The yogin/i who acts as she pleases
Abides in the stage of communion.

Freed from attachment and detachment,
Having the body of supreme joy,
Living in the samsaric state,
He manifests this communion. . . .

The creation stage is one,
And the perfection stage another!
Where these two become one,
That is called "communion.". . .

That is the nondual intuition,
The unlocated Nirvana.
It is the Buddha Vajrasattva himself,
And the Lord Master of all.

Whatever expressions, such as "birthlessness,"
That teach the nondual intuition,
All of them are expressions of this;
There no other is explained.

The Buddhas, quite as numerous
As the sands of the Ganga River,
Realized this very thing, and,
Abandoning being and nothing,
Attained this essence of the Great Seal.

This supreme fifth stage,
By the merit gained from teaching it,
May the whole world sport with this samadhi of communion!

The Natural Liberation Through Naked Vision, Identifying Intelligence

by Padma Sambhava

EMA HOH!
The one mind that pervades all life and liberation,
Though it is the primal nature, it is not recognized,
Though its bright intelligence is uninterrupted, it is not faced,
Though it ceaselessly arises everywhere, it is not recognized.
To make known just this objective nature,
The three-times victors proclaimed the inconceivable
Eighty-four thousand Dharma teachings,
Teaching none other than this realization.
Though Scriptures are measureless as the sky,
Their import is three words identifying intelligence.
This direct introduction to the intention of the Victors—
Just this is the entry into freedom from progression.

KYAI HO!
Fortunate children! Listen here!
"Mind"—though this great word is so well known—
People do not know it, know it wrongly or only partially;
And by their not understanding its reality precisely,
They come up with inconceivable philosophical claims.
The common, alienated individual, not realizing this,
By not understanding her own nature on her own,
Suffers roaming through six life-forms in three realms.
Such is the fault of not realizing this reality of the mind.

Disciples and hermit Buddhas claim realization
Of a partial selflessness but do not know this exactly.
Bound up in claims from their treatises and theories,
They do not behold clear light transparency.

Disciples and hermits are shut out by clinging to subject and object,
Centrists are shut out by extremism about the two realities,
Ritual and performance Tantrists, by extremism in service and
    practice,
And great (Maha) and pervasive (Anu) Tantrists,
By clinging to the duality of realm and intelligence.
They err by remaining dualistic in nonduality,

By not communing nondually, they do not awaken.
All life and liberation inseparable from their own minds,
They still roam the life-cycle on vehicles of quitting and choosing.

Therefore, absorbing all created things in your free inaction,
Realize the great natural liberation of all things from this teaching
Of natural liberation through naked seeing of your own intelli-
    gence!
Thus in the great perfection, everything is perfect! . . .

"Mind," this bright process of intelligence,
In one way exists and in another way does not.
It is origin of the pleasure and pain of life and liberation.
It is accepted as essential to the eleven vehicles of liberation.

Its names are countless in various contexts.
Some call this mind "the mind-reality."
Some fundamentalists call it "self."
Some disciples call it "selflessness."
Idealists call it by name of "mind."
Some call it "Transcendent Wisdom."
Some call it "the Buddha nature."
Some call it "the Great Seal."
Some call it "the Soul Drop."
Some call it "the Truth Realm."
Some call it "the Foundation."
Some call it "the Ordinary."

To introduce the three-point entrance to this itself—
Realize past awareness as trackless, clear, and void,
Future awareness as unproduced and new,
And present awareness as staying natural, uncontrived.

Thus knowing time in its very ordinary way,
When you nakedly yourself regard yourself,
Your looking is transparent, nothing to be seen.
This is naked, immediate, clear intelligence.

It is clear voidness with nothing established,
Purity of clarity-voidness-nonduality;
Not permanent, free of any intrinsic status,
Not annihilated, bright and distinct,
Not a unity, multidiscerning clarity,

Without plurality, indivisible, one in taste,
Not derivative, self-aware, it is this very reality.

This objective introduction to the actuality of things
Contains complete in one the indivisible three bodies.
The Truth Body, the voidness free of intrinsic status,
The Beatific Body, bright with freedom's natural energy,
The Emanation Body, ceaselessly arising everywhere—
Its reality is these three complete in one.

To introduce the forceful method to enter this very reality,
Your own awareness right now is just this!
It being just this uncontrived natural clarity,
Why do you say, "I don't understand the nature of the mind"?
As here there is nothing to meditate upon,
In just this uninterrupted clarity intelligence,
Why do you say, "I don't see the actuality of the mind"?
Since the thinker in the mind is just it,
Why do you say, "Even searching I can't find it"?
Since here there is nothing to be done,
Why do you say, "Whatever I do, it doesn't succeed"?
As it is sufficient to stay put uncontrived,
Why do you say, "I can't stay still"?
As it is all right to be content with inaction,
Why do you say, "I am not able to do it"?
Since clear, aware, and void are automatically indivisible,
Why do you say, "Practice is not effective"?
Since it is natural, spontaneous, free of cause and condition,
Why do you say, "Seeking, it cannot be found"?
Since thought and natural liberation are simultaneous,
Why do you say, "Remedies are impotent"?
Since your very intelligence is just this,
Why do you say, "I do not know this"?

Be sure mind's nature is groundless voidness;
Your mind is insubstantial like empty space—
Like it or not, look at your own mind!
Not fastening to the view of annihilative voidness,
Be sure spontaneous wisdom has always been clear,
Spontaneous in itself like the essence of the sun—
Like it or not, look at your own mind!

Be sure that intelligent wisdom is uninterrupted,
Like a continuous current of a river—
Like it or not, look at your own mind!
Be sure it will not be known by thinking various reasons,
Its movement insubstantial like breezes in the sky—
Like it or not, look at your own mind!
Be sure that what appears is your own perception;
Appearance is natural perception, like a reflection in a mirror—
Like it or not, look at your own mind.
Be sure that all signs are liberated on the spot,
Self-originated, self-delivered, like clouds in sky—
Like it or not, look at your own mind! . . .

Vision-voidness natural liberation
Is brilliant void Body of Truth.
Realizing Buddhahood is not achieved by paths—
Vajrasattva is beheld right now. . . .

Therefore, to see intuitively your own naked intelligence,
This *Natural Liberation Through Naked Vision* is extremely deep.
So investigate this reality of your own intelligence.

Profound! Sealed!

EMA!

CHAPTER 9

Various Treasures of Tibetan Spiritual Culture

Instruction in the Great Science of the
Six-Syllable Mantra

(from The Jewel Case Array Sutra, Chapter 5)

Then the Transcendent Lord Padmottama, the Saint, the perfectly enlightened Buddha, spoke to the Bodhisattva Avalokiteshvara: "Give me, gentle son, the queen, the great science of the six-syllable mantra with which I may liberate from suffering hundreds of thousands of millions of billions of various beings, so that I may cause them to reach unexcelled perfect enlightenment as swiftly as possible."

Then the Bodhisattva Avalokiteshvara, the great spiritual hero, gave the great science, the six-syllable mantra to the perfectly enlightened Buddha, the Transcendent Lord, the Saint Padmottama:

OM MA NI PAD ME HUM.

At that instant, when this great science of the six-syllable mantra was given forth, then the four great continents, along with the heavenly residences of the deities, trembled like a leaf of a banana tree, and the four great oceans were churned up together with all of their demons and obstructors. All of these demons and obstructors were terrified, and the forest demons and the cannibals, and the Great Black One, Mahakala, together with all his great retinue fled away.

Thereupon the Transcendent Lord Padmottama extended his elephant-trunk-like arms and offered the Bodhisattva Avalokiteshvara, the great spiritual hero, a pearl necklace worth many hundreds of thousands, and Avalokiteshvara, receiving that pearl necklace himself, offered it in turn to the Saint, the Transcendent Lord, the perfectly enlightened Buddha Amitabha. He in turn, receiving that necklace, again returned an offering to the Transcendent Lord, the Saint, the perfectly enlightened Buddha Padmottama. Thereupon the Transcendent Lord, the Saint, the perfectly enlightened Buddha Padmottama, receiving this great science, the six-syllable mantra, returned to his Padma buddhaverse.

The Praise of the Twenty-One Taras

Hail Tara! Swift One, Champion,
Your glance like flash of lightning!

You arise the tear-born stamen
From our Savior's lotus face!

All hail! Your face shines splendid
As a hundred full harvest moons,
Ablaze with your laughing light-rays,
Like the host of a thousand stars!

All hail—infinity alive,
Triumphal Buddha-brain-dome Queen,
Honored by all Victor-children,
Showing all transcendent virtues!

Hail! You who fill all space of realms
With fierce HUMG and TUTTARA sounds,
You tread upon the seven worlds,
Controlling them all completely!

Hail you, adored by the All God,
Indra, Agni, Brahma, Maruts,
Honored by all demons, zombies,
Fairies, angels, and the goblins!

Hail, your fierce TRAD and PHAT sounds
Crush enemies' magic diagrams,
Feet planted in the bowman's stance,
Fierce glances blazing searing flames!

Hail you, O great awesome TURE,
Crusher of satanic champions,
Lotus face so fiercely frowning,
Quickly annihilate all foes!

Hail you whose heart is beautiful
With hands in the Three-Jew'l gesture,
Their exquisite royal wheel-marks
Shining their light-rays everywhere!

Hail you—garlands of light cascade
From your diadem aglow with joy,
Smiling, laughing with TUTTARE,
You dominate all devil realms!

Hail you who have power to summon
The whole earth's guardian spirit host,

You dance, you frown, you sound your HUMG,
Deliver us from disasters!

Hail you whose diadem shines brightly,
Moon crescent in dark-lock hairdo,
With Amitabha seated in it
Shining polar constant light-rays!

Hail! You stand wreathed in cosmic flames,
Supernova conflagrations,
In the bowman's stance, joy powered,
Incinerate the wheel of foes!

Hail you who sharply clap your hands
And stamp your foot upon the ground,
Frown fiercely, roar the sound of HUMG,
Shatter all seven underworlds!

Hail you, blissful, gentle, beauty,
Luxurious peaceful in Nirvan',
Glorious with SVAHA and with OM,
Destroy all great atrocities!

Hail you whose pow'r is total joy,
Who rend the bodies of all foes
With your magic syllables ten—
OM TARE TUTTARE TURE SVAHA
And your ferocious spell of HUMG!
OM NAMAS TARE NAMO HARE HUMG HARE SVAHA

Hail you, Swift Lady, stamp your foot,
Springing forth from your HUMG-shaped seed,
You shake the whole threefold planet,
Mounts Meru—Kailash—Mandara!

Hail you who holds the hare-marked moon
Like a divine lake in your hand,
Totally extracts all poisons
Pronouncing TARA TARA PHAT!

Hail you—honored by God Indra,
Brahma, all gods and horse-head fairies,

With armor of joy ecstatic,
You stop all conflict and bad dreams!

Hail you, your shining sun-moon eyes
Penetrate like lightning flashes,
HARA HARA and TUTTARA,
You allay all fatal fevers!

Hail, three-reality created,
Flowing bliss-pow'r Shiva-Shakti,
Best Swift Lady, you overcome
Rushing demons, zombies, ogres!

This mantra-rooted hymn of praise,
Twenty-one-fold salutation,
Sing it ardent, true, and thoughtful,
With devotion to the Goddess!

Remember it well at evening,
Or at dawn upon arising,
It gives safety, stops ev'ry sin,
Reverses all evil fortunes!

One will soon be well anointed
By seventy million victors,
Enjoying thereby much glory,
At last achieving Buddhahood!

Rememb'ring it, one is released
From effects of vilest poisons,
Animal, plant, or mineral,
Whether taken in food or drink!

Reciting its three sevens twice
Completely stops the suffering
Of addictions, demons, fevers,
Poisons, even in other beings;
Who wants a child will soon get one,
Who wants wealth will soon receive it.
One will fulfill all one's wishes
And will not suffer any harm!

Description of the Between

from The *Natural Liberation Through Understanding in the Between*

"Hey, noble one! Listen well, and keep this in your mind! In hell, heaven, and the between, the body is born by apparition. But when the perceptions of the mild and fierce deities arose in the reality between, you did not recognize them. So after five and a half days, you fainted with terror. Upon awakening, your awareness became clearer, and you immediately arose in a likeness of your former body. As it says in the Tantra: 'Having the fleshly form of the preceding and emerging lives, senses all complete, moving unobstructed, with evolutionary magic powers, one sees similar species with pure clairvoyance.'

"Here 'preceding' means that you arise as if in a flesh-and-blood body determined by the instincts of your preceding life. If you are radiant and have traces of the auspicious bodily signs and marks of a mythic hero, it is because your imagination can transform your body; thus, that perceived in the between is called a 'mental body.'

"At that time, if you are to be born as a god, you will have visions of the heavens. If you are to be born as a titan, a human, an animal, a pretan, or a hell being, you will have visions of whichever realm you will be born in. 'Preceding' here means that for up to four and a half days you experience yourself as having a fleshly body of your previous life with its habitual instincts. 'Emerging' means that you begin to have visions of the place where you are heading for rebirth. . . .

"Therefore do not follow after every vision that happens. Don't be attached to it! Don't adhere to it! If you are stubborn and attached to all of them, you will roam in suffering through the six realms. Up until yesterday, the visions of the reality between dawned for you, but you did not recognize them. So you have had to wander here now. So now if, without wavering, you can develop recognition, the spiritual teacher's orientation can open your awareness of the clear light, the naked, pure, vibrant void. Enter into it, relax into the experience of nonholding, nondoing! Without having to enter a womb, you will be liberated.

"If you do not recognize the light, then meditate that your spiritual teacher or archetype deity is present on the crown of your head, and devote yourself totally with a forceful faith. It is so important! Do it without wavering again and again!"

So you should say. If the deceased recognizes the light at this point, she will not wander in the six realms and will be liberated. But if the power of negative evolution still makes this recognition difficult, you should again speak as follows:

"Hey, noble one! Listen without your mind wandering! 'Senses all complete, moving unobstructed' means that even if in life you were blind, deaf, crippled, and so on, now in the between, your eyes clearly discern forms, your ears hear sounds, and so forth. Your senses become flawlessly clear and complete. . . . Recognize this as a sign that you have died and are wandering in the between! Remember your personal instructions!

"Hey, noble one! What is 'unobstructed' is your mental body; your awareness is free from embodiment and you lack a solid body. So now you can move hither and thither everywhere through walls, houses, lands, rocks, and earth, even through Meru, the axial mountain; except through a mother's womb and the vajra throne at Bodhgaya. This is a sign that you are wandering in the existence between, so remember the instructions of your spiritual teacher! Pray to the Lord of Great Compassion!

"Hey, noble one! 'With evolutionary magic powers' means that you, who have no special abilities or meditational magic powers whatsoever, now have magic powers arising from the result of your evolution. In a split second you can circle this four-continent planet with its axial mountain. You now have the power just to think about any place you wish and you will arrive there in that very instant. You can reach anywhere and return just as a normal man stretches out and pulls back his arm. But these various magic powers are not so miraculous; if you don't specially need them, ignore them! You should not worry about whether or not you can manifest this or that, which you may think of. The fact is you have the ability to manifest anything without any obstruction. You should recognize this as a sign of the existence between! You should pray to your spiritual teacher!

"Hey, noble one! 'One sees similar species with pure clairvoyance' means that beings of the same species in the between can see each other. Thus if some beings are of the same species, all going to be reborn as gods, they will see each other. Likewise other beings of the same species, to be reborn in whichever in the six realms, will see each other. So you should not be attached to such encounters! Meditate on the Lord of Great Compassion!

"'With pure clairvoyance' refers also to the vision of those whose pure clairvoyance has been developed by practice of contemplation, as well as to the vision of those whose divine power of merit has developed it. But such

272 ❈ ESSENTIAL TIBETAN BUDDHISM

yogis or deities cannot always see between beings. They see them only when they will to see them, and not when they do not, or when their contemplation is distracted.

"Hey, noble one! As you have such a ghostly body, you encounter relatives and familiar places as if in a dream. When you meet these relatives, though you communicate with them, they do not answer. When you see your relatives and dear ones crying, you will think, 'Now I have died, what can I do?' You feel a searing pain, like a fish flopping in hot sand. But however greatly you suffer, tormenting yourself at this time does not help. If you have a spiritual teacher, pray to your spiritual teacher. Or else pray to the compassionate archetype deity. Don't be attached to your loved ones—it is useless. Pray to the compassionate ones, and do not suffer or be terrified!

"Hey, noble one! Driven by the swift wind of evolution, your mind is helpless and unstable, riding the horse of breath like a feather blown on the wind, spinning and fluttering. You tell the mourners, 'Don't cry! Here I am!' They take no notice, and you realize you have died, and you feel great anguish. Now, do not indulge in your pain! There is a constant twilight, gray as the predawn autumn sky, neither day nor night. That kind of between can last for one, two, three, four, five, six, or seven weeks—up to forty-nine days. Though it is said that for most people the suffering of the existence between lasts twenty-one days, this is not always certain due to people's different evolutionary histories.

"You think, 'How nice it would be to have a new body!' Then you will have visions of looking everywhere for a body. Even if you try up to nine times to enter your old corpse, due to the length of the reality between, in the winter it will have frozen, in the summer it will have rotted. Otherwise your loved ones will have burned it or buried it or given it to birds and beasts, so it affords no place to inhabit. You will feel sick at heart and will have visions of being squeezed between boulders, stones, and dirt. This kind of suffering is in the nature of the existence between. Even if you find a body, there will be nothing other than such suffering. So give up longing for a body! Focus yourself undistractedly in the experience of creative nonaction!

". . . Your body is mental, so even if it is killed and cut up, you cannot die. In fact, your form is the void itself, so you have nothing to fear. The yamas are your own hallucinations and themselves are forms of the void. Your own instinctual mental body is void. Voidness cannot harm voidness. Signlessness cannot harm signlessness. You should recognize that there is nothing other than your own hallucination. There is no external, substantially existent yama, angel, demon, or bull-headed ogre and so on. You must recognize all this as the between!

"Meditate on the samadhi of the Great Seal!

"If you don't know how to meditate, examine carefully whatever terrifies you and see the voidness that is its lack of objective status. That is the Natural Body of Truth. And that voidness is not merely an annihilation. Your triumphant, distinct awareness of the terror of the void is itself the blissful mind of the Body of Beatitude. Voidness and clarity are indistinguishable; the actuality of the void is clarity, the actuality of the clarity is the voidness. Your awareness of voidness-clarity-indivisible is stripped naked, and now you abide in the unfabricated experience. That is the Wisdom Body of Truth. And that spontaneously and unobstructedly arises anywhere. And that is the Body of Compassionate Emanation.

"Hey, noble one! Behold this without wavering! Recognize it! You will definitely become a Buddha, the perfection of the four bodies. Do not be distracted! This is the borderline between a Buddha and an ordinary being. Now is the time described as 'One instant alienated, one instant perfectly enlightened.'

"Until yesterday you were given to distraction, you did not recognize what arose as the between, and you were gripped by so much terror. If you again surrender to distraction, the cord of compassion will be cut, and you will go into the abodes that lack all freedom; so be careful!

"Hey, noble one! If you don't know to meditate thus, then remember and pray to the Buddha, the Dharma, the Sangha, and the compassionate lords. Contemplate all the terrors and visions as the Compassionate Lord or your own archetype deity. Remember your esoteric initiation name and the spiritual teacher who gave you the initiations you received in the human realm; proclaim them to yama, the Lord of Truth! You won't be injured even if you fall off cliffs, so abandon fear and hate!

"Hey, noble one! In short, since your present between-consciousness is highly unstable, volatile, and mobile, and virtuous or vicious perception is very powerful, don't think at all about any unvirtuous evolution, and remember your own virtuous practice. If you have no virtuous practice, then adopt a positive perception and feel faith and reverence. Pray to your archetype deity and to the Lord of Compassion! With an intense willpower, perform this prayer!

> Now that I wander alone, without my loved ones,
> And all my visions are but empty images,
> May the Buddhas exert the force of their compassion
> And stop the fear and hate-drawn terrors of the between!

> Now when I suffer by the power of negative evolution,
> May my archetype deities dispel my suffering!

When reality crashes with a thousand thunders,
May they all become OM MANI PADME HUM!

When I'm pulled by evolution without recourse,
May the lords mild and fierce dispel my suffering!
When I suffer due to evolutionary instincts,
May clear light bliss samadhi arise for me!

"Thus perform this fervent prayer! It will surely guide you on the path. It is crucial that you decide it is sure not to let you down! . . .

"Again, meditate long and carefully that whoever your archetype deity, he or she appears like a magic illusion, lacking intrinsic reality. It is called the pure Magic Body. Then contemplate that archetype deity as dissolving from the edges inward, and enter the experience of not holding rigidly to the insubstantial, the clear light of voidness. Again contemplate that as the archetype deity! Again contemplate it as clear light! Thus meditating deity and clear light in alternation, then let your own awareness dissolve from the edges; where space pervades, let awareness pervade. Where awareness pervades, let the Truth Body pervade. Enter comfortably into the experience of the ceaseless nonproliferation of the Truth Body."

Praises of Various Fierce Protectors

Praise to Mahakala
HUM!
Homage to the swift Lokeshvara!

O Great Black Mahakala! You wear a tiger skin!
Your ankleted feet trample an obstructor!
Your six arms are adorned with snakelets;
The rights hold chopper and rosary
And fiercely rattle a damaru drum!
The lefts hold a skull bowl and a trident
And a noose with which you bind all demons!

Your face is fierce, you gnash your fangs!
Your three eyes bulge, your hair burns upward!
Forehead anointed with red lead powder,
Your crown is sealed with Akshobhya Buddha!
Your garland, fifty blood-soak'd human heads,
Your diadem, five bejeweled human skulls!

Come here from your heaven, accept my cake!
I bow to you, Glorious Six-Armed One!
Fiercely guard the Buddha Teaching!
Fiercely praise the exalted jewels!

We teachers, disciples, and associates—
Wipe out our obstacles and bad conditions,
Quickly grant us the attainments we desire!

Praise to Shri Devi

BHYOH!
Mind-essence working the four miraculous activities,
Not deviant from the essence, neither being mind alone,
Absolute indivisible, free of color or form,
Her miracles mere magic, fitting each being's mind;
She manifests, she the peaceful Glory Goddess!

Peacemaker, Peace Being, her reality is peace,
Chief Lady of the retinue of peace,
Her symbolic body a perfectly pure white!
I bow to the all-peacemaking Mother Goddess!
Pray cease all disease, demons, and obstructions!

BHYOH!
Mind-essence working the four miraculous activities,
Not deviant from the essence, neither being mind alone,
Absolute indivisible, free of color or form,
Her miracles mere magic, fitting each being's mind;
She manifests, she the prospering Glory Goddess!

Growthmaker, Growth Being, her reality is growth,
Chief Lady of the retinue of growth,
Her symbolic body a perfect golden yellow!
I bow to the all-prospering Mother Goddess!
Please expand my life span and my merit!

BHYOH!
Mind-essence working the four miraculous activities,
Not deviant from the essence, neither being mind alone,
Absolute indivisible, free of color or form,

Her miracles mere magic, fitting each being's mind;
She manifests, she the powerful Glory Goddess!

Powermaker, Power Being, her reality is power,
Chief Lady of the retinue of power,
Her symbolic body a perfect passion red!
I bow to the all-dominating Mother Goddess!
Please bring under control all beings of three realms!

BHYOH!
Mind-essence working the four miraculous activities,
Not deviant from the essence, neither being mind alone,
Absolute indivisible, free of color or form,
Her miracles mere magic, fitting each being's mind;
She manifests, she the ferocious Glory Goddess!

Fierce-maker, Fierce Being, her reality is ferocious,
Chief Lady of the retinue of the fierce,
Her symbolic body a glistening dark black!
I bow to the all-terrifying Mother Goddess!
Fiercely pray free of diseases, demons, foes, and obstructions!

BHYOH!
Though your nature is not at all substantial,
By appearing with such variety of natures,
You accomplish beings' aims with four miracle workings,
And we praise you heartily with intense attention!
Let us effortlessly achieve the four activities,
Striving with you for the sake of beings!

Tsong Khapa's Praise of the Inner Yama

The slightest stamp of your bowman's feet
destroys the world with its four prime elements!
Your intensely fierce buffalo face blazes intensely,
your great roar fills the three-realm universe!
Lord Yamantaka, terrible form that tames all evil,
manifest by Manjushri, sole father of Buddhas,
I bow reverently to you!

Now I praise you, Yamaraja—
it's time for every devil to watch out!

Ever sounding the great roar
that shatters mountains and churns up oceans,
dense fierce flame-mass amid billowing black smoke
like lightning flashing in a thunderhead,
your head radiates unbearable heat!

Surrounded with halos of rainbow light;
upon a triangle, blackened as if by a million fogs,
filled with a swirling ocean of blood and fat,
standing on a black ogre prostrate on a solar disk,
there you are, O Yamaraja!

Your short, thick body black as kohl,
right leg outstretched, left drawn up,
in the stance that shakes the earth,
your hair flaming up earthy yellow,
adorned with five-skull diadem,
your crown is adorned with the fiercest vajra bolt!

Necklaced with bloody, freshly-severed-head garland,
your three eyes flash and bulge and dart about,
your mouth gapes with sharp fangs gnashing,
its breath panting constantly with poisonous snake vapors!
Your right hand brandishes the blazing chopper knife
to mince the brains of the demon host,
your left hand fondles the bloody skull bowl,
your tiger-skin skirt shows the power of your fury!

Swiftly recall your vow to Lord Yamantaka!
Never waver, never waver,
accomplish all that I the yogin do command!

More, let all your host of great white, yellow, red, black yamas,
buffalo faces furious wild, adorned with death-ground ornaments,
mouths ablaze, eyes bloodshot, boldly mounted with warrior's
 .stance
atop fierce buffaloes with piercing horns and razor throats,
conquer the host of devils spread out in the four directions!

May the vajra thunder of my praise
accomplish all deeds of peace, growth, power, and terror!
'Til I attain, for the sake of beings as infinite as space,
the supreme state of world-famed Manjughosha,
always praised by all the Buddhas!

So long may Dharmaraja with your yama host
respectfully follow Yamantaka's command!
Effectively conquer the dark-side armies who always struggle
to steal our supreme treasure—the reality path!

Praise of Vaishravana, Deity of Wealth

HUM
O, Savior, arisen from the syllable VAI,
You sit at ease with your massive force
Astride the lion of fearlessness—
We bow to you, lord of the stage immovable!

We make offering, give praise, and bow in homage,
To your four queens and four princes,
Your eight ogres who accomplish special missions,
Your eight dragons who bestow treasures,
Those eight deities and demons with their retinues!

Conquer all the foes and demons,
Perfect our enjoyment of prosperity,
Fulfill all our wishes completely—
Effortlessly accomplish others' aims!

Activation Prayer for the Protector Setrabjen

by Nyare Kentrul Gelek Rinpoche

From the bliss-void reality wherever you are,
Our powerful protector, Great Setrabjen,
Your emanations and their myriad minions—
We heartily invite you—please come here!

In your palace, here in space before us,
On your lotus sun seat that flattens demons,
Great Emanation Dharma King with your armies,
Please stay here while we concentrate!

To you, bliss-guardian Great Setrabjen,
We fervently offer in the bliss-intensifying vase

Oceans of clouds of great-bliss-wisdom offerings.
Please accept them in the bliss-void-indivisible realm!

Great Dharma King arisen from nondual wisdom,
I repent in inconceivability whatever offends you,
Praying with total trust, the all-good offering clouds
And the sacred energizing substances—I offer you!

I offer the great red offering cakes
Purified, transformed, and magnified,
And the inexhaustible elixir medicine, filling the universe,
With your magical power please enjoy them!

Deerskin-clad Lokesha, Buddhas' compassion alive,
Manjushri, wisdom bodied, garbed as eternal youth,
Vajrapani Lord of Secrets, magical power deity—
Inseparable from these, I praise you, ferocious form!

You are the great foe-deity of yoginis,
Master of glory of power and magical feats,
Miraculously guard the life span of glorious mentors,
Widely spread the good tradition of virtue practice!

The Jewel Heart teachings in their good glory,
Teachers and students of our Dharma college,
Please support their spiritual life and happiness,
Make all contact with them ultimately worthwhile!

O deity who has been with us over many lives,
We pray to you wholeheartedly not to leave
From now until we reach enlightenment,
Be our savior, supporter, and friend!

HOH
O Setrabjen, great foe-deity,
Your six main emanations such as Neu Lutsen,
King Jey, all your subemanations,
And the host of your oath-bound retinue—

We pray to you and make offerings!
Please accept this responsibility!
We imagine you! We summon you! Don't delay!
We beg you! We urge you! Don't be idle!

We commission you! Don't be careless!
Especially whatever we will in mind,
Make it happen spontaneously!
Bestow on us all accomplishments!

Prayer of the Word of Truth—

by His Holiness the Fourteenth Dalai Lama

O all-time Buddhas with your children and disciples,
Your glory an ocean of boundless virtues,
You think of poor beings as each an only child;
Please attend to my truthful lamentation!

May you magnify the ten virtuous practices
Of the wise, adept upholders of the Buddha teaching,
And spread the glory of its benefit and bliss the whole world over
As it abolishes the miseries of existence and extinction!

May you rescue wretched beings, ceaselessly tormented
By the fierce push of unbearably vicious evolutionary acts,
Prevent the horrors of their dread diseases, wars, and famines,
And restore their spirits in your ocean of bliss and happiness!

Please look upon the religious people of the Land of Snows,
Ruthlessly conquered with harsh tactics by malevolent invaders;
May your compassion exert itself with miraculous speed
To stop the torrent of their blood and tears!

Ah! Those cruel people defeat themselves as well as others,
Driven to insane behavior by the devil of addictive passions;
Have mercy and restore their decent insight of right and wrong,
Use love and kindness to reunite them in the glory of human
    friendship!

Bring us our deep desire, so long held in our secret hearts,
The natural glory of the perfect freedom of the whole of Tibet,
And grant us the good fortune to enjoy once more
The millennial feast of the union of secular and sacred!

May Chenraysig, the Messiah of the Potala,
Compassionately protect these people who have suffered so many
  ordeals,
Who have given up body, life, and all of their possessions
For the teaching, its holders, their fellows, and sacred/secular rule!

After all I pray there soon may come the brilliant dawn,
The good fruition of the magnificent vow to maintain Tibet
Sworn by the Messiah, Chenraysig the Lord,
In the presence of all Buddhas and Bodhisattvas!

By the power of deep relativity, reality of world and void,
The might of mercy of the Three Jewels, the force of this word of
  truth,
And by the force of the truth of the inexorable effects of evolution—
May our prayer of truth be realized swiftly without interference!

The Nobel Peace Prize Lecture

Tenzin Gyatso,
His Holiness the Fourteenth Dalai Lama of Tibet

OSLO, DECEMBER 10, 1989

Brothers and Sisters:

It is an honor and a pleasure to be among you today. I am really happy to see so many old friends who have come from different corners of the world, and to make new friends, whom I hope to meet again in the future. When I meet people in different parts of the world, I am always reminded that we are all basically alike: we are all human beings. Maybe we have different clothes, our skin is of a different color, or we speak different languages. This is on the surface. But basically, we are the same human beings. That is what binds us to each other. That is what makes it possible for us to understand each other and to develop friendship and closeness.

Thinking over what I might say today, I decided to share with you some of my thoughts concerning the common problems all of us face as members of the human family. Because we all share this small planet earth, we have to learn to live in harmony and peace with each other and with nature. That is not just a dream but a necessity. We are dependent on each other in so many ways that we can no longer live in isolated communities and ignore what is happening outside those communities. We need to help each other when we have difficulties, and we must share the good fortune that we enjoy. I speak to you as just another human being, as a simple monk. If you find what I say useful, then I hope you will try to practice it.

I also wish to share with you today my feelings concerning the plight and aspirations of the people of Tibet. The Nobel Prize is a prize they well deserve for their courage and unfailing determination during the past forty years of foreign occupation. As a free spokesman for my fellow countrymen and -women, I feel it is my duty to speak out on their behalf. I speak not with a feeling of anger or hatred toward those who are responsible for the immense suffering of our people and the destruction of our land, homes, and culture. They too are human beings who struggle to find happiness and deserve our compassion. I speak to inform you of the sad situation in my country today and of the aspirations of my people, because in our struggle for freedom, truth is the only weapon we possess.

The realization that we are all basically the same human beings, who seek happiness and try to avoid suffering, is very helpful in developing a sense of brotherhood and sisterhood—a warm feeling of love and compassion for others. This, in turn, is essential if we are to survive in this ever-shrinking world we live in. For if we each selfishly pursue only what we believe to be in our own interest, without caring about the needs of others, we may end up harming not only others but also ourselves. This fact has become very clear during the course of this century. We know that to wage a nuclear war today, for example, would be a form of suicide; or that to pollute the air or the oceans, in order to achieve some short-term benefit, would be to destroy the very basis for our survival. As individuals and nations are becoming increasingly interdependent we have no other choice than to develop what I call a sense of universal responsibility.

Today we are truly a global family. What happens in one part of the world may affect us all. This, of course, is not only true of the negative things that happen, but is equally valid for the positive developments. We not only know what happens elsewhere, thanks to the extraordinary modern communications technology, we are also directly affected by events that occur far away. We feel a sense of sadness when children are starving in eastern Africa. Similarly we feel a sense of joy when a family is reunited after decades of separation by the Berlin Wall. Our crops and livestock are contaminated and our health and livelihood threatened when a nuclear accident happens miles away in another country. Our own security is enhanced when peace breaks out between warring parties on other continents.

But war or peace; the destruction or the protection of nature; the violation or the promotion of human rights and democratic freedoms; poverty or material well-being; the lack of moral and spiritual values or their existence and development; and the breakdown or the development of human understanding, are not isolated phenomena that can be analyzed and tackled independently of one another. In fact, they are very much interrelated at all levels and need to be approached with that understanding.

Peace, in the sense of the absence of war, is of little value to someone who is dying of hunger or cold. It will not remove the pain of torture inflicted on a prisoner of conscience. It does not comfort those who have lost their loved ones in floods caused by senseless deforestation in a neighboring country. Peace can last only where human rights are respected, where the people are fed, and where individuals and nations are free. True peace with ourselves and with the world around us can be achieved only through the development of mental peace. The other phenomena mentioned above are similarly interrelated. Thus, for example, we see that a clean environment, wealth, or democracy means little in the face of war, especially nuclear war, and that material development is not sufficient to ensure human happiness.

Material progress is of course important for human advancement. In Tibet we paid much too little attention to technological and economic development, and today we realize that this was a mistake. At the same time, material development without spiritual development can also cause serious problems. In some countries too much attention is paid to external things and very little importance is given to inner development. I believe both are important and must be developed side by side so as to achieve a good balance between them. Tibetans are always described by foreign visitors as being a happy, jovial people. This is part of our national character, formed by cultural and religious values that stress the importance of mental peace through the generation of love and kindness to all other living sentient beings, both human and animal. Inner peace is the key: If you have inner peace, the external problems do not affect your deep sense of peace and tranquillity. In that state of mind you can deal with situations with calmness and reason, while keeping your inner happiness. That is very important. Without this inner peace, no matter how comfortable your life is materially, you may still be worried, disturbed, or unhappy because of the circumstances.

Clearly it is of great importance, therefore, to understand the interrelationship among these and other phenomena and to approach and attempt to solve problems in a balanced way that takes these different aspects into consideration. Of course it is not easy. But it is of little benefit to try to solve one problem if doing so creates an equally serious new one. So really we have no alternative; We must develop a sense of universal responsibility not only in the geographic sense but also in respect to the different issues that confront our planet.

Responsibility lies not only with the leaders of our countries or with those who have been appointed or elected to do a particular job. It lies with each of us individually. Peace, for example, starts within each one of us. When we have inner peace, we can be at peace with those around us. When our community is in a state of peace, it can share that peace with neighboring communities and so on. When we feel love and kindness toward others, it not only makes others feel loved and cared for but it helps us also to develop inner happiness and peace. And there are ways in which we can consciously work to develop feelings of love and kindness. For some of us, the most effective way to do so is through religious practice. For others it may be nonreligious practices. What is important is that we each make a sincere effort to take seriously our responsibility for each other and for the natural environment.

I am very encouraged by the developments that are taking place around us. After the young people of many countries, particularly in northern Europe, have repeatedly called for an end to the dangerous destruction of the environment that was being conducted in the name of economic development, the world's political leaders are now starting to take meaningful steps to address this problem. The report to the United Nations Secretary General by the World Commission on the Environment and Development (the Brundtland report) was an important step in educating governments on the urgency of the issue. Serious efforts to bring peace to war-torn zones and to implement the right to self-determination of some peoples have resulted in the withdrawal of Soviet troops from Afghanistan and the establishment of independent Namibia. Through persistent nonviolent popular efforts, dramatic changes, bringing many countries closer to real democracy, have occurred in many places, from Manila in the Philippines to Berlin in East Germany. With the cold-war era apparently drawing to a close, people everywhere live with renewed hope. Sadly, the courageous efforts of the Chinese people to bring similar change to their country was brutally crushed last June. But their efforts too are a source of hope. The military might has not extinguished the desire for freedom and the determination of the Chinese people to achieve it. I particularly admire the fact that these young people, who have been taught that "power grows from the barrel of the gun," chose instead to use nonviolence as their weapon.

What these positive changes indicate is that reason, courage, determination, and the inextinguishable desire for freedom can ultimately win. In the struggle between forces of war, violence, and oppression on the one hand, and peace, reason, and freedom on the other, the latter are gaining the upper hand. This realization fills us Tibetans with hope that someday we too will once again be free.

The awarding of the Nobel Prize to me, a simple monk from far-away Tibet, here in Norway, also fills us Tibetans with hope. It means that, despite the fact that we have not drawn attention to our plight by means of violence, we have not been forgotten. It also means that the values we cherish, in particular our respect for all forms of life and the belief in the power of truth, are today recognized and encouraged. It is also a tribute to my mentor, Mahatma Gandhi, whose example is an inspiration to so many of us. This year's award is an indication that this sense of universal responsibility is developing. I am deeply touched by the sincere concern shown by so many people in this part of the world for the suffering of the people of Tibet. That is a source of hope not only for us Tibetans but for all oppressed peoples.

As you know, Tibet has, for forty years, been under foreign occupation. Today more than a quarter of a million Chinese troops are stationed in Tibet. Some sources estimate the occupation army to be twice this strength. During this time Tibetans have been deprived of their most basic human rights, including the right to life, movement, speech, worship, only to mention a few. More than one sixth of Tibet's population of six million died as a direct result of the Chinese invasion and occupation. Even before the Cultural Revolution started, many of Tibet's monasteries, temples, and historic buildings were destroyed. Almost everything that remained was destroyed during the Cultural Revolution. I do not wish to dwell on this point, which is well documented. What is important to realize, however, is that despite the limited freedom granted after 1979 to rebuild parts of some monasteries and other such tokens of liberalization, the fundamental human rights of the Tibetan people are still today being systematically violated. In recent months this bad situation has become even worse.

If it were not for our community in exile, so generously sheltered and supported by the government and people of India and helped by organizations and individuals from many parts of the world, our nation would today be little more than a shattered remnant of a people. Our culture, religion, and national identity would have been effectively eliminated. As it is, we have built schools and monasteries in exile and have created democratic institutions to serve our people and preserve the seed of our civilization. With this experience, we intend to implement full democracy in a future free Tibet. Thus, as we develop our community in exile on modern lines, we also cherish and preserve our own identity and culture and bring hope to millions of our countrymen and -women in Tibet.

The issue of most urgent concern at this time is the massive influx of Chinese settlers into Tibet. Although in the first decades of occupation a considerable number of Chinese were transferred into the eastern parts of Tibet—in the Tibetan provinces of Amdo (Chinghai) and Kham (most of which has been annexed by the neighboring Chinese province)—since 1983 an unprecedented number of Chinese have been encouraged by their government to migrate to all parts of Tibet, including central and western Tibet (which the PRC refers to as the so-called Tibet Autonomous Region). Tibetans are rapidly being reduced to an insignificant minority in their own country. This development, which threatens the very survival of the Tibetan nation, its culture and spiritual heritage, can still be stopped and reversed. But this must be done now, before it is too late.

The new cycle of protest and violent repression, which started in Tibet in September of 1987 and culminated in the imposition of martial law in the capital, Lhasa, in March of this year, was in large part a reaction to this tremendous Chinese influx. Information reaching us in exile indicates that the protest marches and other peaceful forms of protest are continuing in Lhasa and a number of other places in Tibet despite the severe punishment and inhumane treatment given to Tibetans detained for expressing their grievances. The number of Tibetans killed by security forces during the protest in March and those who died in detention afterward is not known but is believed to be more than two hundred. Thousands have been detained or arrested and imprisoned, and torture is commonplace.

It was against the background of this worsening situation, and in order to prevent further bloodshed, that I proposed what is generally referred to as the Five-Point Peace Plan for the restoration of peace and human rights in Tibet. I elaborated on the plan in a speech in Strasbourg last year. I believe the plan provides a reasonable and realistic framework for negotiations with the People's Republic of China. So far, however, China's leaders have been unwilling to respond constructively. The brutal suppression of the Chinese democracy movement in June of this year, however, reinforced my view that any settlement of the Tibetan question will be meaningful only if it is supported by adequate international guarantees.

The Five-Point Peace Plan addresses the principal and interrelated issues, which I referred to in the first part of this lecture. It calls for (1) Transformation of the whole of Tibet, including the eastern provinces of Kham and Amdo, into a Zone of *Ahimsa* (nonviolence); (2) Abandonment of China's population transfer policy; (3) Respect for the Tibetan people's fundamental human rights and democratic freedoms; (4) Restoration and protection of Tibet's natural environment; and (5) Commencement of earnest negotiations on the future status of Tibet and of relations between the Tibetan and Chinese peoples. In the Strasbourg address I proposed that Tibet become a fully self-governing democratic political entity.

I would like to take this opportunity to explain the Zone of Ahimsa or peace sanctuary concept, which is the central element of the Five-Point Peace Plan. I am convinced that it is of great importance not only for Tibet but for peace and stability in Asia.

It is my dream that the entire Tibetan plateau should become a free refuge where humanity and nature can live in peace and in harmonious balance. It would be a place where people from all over the world could come to seek the true meaning of peace within themselves, away from the tensions and pressures of much of the rest of the world. Tibet could indeed become a creative center for the promotion and development of peace.

The following are key elements of the proposed Zone of Ahimsa:

1. The entire Tibetan plateau would be demilitarized;
2. The manufacture, testing, and stockpiling of nuclear weapons and other armaments on the Tibetan plateau would be prohibited;
3. The Tibetan plateau would be transformed into the world's largest natural park or biosphere. Strict laws would be enforced to protect wildlife and plant life; the exploitation of natural resources would be carefully regulated so as not to damage relevant ecosystems; and a policy of sustainable development would be adopted in populated areas;
4. The manufacture and use of nuclear power and other technologies that produce hazardous waste would be prohibited;
5. National resources and policy would be directed toward the active promotion of peace and environmental protection. Organizations dedicated to the furtherance of peace and to the protection of all forms of life would find a hospitable home in Tibet;
6. The establishment of international and regional organizations for the promotion and protection of human rights would be encouraged in Tibet.

Tibet's height and size (the size of the European Community), as well as its unique history and profound spiritual heritage, make it ideally suited to fulfill the role of sanctuary of peace in the strategic heart of Asia. It would also be in keeping with Tibet's historical role as a peaceful Buddhist nation and buffer region separating the Asian continent's great and often rival powers.

In order to reduce existing tensions in Asia, the president of the Soviet Union, Mr. Gorbachev, proposed the demilitarization of Soviet-Chinese borders and their transformation into a "frontier of peace and good-neighborliness." The Nepal government had earlier proposed that the Himalayan country of Nepal, bordering on Tibet, should become a zone of peace, although that proposal did not include demilitarization of the country.

For the stability and peace of Asia, it is essential to create peace zones to separate the continent's biggest powers and potential adversaries. President Gorbachev's proposal, which also included a complete Soviet troop withdrawal from Mongolia, would help to reduce tension and the potential for confrontation between the Soviet Union and China. A true peace zone must, clearly, also be created to separate the world's two most populous states, China and India.

The establishment of the Zone of Ahimsa would require the withdrawal of troops and military installations from Tibet, which would enable India and Nepal also to withdraw troops and military installations from the Himalayan regions bordering Tibet. This would have to be achieved by international agreements. It would be in the best interest of all states of Asia, particularly China and India, as it would enhance their security while reducing the economic burden of maintaining high troop concentrations in remote areas.

Tibet would not be the first strategic area to be demilitarized. Parts of the Sinai peninsula, the Egyptian territory separating Israel and Egypt, have been demilitarized for some time. Of course, Costa Rica is the best example of an entirely demilitarized country.

Tibet would also not be the first area to be turned into a natural preserve or biosphere. Many parks have been created throughout the world. Some very strategic areas have been turned into natural "peace parks." Two examples are the La Amistad park on the Costa Rica–Panama border and the Sí a Paz project on the Costa Rica–Nicaragua border.

When I visited Costa Rica earlier this year, I saw how a country can develop successfully without an army, to become a stable democracy committed to peace and the protection of the natural environment. This confirmed my belief that my vision of Tibet in the future is a realistic plan, not merely a dream.

Let me end with a personal note of thanks to all of you and our friends who are not here today. The concern and support that you have expressed for the plight of the Tibetans have touched us all greatly and continue to give us courage to struggle for freedom and justice; not through the use of arms but with the powerful weapons of truth and determination. I know that I speak on behalf of all the people of Tibet when I thank you and ask you not to forget Tibet at this critical time in our country's history. We too hope to contribute to the development of a more peaceful, more humane, and more beautiful world. A future free Tibet will seek to help those in need throughout the world, to protect nature, and to promote peace. I believe that our Tibetan ability to combine spiritual qualities with a realistic and practical attitude enables us to make a special contribution in however modest a way. This is my hope and prayer.

In conclusion, let me share with you a short prayer that gives me great inspiration and determination:

> For as long as space endures,
> And for as long as living beings remain,
> Until then may I, too, abide
> To dispel the misery of the world.

Thank you.

Notes

Shakyamuni, whose name literally means "the sage of the Shakya clan," was the historic Buddha of our era, living from ca. 563 B.C.E. to 483 B.C.E. Tibetan Buddhists consider him the founder of the three main forms or Vehicles of Buddhism, the Monastic or Individual (Hinayana), the Messianic or Universal (Mahayana), and the Apocalyptic or Tantric (Vajrayana) Vehicles.

The **brahmins** were the priests of ancient Indian society, the mediators between humans and the gods of the Vedic world, presiding over the sacrificial ritual that provided the main channel of communication with the divine. Their cosmology was based on a sense of better days in the past, coupled with a sense of the present as a process of deterioration. This buttressed their authoritarian mistrust of new generations, which caused them to resist all change, innovation, and progress.

Tantra comes from a verb meaning "to weave" and a noun meaning "thread." As a religious category it refers to methods of spiritual practice, ways of transforming the ordinary world into a divine one, by weaving an enlightened universe in place of the realm of suffering. It can also refer to a set of texts that describe these methods. A **mantra** is a sacred sound, word, or phrase that is magically creative in the sense that it can alter an old or produce a new state of affairs by being repeated or, in some cases, even visualized as letters. The use of mantras is central in most Tantric practices.

A **Bodhisattva** is a person, who can be animal or divine as well as human, who has conceived the will to enlightenment and vowed to manifest the spirit of enlightenment, thus dedicating all his or her lives to the attainment of perfect Buddhahood for the sake of all beings.

Dharma has eleven main meanings, ranging from "thing," through "quality," "duty," "law," "religion," "doctrine," and "teaching," up to "truth," "reality," "absolute," and even "liberation" or "Nirvana." Whenever it is left untranslated and in upper case, it means the latter meanings, especially "Truth" or "Free Reality." Thus a **Dharma king** is a ruler who acknowledges the primacy of the higher reality of liberating Truth and rules his country within an orientation toward that Truth.

Ganden, literally "the joyous heaven," is the Tibetan name for Tushita, the heaven where Maitreya, the future Buddha, dwells. The residence of the Dalai Lama incarnations in Drepung Monastery was called the Ganden Palace because of the Dalai Lamas' association with the progressive, optimistic outlook of the Buddha who will visit the world in the future, enlightening millions of beings. When the Dalai Lamas became head of the Tibetan government, after 1642, the government as a whole adopted the name.

The **Karmapa Lamas** were the originators of the formal institution of the recognized reincarnation. In the first decade of the thirteenth century a small boy was recognized as the reincarnation of the great lama Karma Dusum Kyenpa and was subsequently enthroned as Karma Pakshi, the Second Karmapa. The seventeenth Karmapa is currently recognized as incarnate in not one but two young boys, who are being trained as spiritual teachers.

Shambhala is a mythical country somewhere in the vicinity of Siberia or the North Pole where most of the population is enlightened and life is generally happy. This land is invisible to the rest of the world, except for a few adepts, until a time a few centuries hence when it becomes visible and the more unhappy people on outer earth try to conquer it. There ensues a sort of Armageddon-like conflict, at the end of which life all over the world becomes as idyllic as Shambhala had been for a lengthy period of centuries. Shambhala is the basis of the modern legends of Shangri-la.

The *Kalachakra* (**Time-wheel**) **Tantra** is practiced by learned yogins and yoginis who must first be initiated into the vision of the "Time-machine Buddha" by entering the palace of this Buddha-deity. The architecture of such a palace is represented by a geometric pattern that uses squares, circles, symbols, and architectural elements to provide a sort of blueprint for the three-dimensional building; this pattern is called a **mandala,** a sphere of essence. For major initiation rituals conducted by lamas for large groups, the monks create such a mandala using particles of fine sand mixed with pure pigment. When you see this mandala, the seed of the vision of the full-blown mandala-palace is planted in the subconscious; years of focused meditation are needed to grow this seed into a stable and transformative vision.

Pali was a literary language developed in Sri Lanka during the early centuries of the common era, based on the up-to-then orally transmitted literature of the monastic Buddhist Scriptures, systematically memorized and preserved since the Buddha's time in a language resembling the spoken language of the Magadha region of central India (present-day Bihar province).

The word **Hinduism** originates from the Arabic and basically means no more and no less than "Indian religion," i.e., religion in the Indian region. It thus covers a great variety of religious forms and institutions, including Indian Buddhism and Jainism. It is also used more narrowly to refer to those forms of Indian religion that subscribe to the divine authorship of the ancient Vedas, which Buddhists and Jains do not. Following this latter usage, one tends to refer to non-Buddhist and non-Jain Indian religions as "Hinduism," even though the various groups of believers in Shiva, Vishnu, Indra, or Brahma had no such word to describe themselves.

The **Mahayana (Universal Vehicle) Scriptures** began to appear in India around the first century B.C.E., starting with the *Transcendent Wisdom Scriptures,* though there are no firm grounds for specific dating. By the time of large-scale translation of these Scriptures into Chinese from the fourth century C.E., there were thousands of texts, roughly the equivalent of forty or fifty Bibles, in addition to a huge Sanskrit literature very similar to the Pali collection of Scriptures.

A key point is that the Tibetan **"Stages of the Path of Enlightenment"** teachings are not simply to be classified as exoteric, or "gradual" teaching, the opposite of esoteric, "subitist," or mystical teachings. The path of enlightenment genre evolved in the apocalyptic or Tantric context, in which the stages of the foundational path are compressed and focused to prepare for entry onto the Tantric Vehicle. In the same way, the Tantric "preliminary practices" are merely prostrations, purifications, offerings, and so on, but their special context and accompanying visualizations make them Tantric prostrations and so on.

Once practitioners have achieved the prerequisite understanding of transcendent renunciation, compassionate commitment to all beings, and the wisdom of selflessness, they have the freedom from programmed drives and habitual self-image rigidity that enables them to begin a conscious process of accelerating their evolution. This begins in initiation into a mandala, a sacred alternative universe of an enlightened being, in this case the Buddha-archetype Hevajra, in order to reshape body and mind methodically according to the dictates of wisdom and compassion. This reshaping process begins in the imagination, in what is called the creation stage, and concludes with rehearsals of actual death, out-of-body voyaging, ordinary body reentry, and so on in what is called the perfection stage.

Morphic resonance is a term coined by the evolutionary biologist Rupert Sheldrake to explain a statistical pattern he observed in primitive life-forms, where the adopting of a particular pattern of behavior and embodiment by a number of individuals of a species accelerates the rate of adoption of that pattern in others. He speculates that this kind of phenomenon can be observed in human communities, which explains shifts in fashion, trends in thinking, and so on. It is quite a controversial hypothesis; but I find it useful in describing the relationship between individual transformation through spiritual cultivation and subsequent social changes in the behavior of groups.

A foundational theme in the stages of the path to enlightenment is the **preciousness of the human evolutionary state,** very hard to achieve from positions among the lower life-forms, quickly lost due to its fragility, and the perfect opportunity for coming to self-awareness and self-control in the midst of the evolutionary processes. Among human life-forms, those endowed with the freedom from survival preoccupations and the opportunity to come to full consciousness due to contact with enlightened beings and their teachings are particularly precious. A Tibetan who considers that he or she has such a life-form is naturally inclined to use its every moment to a beneficial evolutionary end.

The **Three Jewels**—Buddha, Dharma, and Sangha—are the treasured refuges for any Buddhist, their Teacher, His Teaching, and the Community of those engaged in its practice. They give refuge from the dangers of the world of egocentric sufferings.

CHAPTER I: *The Quintessence: The Mentor Worship*

Panchen Rinpoche I, Losang Chökyi Gyaltsen, lived from 1570 to 1662. He was considered the reincarnation of Kedrub Jey (1385–1438), one of Tsong Khapa's foremost disciples. He was the main teacher of the Great Fifth Dalai Lama, who named his reincarnation from then on the "Panchen" (literally, "Great Pandit") Rinpoche, regarded as the emanated reincarnation of Amitabha Buddha, the celestial mentor of the Bodhisattva Lokeshvara, who reincarnates as the Dalai Lamas. For more information on the Panchen Rinpoche and his adept heritage, see J. Willis, *Enlightened Beings* (Boston: Wisdom Publications, 1995).

In this *Mentor Worship* text, perhaps his most famous composition, the Panchen Rinpoche records inherited personal instructions for this meditation, the very heart of Tibetan Buddhism, which descended to him from generations of great adepts who lived and practiced in Tibet during the two centuries since Tsong Khapa. In my translation, I have been helped by versions done previously by Sharpa Tulku and Alex Berzin, Geshe Kelsang Gyatso, Tubten Jinpa, and recently by my close colleague Joseph Loizzo, working under Kyabje Gelek Rinpoche. This particular version I did for my personal use twenty years ago, rediscovering and revising it comparatively for this book.

Mother beings (Tib. *ma sems can rnams*) refers to all beings viewed through the eyes of universal love, which recognizes the beginningless evolutionary link between beings, who have been reborn through an infinite past in all possible relationships with one another, making it certain that every single other being in all possible universes has served in many lifetimes as one's personal mother, giving one life, nourishment, protection, and loving care.

The four phrases set in small capitals are mantras meant to be chanted three times when using this text as a visualization contemplation manual. NAMO GURUBHYOH means "I bow to the Mentors!"

The **five aggregates**, or aggregate processes, are those of bodily forms, sensations, ideas, emotions, and consciousnesses, the five layers of mind and body. As an enlightened being, the Mentor is visualized as having those aggregates constituted by living Buddhas, the Transcendent Buddha Vairochana constituting forms, Ratnasambhava sensations, Amitabha ideas, Amoghasiddhi emotions, and Akshobhya consciousnesses. The four elements are earth (solidity), water (cohesion), fire (heat), and wind (mobility), and in such an enlightened being they are constituted by the female Buddhas Lochana, Mamaki, Pandaravasini, and Tara. All the other parts of the Mentor are envisioned as being manifestations of other archetypal Buddhas and Bodhisattvas.

The **three vajras** or diamond-lightning energy foci, identical to the mantric syllables OM, AH, and HUM, represent the essence of the body, speech, and mind of all enlightened beings.

The **seven major jewel ornaments of royalty** are the precious wheel of power, the wish-granting jewel, the jewel queen, the jewel minister, the jewel horse, the jewel elephant, and the jewel citizen. The minor ornaments are the jewel sword, the jewel dragon hide, the jewel couch, the jewel garden, the jewel mansion, the jewel robe, and the jewel boots.

The **three educations** are the moral, meditational, and intellectual educations that constitute the Buddhist teaching in actual practice of ethics, samadhi, and wisdom. The **five paths** are the paths of accumulation, application, insight, meditation, and mastery that stratify the process of evolution of any individual being from ordinary egocentric existence to Buddhahood. The two stages are the creation stage and the perfection stage of the Unexcelled Yoga Tantras of the Apocalyptic Vehicle.

The saffron-colored **delicate tea** is what is called the inner offering, a complex visualization of all the substances internal to the life processes of beings transmuted into precious elixirs. The five hooks are various types of flesh, such as beef and horse meat, and the five lamps are blood, urine, and so forth, all internal substances usually thought of as impure but here transmuted imaginatively into pure elixir of divine life.

The sixty-four arts of love are a standard set of erotic practices detailed in the *Kama Sutra* literature. These heralds are different kinds of female angels, celestial, from imaginary realms, and from the subtle, subatomic dimensions of bliss and ecstasy. Orgasmic (Skt. *sahaja;* Tib. *lhan skyes*) is usually translated euphemistically by "natural" or "spontaneous," or some such, since erotic language seems out of place in "spiritual" contexts. Bringing in the earthiness of Buddhist spirituality might cause misunderstanding in some, but it is a translator's duty to be as clear as the original. Of course, orgasmic bliss does not refer only to the mechanical climax of ordinary sexuality; it includes the ecstasy of the melting of the sense of rigid boundaries between self and other that develops from the intensity of the wisdom of selflessness, an ecstasy whose intensity departs from and goes way beyond the bliss of ordinary sexual melting. The only other occasion in ordinary sentient life where such bliss is inevitable is in the temporary dissolution of individuation in the process of death, but dying bliss is harder for most beings to remember than sexual bliss.

Tibetan medicine classifies diseases according to their principal causes, which are the three disturbances, wind, bile, and phlegm, and their combinations, which correspond to the three emotional addictions of lust, hate, and delusion and their combinations. Each of the four categories includes a list of a hundred and one diseases, for a total of four hundred and four. Of course, when these are analytically subdivided in diagnosis, there are thousands of different disorders.

Things are naturally free from signs because they have no intrinsic significance in themselves, significance being attributed to them by mental habits of beings. When you look at the letter *A,* it seems to pronounce itself inside your head, making the sound "aey," as if it emerged naturally from the three lines of the letter. But a person who didn't know the roman alphabet wouldn't hear any "aey"; you don't hear it if you turn the letter upside down or on its side. Thus the three lines are free from intrinsically being the sign for the letter *A* or the sound "aey." If you think about this, you enter the realm of understanding the profound and liberating Buddhist insight into signlessness, closely related to selflessness, voidness, identitylessness, and so on.

The three kindnesses of a mentor are the kindness of giving initiations and vows, the kindness of transmitting inherited teachings, and the kindness of giving personal instructions based on his or her own insight and realization.

Communion translates Tibetan *zung 'jug,* which refers to the interpenetrating union of compassion and wisdom, bliss and voidness, magic body and clear light, at the fifth stage of the perfection stage, when the practitioner becomes a perfect Buddha. Vajradhara is the Tantric Buddha Archetype Deity *par excellence.* I also translate Sanskrit *Samaja* in the name of the Buddha of the *Guhyasamajatantra* as communion, as it ultimately comes around to the same thing.

The **ten excellent qualities** of a mentor are mentioned in the *Ornament of the Universal Vehicle Scriptures,* as (1) a just mind, (2) a concentrated mind, (3) a wise mind understanding selflessness, (4) greater knowledge, (5) delight in teaching Dharma, (6) wide textual knowledge, (7) profound realization of voidness, (8) skill in teaching, (9) love for his or her disciples, and (10) enterprise in teaching.

The **ten outer and ten inner abilities** of a vajra mentor constitute a detailed list of a mentor's expertise in visualizing, meditating, creating mandalas, performing rituals, conferring initiation, and so forth.

The **five blissful clans** are the Buddha clans that correspond to the five aggregates, the Transcendent clan (form aggregate), the Jewel clan (sensations), Lotus clan (ideas), Action clan (emotions), and Vajra clan (consciousnesses), whose fathers and mothers are respectively Vairochana and Lochana, Ratnasambhava and Mamaki, Amitabha and Pandaravasini, Amoghasiddhi and Tara, and Akshobhya and Vajradhatvishvari. All the ways of dividing the elements, sense media, and body parts of the mentor correspond to groups of Buddha deities in this visualization practice.

The **hundred clans** is an even more elaborate way of analyzing the components of a Buddha mentor, moving the imagination toward the vision of every atom and subatomic energy as a male or female Buddha or Bodhisattva.

The **four blocks** are the emotional blocks of body, speech, and mind, and the cognitive blocks that prevent omniscience. The **four initiations** are the vase, secret, wisdom science, and word initiations that purify and empower body, speech, mind, and intuitive wisdom and make possible the attainment of the Four Bodies of Buddhahood, the Emanation, Beatific, Wisdom-Truth, and Reality-Truth Bodies.

The **three sufferings** are the suffering of change (ordinary happiness that turns into suffering in time), the suffering of suffering (ordinary suffering), and the suffering of creation (inherent in egocentric existence in any state due to the inevitable dissolution of that state).

The **five forces of the mind-cultivation** (*blo spyong*) tradition are those of positive determination, habituation, eradication, positive accumulation, and focused aspiration. They are elements of the process of conscious evolution from negative states of being toward more positive states.

The **spirit of enlightenment** (Skt. *bodhichitta*) is the will and determination to become perfectly enlightened for the sake of all beings, in order to have the ability to effectively help all beings find happiness. There are two kinds of this spirit, the conventional spirit, which is the will to attain enlightenment, and the ultimate spirit, which is the realization of the selflessness or voidness of all things from ignorance to enlightenment, which is the Bodhisattva's awareness of the ultimate nonduality of enlightenment and unenlightenment.

The **mounting of give-and-take** upon the breath refers to the visualization practice of giving all your own happiness to other beings and taking upon yourself all their suffering, sending them your happiness with your exhalation in the form of rays of light and taking in their suffering with your inhalation in the form of clouds of darkness that are consumed in the radiance of awareness of voidness in your heart and turned into the light of happiness that floods back out to the beings.

The **messianic vows** are the Bodhisattva vows to become a Buddha to free all beings from all sufferings, part of the conventional spirit of enlightenment. The **three ethics** of the Supreme Vehicle are the ethics of restraint of evil, of gathering virtue, and of benefiting others.

Reality is described as ultimately **truth-free** to indicate the nonabsoluteness and therefore sheer relativity of all distinctions and rigid divisions, even those between true and false, black and white, good and evil. Ultimate truthlessness does not lead to the nihilism of relative truthlessness; it simply takes away the absolutist sting of egotistical truth.

Nagarjuna was one of the greatest human teachers of ancient India living a mythic six hundred years from ca. 50 B.C.E. to 550 C.E. He was especially renowned for his discovery of the Universal Vehicle Scriptures, beginning with the *Transcendent Wisdom Scripture* and for writing his profound manual called *Wisdom*. Tibetans also regard him as a founder of a major Tantric tradition of practice, the noble tradition of the *Esoteric Communion*.

The **dhuti or avadhuti** nerve is the central channel of the yogic subtle nervous system of nerve channels and wheel complexes. This channel runs from midbrow up over the crown and down just in front of the spine to the coccyx and thence up to the tip of the genitalia. It has a number of complexes, often five, the most important being that at the heart level, at the height of the breasts. Here the Mentor is invited into the center of that heart-wheel complex, the Tantric seat of the soul, the subtle energy continuum of bodymind existence that is the essence of the selfless individual, migrating from life to life and ultimately reaching Buddhahood. The five forces are the same as those identified on p. 298.

Soul-ejection (*'pho ba*) is a practice of forcefully pushing the subtle bodymind of the practitioner out of the heart center up the central channel and out of the coarse body into a rebirth in a Buddha-land. This is done to ensure a positive rebirth in order to continue your practice of the path of Buddhahood. It can also be done by a skilled yogin or yogini for the soul of a dying person using special rituals and visualizations.

CHAPTER 2: *Seeing the Buddha*

At the beginning of each of the following chapters, I will quote a verse or two from the Quintessence work, to link it, the heart of this *Essential* book, with the texts in these chapters. For example, at the head of this chapter, we see again the refuge formulation from the *Mentor Worship*. The first refuge is the Mentor as indivisible from the Buddha, and so we need to know more deeply what the Tibetan Buddhists think a Buddha is. The chapter goes on to give us a Tibetan vision of the Buddha during his life on earth and beyond.

Tse Chokling Yongdzin Yeshe Gyaltsen (1713–1793) was one of the most famous teachers of the eighteenth century, offered the Ganden throne at the head of the Geluk order, personal tutor of the Eighth Dalai Lama, and a prolific author. Among his most famous works are his biographies of the mentors of the path of enlightenment tradition, beginning with this biography of Shakyamuni Buddha, written in the context of his collection of biographies of all the "Path of Enlightenment" teachers. It is especially useful in our context because he tells the Buddha's story as Tibetans see it, with a view to inspiring the spiritual practice of the audience.

A **buddhaverse** is a universe as seen in its reality by enlightened beings. They are sometimes presented as celestial realms of perfect happiness, such as the Sukhavati buddhaverse of the Buddha Amitabha. Other Mahayana Scriptures make the point that this universe, in all its apparent ordinariness, is the Saha (Barely Tolerable) buddhaverse of Shakyamuni Buddha, presented to us ordinary beings in this way for the sake of our spiritual education and evolution.

Yama is the judge of the dead and the lord of the hells in Buddhist myth. He employs numerous demon minions, called Yama-demons, who inflict tortures on beings whose negative evolutionary habits have brought them into these incarnations of paranoia.

The **Thirty-three heaven** is the heaven presided over by the god Indra, the king of the desire-realm gods in the Indian mythoverse. Like the Greek Olympus, it is on the top of the axial mountain at the center of the flat earth.

Incalculable eons are Indian time spans, billions of years long, measuring the evolution and decay of universes, which have no first beginning, no "big bangs," but do arise and dissolve in extremely long cycles, within a context of an infinite expanse of other universes at other points in their own cycles, that is, in a context of unlimited infinities and eternities of space and time.

The **Akanishta heaven** is the highest heaven of the form realm, that is, of all spatial realms, since the formless realms have no coarse spatial extension. It is in that sense on the event horizon between finitude and infinitude, since the first formless realm is the realm of infinite space. It therefore includes an infinite number of buddhaverses within its core region, known as the Dense Array because it is the realm of immeasurable creativity, the dwelling of various Creator Gods as well as of all Beatific Body Buddhas.

The **five certainties** of the Beatific Body of a Buddha are that its abode is always Akanishta's "Dense Array" region, its time is until the end of cyclic life of all beings, it is adorned with all auspicious signs and marks, its retinue is all enlightened Mahayana Bodhisattvas, and it articulates only the Universal Vehicle teachings.

The **Tushita** (Tib. *Ganden*, "satisfaction") **heaven** is the desire-realm heaven second above Indra's Thirty-three heaven, a heaven of solid pleasure where Bodhisattvas descend to dwell in a staging area for their eventual descent to the earth of human beings. At this point it may be useful to present a table of the Indo-Tibetan cosmology of the heavens, human realms, and lower depths (see the table on the opposite page).

In all these lavish descriptions, which Tibetans inherited from the lush literary imagination of India, there are always **eight** of these and **thirty-two** of those, and so forth, as if these were the invariant patterns that occur when Buddhas are born and so forth.

The **three lower states** are hell, the hungry pretan realm, and the subhuman animal realms. That **the earth moves six ways** means merely that it shook in the four directions and up and down. The significance of this violent but nondestructive quaking is that material solidity is subordinate to the cosmic event of the birth of the great being.

Brahma is referring either to a former life of Buddha, when he was a thousand-headed deity who gave away his life in order to receive a teaching of the Dharma, or, perhaps more likely, to a thousand times when Buddha was a human and gave his life away in order to receive teachings of the Dharma.

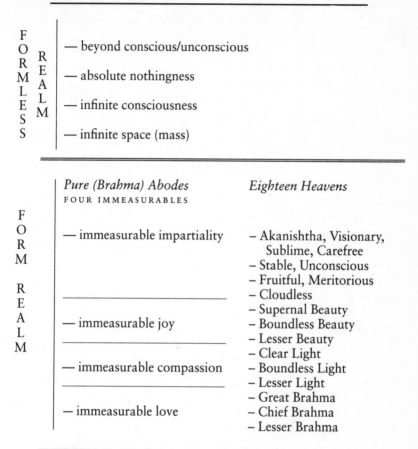

FORMLESS

REALM

— beyond conscious/unconscious

— absolute nothingness

— infinite consciousness

— infinite space (mass)

FORM REALM

Pure (Brahma) Abodes
FOUR IMMEASURABLES

Eighteen Heavens

— immeasurable impartiality

- Akanishtha, Visionary, Sublime, Carefree
- Stable, Unconscious
- Fruitful, Meritorious
- Cloudless
- Supernal Beauty

— immeasurable joy

- Boundless Beauty
- Lesser Beauty
- Clear Light

— immeasurable compassion

- Boundless Light
- Lesser Light
- Great Brahma

— immeasurable love

- Chief Brahma
- Lesser Brahma

DESIRE REALM

SIX HEAVENS

— heaven "control of others' fantasy-emanations"
— heaven "delight of every fantasy"
— heaven "Consummate Joy" (Tushita/Ganden)
— heaven "Struggle-Free" (Yama)
— Indra's "Heaven of the Thirty-three" (heavenly city on the top of Mount Sumeru)
— heaven of the four guardian kings

FIVE MIGRATIONS

— Titan Migration (Asura)
— Human Migration
— Beast Migration
— Preta Migration
— Hell Migration (thirty-two hells)

The **six kinds of beings** are gods, antigods or titans, humans, animals, pretans, and hell beings. The **eighteen great omens** are the usual sort of miracles, lights shining, flowers blooming out of season, angels appearing, jewels appearing, and so on. The **Saha world** is this universe as a buddhaverse, and at such moments the ground becomes smooth and even, soft, luminous, and jewellike. A **kinnara** is a sort of reverse centaur, i.e., a being with a human body and a horse's head. Kinnaras live in the mythical Himalayas and are associated with erotic pleasure, aesthetics, music, magic, and poetry. The **seven treasures** of a noble person are faith, justice, learning, generosity, conscience, consideration, and wisdom.

Various precious offering objects, even mansions, are made of **seven jewels,** the standard list including diamond, ruby, sapphire, emerald, topaz, beryl, and lapis.

The **three wretched or horrid states** are the hells, pretan realms, and animal realms. The vision here is that the light-rays from the Buddha were so powerful that they pulled beings out of these dreadful realms and set them around him in the park.

The spell of **Shankara** (Skt. *dharani*) is for pacifying any disturbance, Shankara meaning "peacemaking." I have not yet found the actual spell.

I have not been able to find the proper Indian spelling of the **Anga** king's name, so I have used the Tibetan transliteration, Shunchidala.

The **Three Baskets** are the three divisions of the exoteric Buddhist Scriptures, the Discipline, the Discourses, and the Sciences (*Vinaya-Sutra-Abhidharma*). The four divisions of the Tantras are the Action, Performance, Yoga, and Unexcelled Yoga Tantra divisions.

CHAPTER 3: *Meeting the Buddha in the Mentor*

This **"Three Body Mentor Yoga"** comes from the *Natural Liberation Through Understanding in the Between*, originally written in the eighth century by Padma Sambhava and rediscovered by Karma Lingpa in the fourteenth century. It is from the Nyingma order tradition but shows the same focus on discovering the Buddha, replete with various Bodies, in the living icon of the personal mentor. For further information, see my *Tibetan Book of the Dead* (New York: Bantam, 1995).

The famous **"Atisha's Pith Saying"** comes from a compilation *Sayings of the Kadam Mentors* (Tibetan *Kadam Thorbu*), which I partially translated in 1963 working under the late Venerable Geshe Wangyal, currently available in publication in G. Wangyal, *The Door of Liberation* (Boston: Wisdom Publications, 1995). I have modified the translation to fit my current style.

The three realms of cyclic life are the realms of desire, form, and formlessness; see the cosmology chart in the notes to chapter 2.

The eight worldly concerns are for profit and loss, fame and notoriety, praise and blame, pleasure and discomfort.

This song of Milarepa occurs in the compilation *The Hundred Thousand Songs of Milarepa*. Milarepa lived in the eleventh and twelfth centuries, and his many songs have come down in many recensions. The basis for this translation is the compilation by Tsangnyon Heruka (1452–1507). This was previously translated, rather freely, by G. C. C. Chang, in a seminal publication, *The Hundred Thousand Songs of Milarepa* (New York: University Books, 1962; rpt. Boston: Shambhala, 1994).

The primary mentor of a practitioner, the one upon whom he or she relies as icon to develop awareness of the immediacy of the perfect Buddha, is called the root mentor (Tib. *rtsa bai bla ma*).

The triad, base, path, and fruit is common to all Tibetan path teachings. Milarepa approaches the triad from a fruitional viewpoint, where you project yourself into nonduality at the start, immersing yourself in reality right away; you proceed on the path without considering it apart from the goal, and you deepen your experience of the fruit of intimate, ecstatic union with all beings and things, where your every experience is timelessly sealed with the stamp of bliss-void-indivisible.

Ankay! seems to be a way of saying "wow!" or "whoopee!" in Peldar Boom's local dialect.

Now that Peldar Boom has recognized Milarepa and asked for teachings, note how he gets right down to earth and makes her aware of her day-to-day bad habits. The mentor's instructions are personal in this way, not consisting of highflown secret teachings but exposing the real problems in a person's life.

"Dromtonpa's Outline of the Path" is also from the *Sayings of the Kadampa Mentors*, discussed above. The last few selections in this section provide overviews of the path that proceeds from the recognition of the Buddha through the mentor.

Gampopa (1079–1153) was one of the main disciples of Milarepa. He founded the Kagyu order as a monastic tradition, combining the personal instruction meditation traditions from Marpa and Milarepa with Kadam order monastic curricula. His main way of presenting the path can be condensed into the precious four themes.

Sachen Kunga Nyingpo (1092–1158) was the second important founder of the Sakya order. As a young man he received a direct revelation from the

Bodhisattva Manjushri giving this set of four themes for practice of the basic path.

Tsong Khapa (1357–1419) was considered an incarnation of Manjushri, but he also received a personal revelation from the Bodhisattva in the early 1390s while meditating on the roof of the Jokang Cathedral of Lhasa. The "Three Principles of the Path" then revealed were considered a seed of his massive work, *Lam Rim Chenmo*, the *Great Stages of the Path*.

CHAPTER 4: *Practicing Transcendent Renunciation*

Kunkyen Longchen Rabjam (1308–1363) was the greatest author of the Nyingma order, who formulated the basic curriculum of the school, synthesizing traditions of ancient teachings from the dynastic period of Tibetan Buddhism in the eighth and ninth centuries with the latest developments in Kadam, Sakya, and Kagyu order teachings. In translating this section from his *Treasury of Wish-Fulfilling Gems*, chapters 13–16, I was helped by a preliminary version kindly done for me by my colleague Joseph Loizzo.

The **Holy Ornaments** are the great Mahayana Buddhist masters of classical India, such as Nagarjuna and Asanga and their colleagues and successors.

The **auspicious marks and signs** are physical marks of a highly evolved being, such as a crown dome, a golden complexion, wheel marks on palms and soles, and a tuft of white hair at midbrow. World monarchs have these signs, and perfect Buddhas have them to a much greater degree.

The **three realms,** already mentioned, are the realms of desire, form, and formlessness.

A **pretan** is a life-form ranked between animal and hell being, often translated "hungry ghost," based on the Chinese translation from the Sanskrit *preta*. They are not ghosts but are solidly reborn in a realm whose dominant characteristic is scarcity of food and drink. They are always tormented by hunger and thirst, their grotesque embodiments reflecting insatiable appetites, with gigantic stomachs, long, narrow throats, and so forth.

The **eighteen voidnesses** are the voidnesses of things, nothingnesses, intrinsic realities, perceptions, and so forth up to the voidness of voidness.

The **thirty-seven accessories to enlightenment** are a famous set of faculties developed by the Buddhist practitioner, including the four foci of mindfulness, the four authentic abandonments, the four magic powers, the five spiritual faculties, the five strengths, the seven enlightenment accessories, and the noble eightfold path. Faith, mindfulness, learning, diligence, samadhi, ethics, conscience, authentic speech, livelihood, view, and various forms of wisdom of selflessness—these are the kinds of faculties.

The **six transcendences** are the famous set of virtues, giving, ethics, tolerance, enterprise, meditation, and wisdom.

These **lay and monastic vows** are taken from Tsong Khapa's *Great Stages of the Path of Enlightenment*. I include them here to show the practical outcome of the contemplations so eloquently set forth by Longchen Rabjampa. When people decide to use their human lives to best evolutionary advantage, they naturally seek to commit themselves to a higher level of ethical commitment, simplifying and focusing their lives in order to develop the contemplation and understanding necessary for real transformation.

Purchok Ngawang Jampa Rinpoche (1682–1762) was a famous teacher of the eighteenth century, teaching the Seventh Dalai Lama and many other eminent lamas, such as Jangkya Rolway Dorje. He sets forth in this text on monastic vows the practical instructions for the ceremonies conferring monastic ordination. I discovered in looking through previous anthologies about Tibetan Buddhism that they focused only on the spectacular meditations, exotic rituals, and mystic realizations, while millions of Tibetans over many centuries have been inspired by the Dharma to enter holy orders on one level or another. So many did become religious, in fact, that the high percentage of monastics in the Tibetan population was a distinctive characteristic of its modern (seventeenth to twentieth century) society.

CHAPTER 5: *Practicing the Loving Spirit of Enlightenment*

Asanga (ca. fourth century C.E.) was one of the eight greatest saints, sages, and authors of classical Buddhist India. His sevenfold cause-and-effect precept for developing the spirit of enlightenment through recognition of the motherhood of beings is what is called an oral tradition precept. Asanga himself received it directly from Maitreya Bodhisattva, and he handed it down to his disciples. Atisha brought it to Tibet, and it descended in various lines to Tsong Khapa, from whom it descended through the "Ganden" or "Ensa" oral tradition even to the present, especially to the Fourteenth Dalai Lama. The original text of this selection is a commentary on Tsong Khapa's *Three Principles of the Path* by the Fourth Panchen Lama, Tenpai Nyima (1781–1853), which I translated thirty-two years ago under the guidance of Venerable Geshe Wangyal; indeed the translation is ornamented by Geshe Wangyal's own inimitable oral-commentary style. It is also available in G. Wangyal, *The Door of Liberation* (Boston: Wisdom Publications, 1995). I have modified the translation considerably for the present edition, going back to the Tibetan original.

The **"Eight Verses on Mind Development"** were written in the Kadampa tradition by Geshe Langri Tangpa Dorjey Sengey, who lived in the late eleventh and early twelfth century. They are a most concise version of the exchange of self and other precept for developing the spirit of enlightenment of love and compassion. This precept for conceiving the spirit is believed to have been given by the Bodhisattva Manjushri to Shantideva, who passed it down through successors in India until the time of the Guru Dharmakirti of Suvarnadvipa (Java), when the transmission left India, in the early eleventh century. Atisha went to Java to recover this precept, then took it to Tibet with him, handing it on to Dromtonpa. Dromtonpa's main successor was Potowa, who in turn handed the main transmission to Langi Thangpa. For previous translation and commentary, see G. Rabten and G. Dhargyey, *Advice from a Spiritual Friend* (London: Wisdom Publications, 1984).

Shantideva was a great Indian master who lived in the eighth century. His story tells of a strange monk who seemed very lazy and nonconforming to his teachers and fellow students. Derisively they called him Bhusuku, literally "he who eats, sleeps, and defecates." He slept in classes, slept a lot in the daytime, and had a good appetite. Finally it came his turn to present his knowledge to the monastery or face expulsion. The whole community turned out for the farce of Bhusuku giving a lecture. He prayed the night before to Manjushri, the Bodhisattva of incisive wisdom. When he mounted the podium, he asked the audience if they wanted a recital of teachings they were familiar with or something unprecedented. "Oh, the latter by all means!" they said. He then recited the eight hundred or so verses of the *Guide to the Bodhisattva Way of Life*, profound in meaning and beautiful in expression, one of the greatest classics in India or Tibet. Its Sanskrit original still exists, with several commentaries, and its Tibetan translation is universally used in the practice of Tibetan Buddhism. This selection, the passages on cultivating tolerance, the remedy for hatred (from chapter 6), and compassion through the precept of exchanging self and other (from chapter 8), are considered the *locus classicus* for the transmission of this special precept, the foremost upholder of which in the present day is His Holiness the Dalai Lama. For previous translations, see Shantideva (S. Batchelor, trans.), *Guide to the Bodhisattva Way of Life* (Dharamsala, India: Library of Tibetan Works and Archives, 1979); the Dalai Lama, *A Flash of Lightning in the Dark of Night* (Boston: Shambhala Press, 1994).

The section on cultivating compassion through the exchange of self and other occurs in chapter 8 of Shantideva's great work. After exchanging self and other, one looks upon oneself with the other's eyes and imagines seeing oneself as inferior, equal, and superior with eyes of contempt, rivalry, and jealousy. This is a powerful method of cultivating the ability to substitute other-concern for self-concern. I do not quote the verses on this practice because this selection has become so long. Please consult the original work.

The instruction on how to confer **the Bodhisattva commitment** on an aspirant Bodhisattva comes from Tsong Khapa's masterpiece, *The Great Stages of the Path of Enlightenment*, a full translation of which is soon to be published from the Library of Tibet.

The **sevenfold preliminary prayer** has already been described above; it includes bowing, offering, confessing, congratulating, requesting teaching, requesting the enlightened ones not to depart, and dedicating one's merit to Buddhahood for the sake of all beings.

The **Bodhisattva vow ceremony** is another more concise version of the ceremony to undertake the activated spirit of enlightenment—it also comes from Tsong Khapa's masterpiece.

Shantideva's Bodhisattva vow comes from the third chapter of his greatest work, *Guide to the Bodhisattva Way of Life*. It is often recited when taking the vow in a ceremony for its beauty and the sheer good omen of it.

This last selection of this chapter, **"The All-Good Prayer,"** is the famous "Prayer of the All-good Bodhisattva, Samantabhadra," which originally comes from the *Garland Sutra* and is considered a quintessential expression of the Bodhisattva spirit of universal responsibility. I originally translated it for an anthology of Tibetan prayers published by the Library of Tibetan Works and Archives in Dharamsala, though I have abbreviated and altered it substantially here. It has also been translated from the Chinese by Thomas Cleary in his masterpiece *The Flower Ornament Sutra* (Boston: Shambhala, 1994). I include this because hundreds of generations of Indians, Tibetans, Chinese, Koreans, Japanese, and Mongolians have memorized and chanted this prayer. Its pattern of "all-good dedication" underlies the positiveness and benevolence we can find in the acts and teachings of a teacher such as His Holiness the Dalai Lama and his many enlightened colleagues.

CHAPTER 6: *Practicing the Liberating Wisdom*

Along with the emblematic segment from the "Quintessence," I repeat these four extraordinary verses from Tsong Khapa's **"Three Principles of the Path"** (see chapter 3) because they are so seminal in the practical way wisdom is cultivated in the Tibetan curriculum.

The *Transcendent Wisdom Heart Sutra,* known as *The Heart Sutra* in all Mahayana Buddhist countries, and *The Heart of Wisdom* in Tibet, is a concise expression of the profound vision of reality that is the root of liberation from suffering. Tibetan religious all know this by heart and chant it solemnly at the beginning of every ceremony. In addition to a prescription for enlightenment, they consider it the most powerful exorcism, purifier, and developer of merit as well as wisdom.

The **five body and mind processes** are the five aggregate constituents of body and mind already encountered above; to repeat, forms, sensations, ideas, emotions, and consciousnesses.

"Establishing the Nature of Reality" is the eighteenth chapter of *The Treasury of Wish-Fulfilling Gems* by the great Nyingma Lama Longchen Rabjam discussed above (see notes to chapter 4).

Datura is the notorious "loco weed" that stimulates hallucinations in cows and even humans, though it is used by shamans in the American southwest to teach to vision-questers the illusoriness of habitual objective reality.

"The wish-granting gem that fulfills both aims": both aims are aims of self and other; enlightenment fulfills self-interest by being a state of perfect and stable bliss, the highest happiness, unimaginable by those addicted to fleeting pleasures, and fulfills other-interest by effortlessly extending itself with the energy of such bliss to relieve the tensions of others and introduce them to their own deeper blissful nature.

Late in life, around 1414 C.E., Tsong Khapa wrote a more concise version of his *Great Stages of the Path of Enlightenment*, called, naturally enough, the *Short Stages of the Path*. The next selection, **"Tsong Khapa's Medium-Length Transcendent Insight,"** includes portions of the third section of this text, the section dealing with transcendent insight (Skt. *vipashyana*), the critical, analytic meditation used to develop transcendent wisdom that understands the nature of reality. **Quiescence** is the other main type of meditation, one-pointed, noncritical, thought-free meditation, used to calm and sharpen the focus of the mind but unable by itself to provide the meditator with new insight or deeper understanding. Enlightenment and liberation must thus be achieved by an integrated approach, an approach that focuses the acuity of the one-pointed mind on the task of critical penetration of the true nature of reality. I published an earlier version in *The Life and Teachings of Tsong Khapa* (Dharamsala, India: Library of Tibetan Works and Archives, 1983). I have here gone back to the original and retranslated it to accord with my current translation usage.

Thatness is a Buddhist way of referring to the immanent ultimacy of all things, perceived by wisdom as each thing's unique nonduality with the infinite, called its thatness since its conventional name seems inadequate to express its reality. It is sometimes opposed to "suchness," which designates the transcendent ultimacy of all things, the fact that each thing's reality transcends its conventional name and can appear only as if "such" as itself, i.e., not quite only itself.

The **Transcendence Vehicle** is a way to refer to the exoteric Universal Vehicle in a context where the Tantra Vehicle is understood to be the esoteric Universal Vehicle.

The **three lower Tantra divisions** are those of Action, Performance, and Yoga Tantras.

The philosopher-yogin-saints mentioned in **"Conditions Necessary for Transcendent Insight"** constitute the pantheon of the Tibetan curriculum: Nagarjuna (ca. 50 B.C.E.–550 C.E.!), Aryadeva (ca. second–fourth century), Buddhapalita (ca. fifth century), Bhavaviveka (ca. fifth–sixth century), Chandrakirti (ca. sixth–seventh century), Shantarakshita (ca. eighth century), and Kamalashila (eighth–ninth century) were the greatest teachers of the centrist (Madhyamika) tradition of critical philosophy within which Tsong Khapa here writes.

I use **addiction** to translate Tibetan *nyon mongs*, which means a distorted emotional or conceptual state, such as hatred or confusion, which takes over your mind and drives you to involuntary thoughts and acts. They are addictive in that they trick you into thinking your following their dictates will bring you satisfaction, yet they actually put you in states where you feel all the more unsatisfied. Addictive misknowledge is the instinctual level of delusion described below, contrasted with cognitive misknowledge, which is simply the failure to know realities.

The following discussion may seem rather technical in nature, but I cannot emphasize enough the importance of this type of teaching within the Tibetan curriculum, a teaching that demonstrates the supremely intelligent approach the Tibetan Buddhists have developed, building on the knowledge of their Indian ancestors, for dealing with the psychology of identity. The misknowledge described in such detail is basically the misappropriation of identity—the reification and rigidification of identity, of self, in subjects and objects—that traps conscious beings in an oppressive world in which the self-absolutized subjectivity is constantly being overwhelmed by a massive and inescapable universe of objectivities. Overcoming this misknowledge leads to the wisdom that sees through the alienation and discovers the freedom and relationality revealed when the intrinsic identity habit is discarded. For further details about this, see my *Central Philosophy of Tibet* (Princeton, N.J.: Princeton Univ. Press, 1984); and my *Life and Teachings of Tsong Khapa* (Dharamsala, India: Library of Tibetan Works and Archives, 1983).

It may be useful to list the types of misknowledge Tsong Khapa discusses in a single list:

1. Conscious or theoretical, personal or subjective self-habit or I-habit
2. Unconscious or instinctive, personal or subjective self-habit or I-habit
3. Conscious or philosophical property-habit or mine-habit

4. Instinctive or natural property-habit or mine-habit

5. Conscious objective self-habit, identity-habit, truth-habit, objectivity-habit, reality-habit

6. Instinctive objective self-habit, etc.

The more deeply you can identify your inner identity-habits, the more thoroughly you can free yourself from their compulsive aspect, and the more supple, flexible, and connected is your sense of relational self.

Negatee refers to that which is negated by negative expressions such as voidness and selflessness. To understand a negation, you have to understand what is being negated. Thus meditation on selflessness is not a mindless, thoughtless fixation on a contentless mind and reality; it is an active investigation of your whole being, body, and mind in the attempt actually to discover the self you habitually assume to be there. Only in looking for the self as hard as you can and failing to find it do you begin to feel free of the rigid self-image that the Buddhists say you have been driven by and carrying for beginningless lifetimes. So the negatee of this most liberative of negations, the negation that is freedom, is self, intrinsic reality, intrinsic identity, and so on.

The four key procedures for determining selflessness can be summarized in a list:

1. The key of ascertaining the negatee—identifying the presumed self that misknowledge and self-habits assume to exist substantively as their core concern

2. The key of ascertaining logical pervasion—determining that such a presumed self must either be the same as the bodymind processes or different from them, and that there is no third option

3. The key of ascertaining the lack of true sameness

4. The key of ascertaining the lack of true difference

"Praise of Buddha Shakyamuni for His Teaching of Relativity" was written by Tsong Khapa on the morning of his final enlightenment, in 1398, in his retreat cave on Oede Gungyel Mountain above Olkha. For further information, see my *Central Philosophy of Tibet* (Princeton, N.J.: Princeton Univ. Press, 1984), wherein I published an earlier version of my translation, along with considerable biographical detail and commentary in an introduction.

"Discovery of Mother Voidness" was written at the sacred mountain Wu Tai Shan in Shensi province of China by the great Mongolian lama Jankya Rolway Dorje (1717–1786). Like the previous poem written by Tsong Khapa, it fits into the literary category of "Enlightenment Song" (Tib. *lta* *mgur*), being an expression of joy and appreciation in the euphoria and lucidity of just having attained a comprehensive freedom from ageless suffering and anxiety. The Mother symbolism here is poignant, building on ancient traditions. Transcendent Wisdom herself is called Mother of all Buddhas; wisdom is associated with female, and compassion with male.

"**Some of the bright ones of our school . . .**": here Rolway Dorje critiques his colleagues in the Geluk order for overintellectualizing the matter and not putting the vital point of selflessness into practice.

"**The systematists . . .**": here he critiques various Indian Buddhist philosophers and those in Tibet still caught up in their theoretical postures, misperceiving the white elephant of reality as tiger, monkey, and bear.

"**The many sages . . .**": here he teases the many Tibetan sages in various orders, repeating their many highflown phrases for ultimate reality, conceding their correctness, but then challenging them to press themselves internally (symbolized by pressing their fingers on their own noses), "Do I really understand it all that well myself?"

From "**Cheer up**" on he proceeds, not to reject any of the Indian or Tibetan sages he has named, but rather to agree with them all, embracing all their understandings in the ecstasy of his own fresh vision of reality, concluding with apologies for any brusqueness of manner.

CHAPTER 7: *Practicing the Creation Stage*

Glorious Esoteric Communion Self-Creation Yoga, a visualization and recitation manual for the creation stage yoga of the Esoteric Communion Archetype Deity, was arranged by Tsong Khapa, combining the Indian Guhyasamaja literature with the personal instructions of the Adepts descending from Nagarjuna and disciples through the agency of the great Adept Naropa and the Tibetan translator Marpa. It was polished and refined in subsequent centuries in the Tantric monasteries of the Geluk order. The version here translated in abbreviated form is that used by the Namgyal Monastery of the Potala, currently in exile in Dharamsala; it shows by the mentors listed in its spiritual salutation that it was fixed in the late eighteenth century, in the time of the Eighth Dalai Lama.

The contents of this manual are meant for recitation in a slow chant, punctuated by musical interludes during the sense-offering sequences, while the detailed visualizations of body and mind, self and others in this celestial mandala environment are to be vividly contemplated in the mind's eye. You should not try to visualize these deities, and especially not project yourself into being the main deity, unless you are initiated into the practice.

I include this manual here to show the reader the essence of the Tibetan Buddhist Unexcelled Yoga Tantra creation stage practice, since hundreds of thousands of lamas over millennia have assiduously performed it and have developed the ability to see with the inner eye these elaborate alternative dimensions in all their jeweline beauty and detail.

The main point of the creation stage is given in the "Quintessence" verse repeated at the head of the chapter, to use the disciplined imagination in meditation to cleanse one's habits of perception and conception of the solidity of the suffering-bound ordinary world and the ordinary self. One thereby creates an imaginative, holographic blueprint for an enlightened, divine world where self and others may enjoy the perfect happiness of wisdom and compassion. Environment is visualized as divine residence, and self is visualized as Buddha-deity, death is visualized as Truth Body of the absolute, between state is visualized as Beatific Body, and life-state is visualized as Emanation Body. Once persistent meditation, visualization, and focused stabilization have enabled you to enter such a world completely in imagination, you are ready to enter the perfection stage practices, where you begin a process of transformation to develop the ability actually to enter such dimensions, to change your embodiment, and to change your mentality, traversing at will the realms of death, between, and alternative life-worlds.

In the benedictory verses at the end, there are numerous allusions to practices and lists of items that may pique the reader's curiosity. I include the verses for their beauty and the outline they provide of the path of Unexcelled Yoga Tantra. There is no space here to annotate these allusions thoroughly.

The **Inner Sacrifice** is a visualizational and ritual simulation of a holy grail, a grail with the magical power to transmute the ordinary poisons of egocentric life into elixirs of enlightened immortality.

The meditator as **Akshobhyavajra** in the center of the mandala visualizes that the deities sitting and standing around the jewel mansion are drawn on light-rays into positions on his (even if the meditator is a woman in ordinary life, she visualizes herself here as male) body, and then those miniaturized deities in those spots dissolve into light as one's body dissolves into light as the death-dissolution sequence ensues. With the mantra OM SHUNYATA, etc., one imagines oneself as dissolved into the absolute as at death, but here one's infinite awareness is the Truth Body of all Buddhas.

The **Supreme Triumph over Evolution** visualization is very complicated, involving a sending out of the deities visualized within the micro-mandala in the drop in the sexual center of the male-female union where they go out into the ordinary world as light-rays and transform all its negative aspects into positive ones, thus making the bliss-void-wisdom of the mandala triumph over the miserable ignorance of the evolutionary world. It is not necessary to elaborate more here, as anyone trying actually to do this visualization would have to receive initiation and formal training.

The **triply enfolded spiritual heroes** refers to visualizing oneself on the coarse level as Akshobhyavajra with three faces, six arms, and so on in the ordinary scale of the mansion and others, here called the Devotee Hero. In one's heart is again oneself as a thumb-size Guhyasamaja deity with one face and two arms, called a Wisdom Hero. In his heart again is a mustard-seed-size dark blue HUM letter, shining with rainbow light-rays, called a Samadhi Hero.

CHAPTER 8: *Practicing the Perfection and Great Perfection Stages*

The realm of the perfection stage, or of the great perfection, depending on which system you use to approach it, is the realm of the deepest mystery and the most incredible magic in the Tibetan tradition. It is the realm of practice of the Tibetan Adepts, whom I have called psychonauts, by analogy with our astronauts—i.e., those highly trained scientists who are also courageous explorers of the most far-out dimensions of reality as they have discovered it. I have discussed their world somewhat in the introduction to my recent translation of *The Tibetan Book of the Dead* (New York: Bantam, 1994). In this chapter I present a glimpse of the vast literature of this most advanced region of the Tibetan evolutionary path.

The first work is an excerpt from *Five Stages of the Perfection Stage* by Nagarjuna, considered by Tibetans to be the same Nagarjuna as the great centrist philosopher, though modern scholars do not accept this, since it involves crediting the Indo-Tibetan belief in the six-century longevity of Nagarjuna. Though a work originally produced in India, it is considered a fundamental codification of the yogic instruction in the practice of the perfection stage. It serves as the basis of numerous Tibetan works on the perfection stage, the most important of which is Tsong Khapa's *Extremely Brilliant Lamp of the Five Stages*, which I have been working on for ten years and hope to finish in 1996. After much deliberation, I decided it is perfect to excerpt for this chapter to convey the essence of this most advanced dimension of essential Tibetan Buddhism. An extra advantage is that it also connects with the *Esoteric Communion,* which was presented as the example of the creation stage.

The **five stages of the perfection stage** are counted in various ways; here they are counted as (1) vajra repetition (sometimes called speech isolation), (2) mind-objective (or mind isolation), (3) self-anointment (sometimes called magic body), (4) universal enlightenment (sometimes called clear light), and (5) communion, which is the same as perfect Buddhahood. The great perfection teaching, preserved especially in the Nyingma tradition, sometimes is presented as something even more advanced than all five of these stages but more often as the three upper stages of the five, since it is hard in Tibetan Buddhism to maintain that there is anything more advanced than perfect Buddhahood.

The **five main neural winds** are the vitalizing, the evacuating, the elevating, the digesting, and the pervading winds. The **five branch winds** are variously named and connect particularly with the five sense organs. The **vajra repetition** trains the yogin/i to develop voluntary control of these subtle energies within the circulatory and nervous systems.

Throughout this translation, I have added a nonsexist particle to the generic masculine case that is assumed in much translation (probably in many of the originals as well) from inflected languages like Tibetan and Sanskrit, since I feel that the uninflected English, where there are different words for male and female, makes the sexist subtext more pronounced than in the original. Hence, when yogin is mentioned, I put yogin/i, and when pronouns are used, I alternate male and female.

This lengthy quote from the *Magnificent Play Sutra* (Skt. *Lalitavistara*) is not found in the version remaining in the Tibetan translation of this scripture (the Sanskrit original is lost). It shows vividly how the Tibetan apocalyptic Buddhists saw the interfusion of exoteric and esoteric Buddhisms, as the esoteric and exoteric biographies of Shakyamuni interfuse in the depictions of his attainment of enlightenment.

In this quote again we encounter the paradox of Tibetan Buddhism. The role of the mentor emerges again as central in the rebirth of the yogin/i in this context, something beyond father, mother, beloved, or deity. Yet all the intensity of this relationship, where the mentor is envisioned as all-in-all and all devotion is mobilized, the mentor himself or herself focuses all that authority on empowering the disciple to empower himself or herself to be self-sufficiently the abode of all Buddhas, the agent of all enlightenment, the enjoyment of all perfection and bliss.

The direction in this ancient text that one should be ready to offer one's mate could be misunderstood. The couple's relationship at this level of practice is something different. The mate is not simply a tool, an instrument for the yoga of the practitioner. It is clearly stated in many sources that no yogini can serve effectively as consort for a yogin (and no yogin can be effective consort for a yogini) beyond the vajra repetition stage unless that yogini or yogin has attained at least the same stage as the partner. At the objective or isolation stage of mind, both yogin and yogini, who need each other to traverse the stage, must undergo the death-dissolution processes completely.

Indeed, this is why they need each other, since the stabilization of a specially balanced contemplative sexual union is the only state other than actual death through which all of the ten neural winds can be forced to dissolve in the central channel, thereby breaking the compulsive connection of the yogin and yogini with their habitual coarse body. After having attained that stage and thus being ready for the self-empowerment teaching, yogin and yogini, though they love each other totally and universally, are colleague psychonauts, not merely pair-bonded ordinary egocentric mates. Thus, in the process of going further into the realm of subtle body practice, voyaging into out-of-body practices of magic body and clear light, they are naturally willing to give each other away, especially to the all-important mentor, at the moment of receiving the "jumping-off" instructions in the magic body. For a fascinating discussion of this issue, see Miranda Shaw, *Passionate Enlightenment* (Princeton, N.J.: Princeton Univ. Press, 1994).

The **three luminances** (Skt. *aloka*) are the three intuitive wisdoms that occur when the yogin/i enters the final phase of the dissolution process. It has eight stages: (1) earth dissolves into water, (2) water into fire, (3) fire into wind, (4) wind into gross consciousness, (5) gross consciousness into luminance, (6) luminance into luminance-radiance, (7) luminance-radiance into luminance-imminence, and (8) luminance-imminence into clear-light translucency, the ultimately subtle state. The subjective signs of these dissolutions are, respectively, (1) mirage, (2) smoke, (3) fireflies, (4) candle flame, (5) moonlit sky, (6) sunlit sky, (7) blacklit sky, and (8) predawn gray-lit twilight sky. The three luminances, or luminance intuitions, are states (5), (6), and (7).

"The Natural Liberation Through Naked Vision" is an important formulation of the Nyingma tradition's Great Perfection teachings, attributed to Padma Sambhava, later discovered by the treasure-finder Karma Lingpa. I take this excerpt from my full-length translation, published as an appendix to my *Tibetan Book of the Dead* (New York: Bantam, 1994). It is clear that this teaching very much resembles the communion teachings of the perfection stage. It teaches the most advanced, radical vision of nonduality, the Buddha-vision accessible to the psychonaut once he or she has been able consciously to traverse the death experience and can remember the clear-light translucency of ultimate mind.

CHAPTER 9: *Various Treasures of Tibetan Spiritual Culture*

I include **"Instruction in the Great Science of the Six-Syllable Mantra,"** an excerpt from the *Jewel Case Array Sutra,* to introduce the archetypical mantra of Tibet, OM MANI PADME HUM. It is a good omen, perhaps, in the light of Tibetan myth, since this Sutra is one of the first Buddhist texts to come to Tibet. Legend has it arriving miraculously from the air on the roof of the palace of King Lha Totori Nyentsen. It was kept there and revered, and three generations later Tibetans learned to read it!

This eulogy to the **Twenty-one Taras** must be included, since so many Tibetans of all walks of life have it memorized and recite it up and down the mountains, day in and day out. Tara is the Mother Mary figure for all Tibetans. So all-encompassing is her presence, she is invoked daily in these main twenty-one forms, though Tibetans believe her to be functioning in limitless forms, for the sake of all beings. For an earlier translation of this homage, see M. Willson, *In Praise of Tara* (London: Wisdom Publications, 1982). For the iconography of Tara, see Rhie and Thurman, *Wisdom and Compassion: The Sacred Art of Tibet* (New York: Abrams, 1991).

"Description of the Between" comes from my translation of *The Tibetan Book of the Dead* (New York: Bantam, 1994). I include it to give the reader a brief description of the between (Tib. *bardo*; Skt. *antarabhava*) state, the subjective experience of beings after death and before the next rebirth. Though this idea was inherited from Indian Buddhism, the Tibetans developed it carefully and incorporated it in the very heart of their culture, which helped them cope with death, both of loved ones and of themselves, and gave their lives the dimension of being open both to the subtle dimension and to a limitless future.

Mahakala was a demon who was once unleashed upon the world and was tormenting even the gods with his greed and aggression, as the god Brahma had given him the boon that no outside enemy could defeat him. The Bodhisattvas Manjushri and Avalokiteshvara teamed up, transformed themselves into a horse and a pig, entered his mouth and anus, and then began to expand in size. When the demon, about to explode, begged to surrender, the Bodhisattvas chained him up and then began a process of converting him to gentleness and compassion. Eventually he became a protector of the Dharma, a fierce cherubim or seraphim, using his demonic strength to keep lesser evil spirits and calamities at bay. He is propitiated by most Tibetans in one of his many forms. This short invocation, **"Praises of Various Fierce Protectors,"** is from the equivalent of the "Book of Common Prayer," published in Dharamsala.

Shri Devi is the fiercest form of Tara. Art historians and mythographers associate her with the Hindu goddess Kali. She has become thoroughly domesticated in Tibet, serving as special protectress of the Dalai Lamas and the nation. Her "soul-lake" is in central Tibet, and is used as an oracular mirror by high lamas when they go to search for the reincarnation of a Dalai or a Panchen Lama.

Yama is the god of death, inherited from India by the Tibetans. Tsong Khapa was considered an incarnation of Manjushri, who himself adopts his fiercest form of Yamantaka (Killer of Death) when he confronts Death and overwhelms him so that all beings, including Death, can become immortal. Tsong Khapa had a vision of Yama, now redeemed as a protector of the Dharma, and left this famous invocation.

Vaishravana is the guardian deity of the north and the jolly god of wealth (perhaps an Indo-Tibetan archetype of Santa Claus!). He is constantly invoked by Tibetans, who ask his help to keep the economy in good shape so that the spiritual institutions may be handsomely supported.

Setrabjen (Rhino Breastplate Wearer) is a typical Tibetan fierce deity, one who can be invoked to protect against more local, not only spiritual, difficulties. The author of this invocation is a lama who lives and teaches in the United States, the reincarnation of an abbot of the Tantric University of Upper Lhasa, which was located in the Ramochey National Cathedral.

"Prayer of the Word of Truth," written by the Dalai Lama some years after his escape from the Chinese Red Army into exile in India, has become something of a hymn for the Tibetan exile community around the world. The Word of Truth is a Buddhist concept, indicating the Buddhist faith that if one sincerely upholds the truth, its simple power will eventually overwhelm injustice, the might of arms and numbers, and lies and negativity, and the good, the right, and the innocent will prevail. It is closely associated with the Gandhian idea of "truth upholding" (*satyagraha*), which is the heart principle underlying nonviolent social action. This is a principle that the Dalai Lama and the majority of Tibetans have steadfastly clung to, in spite of the lethal persecution and official neglect they have suffered for nearly half a century.

I close this *Essential* book with this last selection, the very moving speech given by His Holiness the Dalai Lama in Oslo, on the occasion of his being awarded the Nobel Prize for Peace, which I include by kind permission of Snow Lion Publications, Ithaca, New York, who originally published it in America in the Dalai Lama, *A Policy of Kindness* (1990). In it we can hear the echo of the compassion and universal responsibility teachings given here in chapter 5, as well as the wisdom teachings in chapter 6. It also concludes our journey in this book on a positive note, on the manifestation of the wisdom and compassion of Tibet. He reaches out from Tibet's own darkest hour into our modern world and offers all of us from all nations a vision of a positive twenty-first century, at a time when things still seem quite worrisome.